100 THINGS LSU FANS SHOULD KNOW & DO BEFORE THEY DIE

Ross Dellenger and Ron Higgins

TRIUMPH
BOOKS

Copyright © 2020 by Ross Dellenger and Ron Higgins

No part of this publication may be reproduced, stored in a retrieval system, or transmitted in any form by any means, electronic, mechanical, photocopying, or otherwise, without the prior written permission of the publisher, Triumph Books LLC, 814 North Franklin Street, Chicago, Illinois 60610.

Library of Congress Cataloging-in-Publication Data available upon request.

This book is available in quantity at special discounts for your group or organization. For further information, contact:

Triumph Books LLC
814 North Franklin Street
Chicago, Illinois 60610
(312) 337-0747
www.triumphbooks.com

Printed in U.S.A.
ISBN: 978-1-62937-810-7
Design by Patricia Frey

To my wife, Elizabeth; parents, Stan and Rose; and other family members. I am lost without them.

—R.D.

This is dedicated to my wife, Paige, and sons, Carl and Jack, all of whom have had infinite patience throughout my career.

—R.H.

Contents

Foreword

Ross Dellenger and Ron Higgins have created *100 Things LSU Fans Should Know & Do Before They Die*, a behind-the-curtain look into LSU athletics that is a must-read for all Tigers fans. The duo covers all the historic moments and personalities that make up one of the most substantial athletic departments in college athletics. You'll get an exhaustive glance into Hall of Fame coaches, generational athletes, and—yes—Louisiana politics.

When I think of LSU athletics and its history, the one word that always comes to mind is *unique*. It doesn't matter if it's a Saturday night in Death Valley or a Sunday afternoon at Alex Box Stadium; you can feel the uniqueness in every moment. It's something you learn at a very early age growing up in Louisiana. I can remember asking my parents, "Does everybody do it like this?" The answer was always the same: "Not even close." It can often be tough to explain that uniqueness, but that's exactly what you get in *100 Things LSU Fans Should Know & Do Before They Die*.

In my lifetime I've seen the LSU football program go from celebrating an Independence Bowl berth in 1995 to hoisting three national championship trophies in the 25 seasons that followed. One of the more impressive things about LSU's turn of fortune was the fact that it was done by three different head coaches. The authors do a fantastic job of diving into the three contrasting personalities who have led the Tigers since the turn of the millennium. You'll not only learn how that transformation took place in this book, but you'll also get a history lesson about LSU's mid-century success, which many Tigers fans continue to hold in high esteem.

For more than 60 years there was one significant name that went along with LSU football: 1959 Heisman Trophy winner Billy Cannon. Every Tigers fan young and old has seen the Halloween

Run against Ole Miss from 1959. It's the first thing shown in LSU Fandom 101. Before every home game, the team plays a video of Cannon's punt return from that Halloween night on the Jumbotron in Tiger Stadium. That one punt return might be the first thing you learn about Dr. Cannon (he became a dentist after football), but it certainly won't be the last. The authors cover every aspect of Cannon's rise, fall, and redemption.

While LSU football might be the crown jewel of LSU athletics, it's not the only show in town. The LSU baseball program keeps the sports needle moving in Baton Rouge from February to Omaha. I say Omaha because that's where the LSU baseball team is expected to end every season. They created what the standard is in college baseball, and it all started with legendary coach Skip Bertman. This book covers the complete dominance Bertman and the Tigers had throughout the 1990s as well as the challenge of replacing the legendary coach. The authors also highlight some of the unforgettable moments from the diamond. Every LSU fan knows exactly where he or she was when Warren Morris walked off Miami, when Gorilla Ball took over the 1997 College World Series, and when Ryan Theriot slid across home to bring the title back to Baton Rouge in 2000. You'll get to relive those moments in their entirety throughout the many chapters dedicated to LSU baseball.

Before a guy named Joe Burrow got to Baton Rouge in 2018, the only player whose name could stand next to Billy Cannon's in LSU athletics lore was Shaquille O'Neal. It never fails: Every time I walk in to watch an LSU basketball game, someone will say, "You should have seen this place when Shaq filled it to the rafters." From 1989 to 1992 LSU fans were treated to something that no one had ever seen before. Shaq was considered a unicorn for the sheer size of his body and everything he could do on the basketball court. Shaq's personality off the court is something that has made him a basketball icon for eternity. The authors give you a look into his days dominating college basketball as well as what makes him—in his own words—Shaquille "the Big Aristotle" O'Neal.

LSU football is not a program that retires jersey numbers for every All-American or NFL first-round draft choice. In the long and distinguished history of the program, there have been only three retired numbers. For almost 50 years Billy Cannon was the only player with his number retired, until Tommy Casanova joined him in 2009, and he was LSU's only three-time All-American. The runner-up for the 1962 Heisman Trophy, Jerry Stovall, didn't have his number at the top of Death Valley until 2018. This scarcity of retired numbers makes jersey traditions that much more important at LSU.

The biggest honor I had in my football career was when 2003 national championship quarterback Matt Mauck asked me to wear No. 18 for the Purple and Gold. The number 18 has a lot of meaning in the state of Louisiana. For one, Louisiana was the 18th state to join the Union of the United States. When I was approached to wear such an honor, I was honestly surprised. I was a two-star recruit who was the 795th prospect coming out of high school. I was the lowest-rated prospect in the 2004 LSU signing class, but Mauck, head equipment manager Greg Stringfellow, and head athletic trainer Jack Marucci thought I would be the ideal choice to start the No. 18 tradition. I wasn't sure how they came to that decision. Was it something I did on my official visit? Did Nick Saban mention something to them? I didn't want to ask, because I didn't want them questioning their thinking.

I truly think the number was a big part of my career. I thought it brought with it a high expectation level for me and my career. I never thought of it as a pressure situation. It held me accountable throughout my four years in Baton Rouge, and honestly it still does in my everyday life. I never wanted to let Matt Mauck down. I wanted to win every day and play well enough that the tradition didn't die with me. I wanted to be able to pass it down to another

Tiger who embodied what it meant to be an "Ultimate Tiger" on and off the field.

I can't describe what it means for my family and me to be a part of such an amazing tradition. There have been 14 players from all over the map with completely different backgrounds who have worn No. 18 and represented LSU in their everyday lives. Wearing 18 at LSU isn't a one-year thing or even a four-year thing in my case; it's a lifetime thing. When you're chosen to wear No. 18, the conversations are, "Will this guy represent the number beyond his playing career and continue to represent the group in a positive way?" The tradition of who wears the number is something that now is anticipated on the first day of fall camp each year. People across the college football world have picked up on the tradition. I can't explain what it means to see the LSU 18 jersey that hangs in the College Football Hall of Fame in Atlanta. It even made its way to the National Football League: when Bennie Logan was in the NFL Draft process, one team's GM was in communication with LSU and made the comment, "I don't need to ask any character questions. He wore No. 18." To be a small part of such an incredible group of men is something that humbles me every time someone mentions it. It has also created a brotherhood of former Tigers that now spans almost 20 years. We might not have all had the opportunity to play alongside each other, but it's a bond that will connect us for a lifetime.

Growing up in Louisiana, there is only one team you dream of playing for. Louisiana isn't like other states in the South. Florida has UF, FSU, and Miami. Georgia has UGA and Georgia Tech. Mississippi has MSU and Ole Miss. South Carolina has USC and Clemson. Texas has five Power 5 universities. In the state of Louisiana it's the LSU Tigers from Shreveport to Galliano. In every backyard football game growing up, we fought over who was going to get to be the Tigers. When schools across the state have college spirit days, it isn't a question of which team you're wearing, it's,

"Are you wearing purple or gold?" I'm sure other collegiate athletes have a lot of state pride, but I'll argue that none are as prideful as a kid from Louisiana one day suiting up for the Bayou Bengals. That was the offer I waited for in high school. I can remember the disappointment I felt thinking LSU wasn't going to offer me a scholarship. I had other SEC and Power 5 offers, but it was that call from Nick Saban that I was waiting on.

That call never came. The way I was discovered by LSU was different than most. It has led me to live by the mantra "You never know who's watching." Nick Saban was at a spring football practice at my high school, and he was there to watch six other D-1 athletes. I had no idea Coach Saban was in attendance; I just went out and practiced like it was a normal day. We finished up practice and I was running into the locker room to jump into my baseball uniform for that night's game when I got asked by my coach, Chris Tilley, to come into the coaches' office. I was thinking we were about to make a correction from practice or Coach was drawing up a new play. I walked in and saw Coach Saban watching tape of my practices from early in that spring. I was lost at that point. Coach Saban stood up and said something I'll never forget. He said, "Son, I had no idea who you were before I got to Shreveport today, but I do now, and I'd like to offer you a scholarship to play football at LSU." It was at that moment that my mind went back to every backyard football game fighting with my brothers over who was going to be the Tigers. I thought about wanting to be Kevin Faulk in the 1995 Independence Bowl, wanting to score against the Florida Gators like "Touchdown" Tommy Banks did in 1997, or how many times I read about Jimmy Taylor and his grit when he wore the Purple and Gold. Growing up in the state of Louisiana and hearing a coach say to you, "LSU wants you to be a Tiger"—no greater words can ever be spoken.

100 Things LSU Fans Should Know & Do Before They Die covers every unique tradition, every dynamic playmaker, every high-profile coach, and every storyline that has created one of the most successful, profitable, and celebrated programs in college athletics. There is no detail that is left uncovered in this book. Even the most passionate Tigers fan will walk away having learned something he or she didn't know prior to reading *100 Things LSU Fans Should Know & Do Before They Die.* It doesn't matter which sport fuels your LSU fandom, the authors pull you in with every chapter. From Skip Bertman and Gorilla Ball to the first LSU football coach without an accent to Governor Huey P. Long's major impact on LSU athletics, it's all covered here in great detail and with inside information.

Geaux Tigers!

—Jacob Hester, fullback and team captain
on LSU's 2007 BCS National Championship team

1 Joe Burreaux

Joe Burrow arrived in Louisiana in the summer of 2018 as a midwesterner born and raised in Ohio and reared on Nebraska football. His new environs took some getting used to. His first trip to LSU's dining hall ended with his new teammates shaming him for eating a salad and recommending items such as fried chicken and étouffée (Burrow proceeded to gain 10 pounds in his first six weeks on campus). The Louisiana heat forced him to trim his shoulder-length locks, and it also melted his very first pair of cleats, as LSU's outdoor artificial turf climbed well above 100 degrees in the summer. "It's like having a hairdryer blowing in your face," Burrow explained.

The quarterback quickly crossed these cultural hurdles, won the starting job during fall camp, and finished his first season on such a hot streak that it ultimately triggered head coach Ed Orgeron to overhaul his offense into a spread-centric unit. A year later Burrow capped one of the greatest seasons in college football history with a Heisman Trophy victory, emerging as the unquestioned captain in LSU's unblemished march to the 2019 national championship. With unparalleled accuracy, gritty determination, and an audacious personality, Burrow took the nation by storm, endearing himself to LSU fans and others alike with both his play and press conferences. After all, he arrived to his news conference following the national championship win over Clemson with a lit cigar.

He earned it. Burrow toppled dozens of school and national records, setting single-season LSU marks for completions (402), completion percentage (76.3), consecutive passes without an interception (187), passing yards (5,671), and passing touchdowns

(60). Burrow's 60 TDs broke the Football Bowl Subdivision (FBS) record of 58 originally set in 2006 by Hawaii's Colt Brennan, and Burrow holds the FBS all-time passer rating mark too, at more than 204, far outdistancing No. 2 on the list, former Alabama quarterback Tua Tagovailoa. His 2019 completion mark is second all-time nationally, and his passing yards are third-most in college football history.

"To be blunt but accurate, Burrow on Monday night completed the best individual effort by a college football quarterback in the 150 years the sport has existed," wrote CBSSports.com in a story published after LSU's championship win over Clemson.

In a stat that speaks to LSU's passing struggles before Burrow arrived, the Tigers threw for a combined 59 touchdowns in a four-season span from 2014 to 2017. That's one fewer than Burrow completed in his final season alone. Burrow had help, of course; a trio of talented receivers (Ja'Marr Chase, Justin Jefferson, and Terrace Marshall) and a stud tight end (Thaddeus Moss, son to former NFL sensation Randy Moss) made things easier. Also, LSU's 2019 offensive line won the Joe Moore Award, given to the best O-line unit in the country. But maybe the biggest factor was LSU's off-season schematic change on offense. Former New Orleans Saints assistant Joe Brady, hired in January 2019, helped transform the Tigers from a traditional approach to a fast-paced spread offense that eventually led the nation in yards per game (568.4).

"It's been the greatest story in college football," Kirk Herbstreit, a longtime ESPN analyst and former Ohio State quarterback, said during LSU's 2019 campaign. "[Burrow] is basically like a co-offensive coordinator. That's the NFL model when you have a quarterback able to invest and communicate at that level. Joe is the cutting edge of that mold. When I watch LSU, it's not just Joe Brady's offense—it's Joe Brady and Joe Burrow's offense."

Unused at his home-state Ohio State and unwanted at his childhood darling, Nebraska, Burrow's arrival in Baton Rouge was somewhat stunning. Many things unfolded to make it happen. In Columbus, Ohio, he lost the starting job to future first-round pick Dwayne Haskins, a 2018 spring competition that triggered his departure. The Cornhuskers, meanwhile, twice passed on Burrow, once out of high school and then again while transferring. That inflamed some family members. Burrow's father, Jimmy, and his two brothers, Dan and Jamie, played for the Cornhuskers. "They were questioning his arm strength and whatever," Dan said in a 2019 story published in *Sports Illustrated*. "All Joe ever wanted to do is play for Nebraska. It really, really hurt me."

Burrow's career has been filled with enough doubters that he admits to keeping a log of the most egregious of them—"Mental notes," he said. Sometimes Burrow's mental notes are made public, years of frustration exploding outwardly at various parties. For instance, ESPN cameras caught Burrow waving good-bye to the Texas crowd as LSU finished off a win in Austin in September 2019, while in the stands his father, Jimmy, flashed the horns-down hand signal.

The Burrows are a midwestern football family rooted in competition and toughness, but Joe Burrow is also the spawn of educators. Mom Robin is an elementary school principal, and Jimmy is a longtime college and high school coach who played safety under Tom Osborne at Nebraska. The baby of the house-hold—Joey, they call him—is a much younger half-brother to Dan and Jamie, respectively a safety and linebacker at Nebraska in the 1990s and early 2000s. Joey drifted to the offensive side of the ball, but that didn't mean he'd play soft. "He had no choice," Jimmy said. "We weren't going to let him not play physical."

LSU coach Ed Orgeron often described Joe Burrow as a linebacker playing quarterback. "I enjoy getting hit sometimes," Burrow told reporters during the 2019 season. "It makes me feel like a real football player instead of a quarterback. People can look down on quarterbacks if they're not taking hits."

His ability to withstand body blows endeared this midwesterner not only to his teammates but to a rabid fan base in the Deep South. They've embraced Burrow, many of them donning No. 9 jerseys, a slight alteration to his last name crawling across their Cajun backs: BURREAUX. Louisiana loves Joe Burrow, and Joe Burrow loves Louisiana. They've fallen for one another in a perfect marriage, a program that has been one quarterback short of returning to national prominence and a guy who has been one opportunity short of making a big impact on the game.

Few saw it coming. Burrow became one of the most unlikely Heisman winners in recent history, having entered the 2019 season at 200-to-1 odds to win the top individual prize in football. In 2018 he threw for 2,894 yards and 16 touchdowns and completed less than 60 percent of his attempts. "I don't want to call it unprecedented," said Rece Davis, *ESPN College GameDay*'s lead anchor, before pausing for a brief second and adding, "but I can't think of anyone who has made this drastic a leap."

Others draw dark-horse comparisons back to the 1980s, to winners such as Tim Brown, the first receiver to win the Heisman, or Barry Sanders, who burst onto the scene as a little-known junior. In more recent history, there were out-of-nowhere Heisman winners such as Cam Newton in 2010 and Johnny Manziel in 2012.

One NFL scout says Burrow is the single-most-improved player from one year to the next that he's ever scouted. Another said that in June many NFL teams did not even include Burrow on their 2020 draft boards. "It's been an unusual rise," Phil Steele, a college football prognosticator, said during the 2019 season. "I talk to NFL guys. He wasn't really on the radar."

And now, one day, he might just have himself a statue. Burrow will forever live in LSU lore, joining halfback Billy Cannon (1959) as the university's only Heisman winners. Sure, he's a quirky midwesterner, his past rooted in Cornhuskers red and Buckeyes scarlet, but he embraced Louisiana and they embraced him back.

Hours after Burrow helped lead LSU to its first win over Alabama in eight years, hundreds of fans greeted the team at the Baton Rouge airport, their faces peering through a chain-link fence as Burrow raced down its length, his arm extended brushing the fence with his open palm in an emotional scene that the school captured on video.

Not long afterward, Burrow posted on Twitter four words, simple by themselves but strong when strung together: "Louisiana I love you."

2003 National Championship

The play was called Laser Pick, and without it, maybe LSU wouldn't have won the 2003 national championship.

While in the huddle, Skyler Green only heard half of the play call—"Laser"—and so he ran the wrong route. Matt Mauck still found the speedy athlete for a game-winning 34-yard touchdown to send the Tigers to a 17–10 victory over No. 7 Georgia, the most crucial win during the 2003 title-winning run. "That Georgia game put LSU on the map," Mauck said. "It was our coming-out party."

Led by fourth-year coach Nick Saban, quarterbacked by a 24-year-old former minor league pitcher, and anchored by a defense with future pros such as LaRon Landry and Marcus Spears, the Tigers won the program's first title since 1958, a 45-year hiatus that spanned seven head coaches.

It was a return to glory—a place LSU would stay for quite some time. The championship began a stretch known in Baton Rouge as the golden age of LSU football, an 11-year run that included three SEC championships, two national titles, and eight 10-win seasons.

The Tigers had never before experienced the sustained success and championship hardware they did over that time. This was a program that had been very up and down over the previous half century: Johnny Vaught and Ole Miss consistently beat the Tigers in the days of leather helmets, Alabama and Bear Bryant toppled them in the 1970s and '80s, and Steve Spurrier and Florida bludgeoned them for another decade.

Then came the win over Georgia. Then came the national title. "To me, it was the game that turned the tide," Michael Bonnette, an LSU graduate and administrator at the school during that time, told *Sports Illustrated* for a 2018 story. "It proved we belonged."

While that season included a host of memorable games—the lone loss, 19–7 to Florida; a 46-point dismantling of Arizona; and the three-point road win over Eli Manning and Ole Miss among them—the Tigers faced potentially their toughest test on September 20 against the Bulldogs in a top 12 showdown, the rare day game in Tiger Stadium that drew a sellout crowd. They were hostile, too. In fact, while tailgating before the game, a group of LSU fans toppled a Porta Potty with a Georgia fan inside.

"You think about the great Tiger Stadium games, and you almost always think of the great night games," said Charles Hanagriff, a longtime LSU radio personality. "I still believe [the Georgia game is] the most significant day win in Tiger Stadium history,"

The hype for the matchup rivaled even a top 10 meeting at night. *ESPN College GameDay* originated from Baton Rouge that weekend for the first time in six years, and more than 400 media outlets requested credentials, the most ever at that point in Tiger Stadium history.

A column that week in the hometown newspaper the *Advocate* crowned the game LSU's biggest since the days of Coach Paul Dietzel and his crew of Chinese Bandits in the late 1950s. Fans were craving for LSU to become a consistent winner and national title contender. The program had spent just one of the previous 40 seasons in the national championship race (1987). The Tigers were a middling program with a fan base that former athletic director Skip Bertman said couldn't even sell out its ticket allotment to the 2000 Chick-fil-A Peach Bowl without administrators convincing south Louisiana businesses to buy in bulk.

What unfolded on the field that day was a physical battle for the players and a chess match for the coaches: the defensive-minded Saban and his offensive-minded counterpart, Georgia head coach Mark Richt. Saban's club blitzed 40 times that day, sacking quarterback David Greene four times, deflecting seven passes, and snapping his streak of attempts without an interception at 176.

The real heroes of the game, of course, were Green and Mauck, who on third-and-4 with 90 seconds left in a tied game connected for what may be the play of the season. Offensive coordinator Jimbo Fisher called Laser Pick, designed for Green to "pick" the defensive back covering receiver Michael Clayton by running a short in route. Clayton, the motion man, would cross paths with him on a quick out route. "I didn't hear the 'Pick' in 'Laser Pick,'" Green said. "I ran what Laser was. Laser was I ran a deep corner route."

Mauck rolled to the side with Clayton and Green, as the play was designed, but arrived there confused. Clayton was covered and he couldn't find his second option. "I come out and think, 'Where the hell's Skyler?'" said Mauck, who spent three years as a minor league pitcher before enrolling at LSU. "Then I caught a glimpse of him deep and threw it."

Beyond its importance in winning the 2003 national title, LSU's victory in such a crazed environment announced to a national audience that 1) the Tigers could win a big game under the sun and 2) its stadium, nicknamed Death Valley, could rock in the daylight just as it does under the stars. Back then, LSU's reputation in day games was such that the Associated Press, in its projection column the week of the game, chose Georgia to win and gave as a reason the time of kickoff.

Of course, two weeks later, LSU lost on that very field in a day game against an unranked Florida team before rebounding to win the next eight, including a 21–14 victory over Oklahoma in the BCS National Championship Game. The 2003 title wasn't without controversy. In fact, LSU split the national title with USC, who finished No. 1 in the AP poll, the longstanding media rankings that independently anoints its own champion.

How did this happen? It's somewhat complicated. This was year six of the BCS, a computer-based, data-driven poll that pitted its top two teams at season's end in a national championship game. That year presented a real problem for any system with just two participants because there were three, and only three, major conference teams with one loss: LSU (12–1), USC (11–1), and Oklahoma (12–1).

In the BCS's penultimate poll, before Kansas State upset the Sooners in the Big 12 championship, Oklahoma was No. 1, followed by USC and then LSU. The Tigers' SEC Championship Game victory over Georgia (yes, the two met again) was enough to leapfrog them to No. 2 over the Trojans, and despite a 28-point loss to the Wildcats, Oklahoma remained at No. 1.

The BCS used a combination of polls and computerized selection methods that eventually spit out a number by which teams were ranked. Thin margins separated the three in the final poll: 1) Oklahoma 5.11, 2) LSU 5.99, and 3) USC 6.15. According to a 2013 analysis on *Bleacher Report*, had one of the four computers that ranked LSU No. 2 and USC No. 3 switched places for those teams, the Trojans would have gotten the coveted No. 2 BCS slot by .01 percent.

Frustration brewed well into January. In fact, Ted Waitt, CEO of Gateway Computers, actually offered the NCAA $31 million to create a true championship game between the Tigers and the Trojans. The NCAA passed.

In the minds of many Tigers fans, of course, there was no split at all. Their team—a legendary group of players and coaches—won the national championship. That team produced NFL players including Corey Webster, Landry, Joseph Addai, Devery Henderson, Spears, Justin Vincent, and Andrew Whitworth while also cranking out SEC head coaches. Saban's staff included three assistants who eventually landed SEC head jobs: Fisher (Texas A&M), Derek Dooley (Tennessee), and Will Muschamp (Florida and South Carolina), with Kirby Smart (Georgia) joining the group the very next year.

"The thing that made that team special to me was that most of the guys that were recruited on that team came to LSU when we weren't all that great and they came there sort of with a mission to accomplish something special," Saban later said. "I love that team. It's the first team we ever had that had that kind of success."

And it all goes back to Laser Pick and a daytime showdown with Georgia. "There was something about that day," Bonnette says. "It will forever be remembered as the day that got us where we are."

3 Nick Saban

When Nick Saban arrived in Tuscaloosa by private plane in January 2007 after agreeing to become Alabama's coach, he was mobbed by adoring fans. But when he arrived in Baton Rouge in late November 1999, at his introductory press conference announcing him as LSU's coach, the reception was "Who's Nick Saban, and why is LSU paying him $1.2 million a year?"

"I couldn't believe the response and the attitude people had toward me," Saban said. "I felt like there were a lot of questions, a lot of doubts. You have to understand. I was coming from a place [Michigan State] where the people were pretty happy over what had been done. I was shocked. I was thinking, *Maybe I ought to go back where I came from.*" Thankfully for LSU, he didn't.

What he did was save the Tigers' football program with a national championship, two SEC titles, and a 48–16 record (.750) in five seasons from 2000 to 2004 before chasing an NFL dream as the head coach of the Miami Dolphins. He arrived at a time when LSU was thirsting for success, stability, and a coach with his sights set on the elements required to build and sustain a national power.

After LSU had only two head football coaches (Paul Dietzel and Charles McClendon) in a 25-year period from 1955 to 1979, the Tigers had five coaches in 20 seasons from 1980 to 1999. In that period, LSU won SEC championships in 1986 and 1988, but after the 1988 title the Tigers had 8 losing seasons in the next 11 years.

When LSU fired Gerry DiNardo with one game left in 1999, administrators already had a list of coaching candidates they wanted to pursue. But Saban wasn't originally on it. He was a Bill Belichick disciple who worked as Belichick's defensive coordinator for four seasons with the Cleveland Browns and had been a college head coach for six seasons, including five at Michigan State. There, he was basically a .500 coach in his first four seasons before posting a 9–2 record in 1999. When DiNardo got fired at LSU, Saban had interest in the job for one reason: For years the state of Louisiana had produced more NFL players per capita than any state in the nation. Saban saw a rich recruiting base waiting to be plucked.

Saban had his Memphis-based agent, Jimmy Sexton, get in touch with then–LSU athletic director Joe Dean. The conduit was Sean Tuohy, one of Sexton's business partners and a friend of Dean. The negotiations moved quickly. Saban said he would accept the job, but only if LSU built a football operations building and an academic center for athletes and provided better living conditions for the players. When then–LSU chancellor Mark Emmert agreed to Saban's conditions, it marked the commitment that advanced the program to a national championship contender.

None of Saban's assistants followed him from Michigan State, though he offered four of them jobs. He immediately put together an all-star staff that during his LSU years included future head coaches Jimbo Fisher (Florida State, Texas A&M), Will Muschamp (Florida, South Carolina), Kirby Smart (Georgia), Mel Tucker (Colorado), Derek Dooley (Tennessee), and Freddie Kitchens (Cleveland Browns).

Saban never won fewer than eight games in each of his five seasons. He had three bowl wins, one of which was the BCS national title game victory in the Sugar Bowl over Oklahoma. His SEC Championship Game victories came against Tennessee and Georgia. That win against the Vols in the 2001 league title tilt was the victory that lit the fuse for LSU's national championship run two years later. LSU had lost at Tennessee 26–18 earlier in the 2001 season. By the time the teams met again in the Georgia Dome, the No. 2–ranked Vols were a win away from advancing to the Rose Bowl and playing for the national championship. But despite the Tigers losing starting quarterback Rohan Davey and leading rusher LaBrandon Toefield with injuries in the first half, LSU roared back from a 17–7 deficit to score a 31–20 upset.

Two seasons later, after four superb recruiting classes, Saban's 13–1 Tigers delivered the school's first national championship since 1958 by beating Oklahoma 21–14. "The 2003 team had so much character that it didn't need a leader," Saban said. "They thought they would win the championship long before I did." As a result of winning the national title, Saban landed the nation's No. 1 recruiting class. It was a class that would help Les Miles, the next LSU coach, win a national championship in 2007.

At the end of the 2004 season, a contract for $5 million per year and promised control of player personnel decisions lured Saban to become head coach of the Miami Dolphins. "I learned from that experience in hindsight was, it was a huge mistake to leave college football," Saban said in May 2019. "And I know a lot of LSU fans think I left for whatever reasons, but I left because I wanted to be a pro coach, or thought I wanted to be a pro coach. We loved LSU. We worked hard to build the program. If there was one thing professionally that I would do over again, it would've been not to leave LSU."

Saban lasted just two years before he returned to the college game as Alabama's head coach, much to the chagrin of many LSU fans, especially after the Tide's 21–0 win over the Tigers in the Sugar Bowl to win the 2011 BCS National Championship Game. That started a streak of eight wins over the Tigers that ended in 2019. In his first 13 seasons at Alabama, Saban has won five national championships, cementing his legacy as one of the greatest college football coaches in history.

Saban was pleasantly stunned in August 2019 when named to the Louisiana Sports Hall of Fame. He will be inducted in December 2020. "I'm just amazed this has happened," he said after being informed of the honor. "I didn't know Louisiana would do this for me."

Shaq

Shaquille O'Neal is the only LSU player to be selected National College Player of the Year, win the NBA's MVP award, earn a gold medal in the Olympics, and be elected to the Naismith Memorial

Basketball Hall of Fame. From the moment he walked on campus in Baton Rouge in the fall of 1989 as a seven-foot center who could run like a deer, it was obvious he could accomplish just about anything. "I did everything the right way and earned my spot in this game," O'Neal said. "Nothing was given to me."

It was O'Neal's late father, Phillip Harrison, a U.S. Army drill sergeant, who introduced Shaquille to basketball when he was nine years old. "We go to a park," O'Neal said. "And my father said, 'Son, I'm going to teach you how to be like Bill Russell, Wilt Chamberlain, and Kareem Abdul-Jabbar.' I had no idea who those guys were, so I was like, 'OK, Dad.'

"He told me how to block shots and keep it in bounds like [Russell]. He taught me the [Abdul-Jabbar] skyhook, but it was too old-school for me, so I transitioned to the jump hook. He taught me to be dominant like Wilt."

Yet at age 13 O'Neal snuck into a basketball clinic by LSU coach Dale Brown being conducted at a military base where O'Neal's father was stationed in Wildflecken, West Germany, located at the East Germany border. "At that point, I wasn't very good at basketball," O'Neal said. "I was down on myself. My father came in, punched me in my chest, and said, 'There is a coach up at the gym. Maybe if we get him to see you, we can get a scholarship.'"

When the clinic finished, O'Neal approached Brown. "This man about 6'6" with good-looking shoulders and huge feet," Brown recalled of the youngster. "He said, 'Coach, could you recommend me some exercises for my legs? I'm big and I can't dunk.'

"I showed him a couple of exercises, looked at his feet, and asked, 'How long have you been in the service?' He said, 'Coach, I'm only 13 years old.'"

Brown had O'Neal take him immediately to meet his father to begin a relationship that ended with O'Neal growing to seven feet, leading his San Antonio (Texas) Cole High School team to the state championship in 1989, and signing with LSU. "It was the most clean and honorable and simplistic recruiting effort I've ever dealt with," Brown said. "Everything was strict, disciplined, and aboveboard."

O'Neal turned down offers from every traditional college basketball powerhouse to sign with the Tigers. "I chose to come to LSU because Coach Brown knew me when I was nobody and he was always consistent," O'Neal said.

By O'Neal's sophomore season, he was ready for the NBA on the court but not prepared off the court to handle some of life's basic things. "I wanted to come out my sophomore year," O'Neal said. "My father said, 'So you been broke for 18 years; you can be broke for 19 years.' I said, 'Why? It's time for us to get some money.'

"He said again, 'Nah, you been broke for 18 years; you can be broke for 19 years.' I would have to be mentally ready, physically ready, and I would have to know what I was getting into."

College basketball breathed a sigh of relief when O'Neal stayed on, making the move to the NBA after his junior season in 1991–92. O'Neal finished as LSU's fourth all-time leading scorer with 1,941 career points, and he ranks second overall in career rebounds with 1,217. He averaged 21.6 points and 13.5 rebounds and blocked an SEC record 412 shots in his three seasons with the Tigers. O'Neal was a two-time consensus Southeastern Conference Player of the Year and first-team All-American in 1991 and 1992.

In 1991–92 he was the first player to lead the Southeastern Conference in scoring, rebounding, field goal percentage, and blocked shots in the same season. He was the first player to lead the SEC in rebounding for three straight seasons since Charles Barkley of Auburn (1982–84).

As the No. 1 overall pick by the Orlando Magic in the 1992 NBA Draft, O'Neal embarked on a 19-year NBA career that got him elected to the Naismith Memorial Basketball Hall of Fame in 2016, his first year of eligibility. Using his tremendous size (7'1", 325 pounds), he scored 28,596 points, grabbed 13,099 rebounds, won three consecutive NBA Finals MVP awards, was a 15-time All-Star Game selection, and was selected as one of the NBA's top 50 all-time players in 1996. He won three straight NBA championships with the Los Angeles Lakers from 2000 to 2002 and another with the Miami Heat in 2006.

It was after O'Neal won NBA Rookie of the Year that Coach Dale Brown wrote him a letter advising him how to handle the rush of fame coming at him. Part of the letter read:

"Affect mankind. Affect your fellow man and always for good. Shaquille, leave a legacy beyond trophies and statistics…. Be your brother's keeper. Lift him up when he has fallen, bandage him when he is wounded. In body, he may not be as big as you, but in spirit he is.

"Well, that's my advice to you, Shaquille. You really don't need it. You are what you are, a good man full of love."

As O'Neal became a worldwide personality, acting in movies, TV, and commercials as well as dabbling in music, he stuck to the promise he made to his mother of returning to college to earn his degree. He did more than that. After earning his bachelor's from LSU in 2000, he added a master's from the University of Phoenix in 2005 and a doctorate from Barry University in 2012. While becoming an astute businessman and investor as well a TV analyst on TNT's *Inside the NBA*, Shaq never forgot his time at LSU.

LSU named its life skills program for athletes in honor of O'Neal because of his continued time, effort, and support of the program. Every fall in or nearby Baton Rouge during a home football game weekend, O'Neal hosts a golf scramble fund-raiser for the Shaquille O'Neal Life Skills Program. "The joy is that this is where I developed the Shaq character," O'Neal said at one of the recent scrambles. "The people of Baton Rouge have been so gracious to me. I always see old friends, and we're doing a good thing."

5 1958 Championship

For 62 seasons they were the only undefeated national championship team in LSU football history. The 1958 Tigers went 11–0, capping the season with a 7–0 win over Clemson in the Sugar Bowl in New Orleans.

After LSU's 2003 and 2007 national championship teams won titles with one loss and two losses respectively, the 15–0 Tigers of 2019 finally joined the 1958 team in the perfection penthouse. And again it ended in New Orleans against Clemson, in a 42–25 LSU win whose connection with the Tigers' football history didn't go unnoticed by President Donald Trump during the team's ceremonial trip to the White House. "For the first time since the legendary coach Paul Dietzel, a name we all know, and the Fighting Tigers of 1958, LSU had a perfect undefeated season," Trump said. "So rare."

So rare indeed, and extremely unexpected for the 1958 team, which was predicted to finish eighth in the Southeastern Conference. Heading into the season, the Tigers had only 15 lettermen and three seniors returning from a 1957 squad that had to beat Tulane in the season finale to break even at 5–5. But in the off-season, Dietzel made two decisions that were vital to the Tigers coming virtually out of nowhere to win the national championship in 1958.

The first was switching to a Wing T offense, an attack that mixed elements of the single wing (double-team blocks, misdirection, pulling linemen, reverses, and double reverses) and the T formation (deceptive ball handling). The offense played to the strengths of LSU's personnel and covered its weaknesses. LSU had speed in the backfield with quarterbacks Warren Rabb and Durel Matherne and running backs Billy Cannon, Johnny Robinson, and Don Purvis. Powerful Red Brodnax switched from halfback to fullback in the spring. On a line whose heaviest player was 215 pounds, double-team blocking at the point of attack was a godsend; the line had struggled blocking one-on-one the previous year. Rabb was a slick ball hander and underrated runner; Cannon's size, strength, and speed made him an explosive power runner; Robinson was more evasive; and Purvis was aptly nicknamed Scooter because he was a scatback. "This offense was perfect for our ballclub; we were excited about the change," said Rabb in author Bud Johnson's book *The Perfect Season: LSU's Magic Year—1958.*

Then there was Dietzel's way to solve the Tigers' depth problem. It was something he had noticed in 1956 when a 17–14 LSU halftime lead over Ole Miss turned into a 46–17 loss. And again in 1957 he saw several teams beat the Tigers by wearing them out in the second half. Dietzel's first intention was to create two units of players and alternate them. Both units would play on both sides of the ball because substitution rules at that time stated that a player could only reenter the game twice each quarter.

Throughout preseason practice, Dietzel experimented with his personnel. By the season opener, he concluded his best 11 players—the White Team—were good enough to play both ways, but he was unsure about the rest of the team. By the second game of the year, he had created the last two two-way units called the Gold Team (which became the Go Team as nicknamed by a Miami sportswriter), which specialized more on offense, and the Chinese Bandits (named after characters in a comic strip), which became known as defensive stoppers. In Dietzel's 1959 football instructional book, *Wing-T and the Chinese Bandits*, he recalled how he explained to his team in the 1958 preseason how the three units would work: "We planned to play the starting unit half of a quarter and then play the best remaining men on offense or defense the rest of the quarter," Dietzel wrote. "Then, there was the 'Go Team,' which had players stronger on offense and the Chinese Bandits, which had defensive stalwarts."

In the 10-game regular season, the White Team averaged 35 minutes per game. The Go Team and Chinese Bandits averaged 12.5 minutes each. "It was one of the best decisions Dietzel ever made," Bandits middle guard Tommy Lott said of creating three units.

It took LSU six straight wins to climb to No. 1 in the Associated Press poll and two more victories to also get the top spot in the UPI poll. By the season's end, it seemed as if the Tigers always made the clutch play when needed. They were 3–0 in one-possession games, including a 7–6 road win in Game 9 over Mississippi State in Jackson's rain-drenched Hinds County War Memorial Stadium. LSU fumbled four times in the first half before State finally scored a touchdown but missed the extra point. The Tigers escaped with the win on a Rabb-to–Red Hendrix fourth-and-goal five-yard TD pass and Tommy Davis's extra-point kick. "What does it matter—7–6 or 70–6?" said a relieved Dietzel exiting the stadium.

He could have added "7–0 or 70–0" after the Sugar Bowl win over Clemson that closed out the perfect season. After LSU starting QB Rabb broke his right hand in the second quarter, Dietzel ordered no more rollouts when backup QB Matherne entered the game. LSU got its break to win when a bad Clemson third-quarter snap was recovered at the Clemson 11. On third-and-8 from the Clemson 9, Cannon took a handoff from Matherne, ran right, and lofted a TD pass to Mickey Mangham. "It was a pretty good pass," Cannon said, "thrown by the Lord." After one last fourth-quarter defensive stand by the Chinese Bandits, LSU obtained perfection.

When it was said and done, LSU had outscored its 11 victims by a combined 275–47. The Tigers had only four touchdowns scored against them in the third and fourth quarters all season. "It was a tremendous effort by every player [and] by the coaching staff," Cannon said. "The team was like that all year."

6 Charles McClendon

No head coach rode the bucking bronco known as LSU football longer than Charles McClendon. He saddled up in 1962 after Paul Dietzel left the Tigers to coach Army and held on for 18 seasons to become the winningest coach in school history. By the time the LSU Board of Supervisors forced him out after the 1979 season, he had won almost 70 percent of his games (137–59–7), captured an SEC championship, guided the Tigers to 13 bowls, produced 21 first-team All-Americans, was twice SEC Coach of the Year, and was National Coach of the Year once. And he did all that without ever firing an assistant and without committing any NCAA violations. "My mistake at LSU was I didn't cheat when I recruited, and I was proud of the fact," said McClendon, who died of cancer at age 78 in December 2001. "I just made the decision I didn't want to cheat."

His character was unquestioned by his peers. "Charlie Mac is the type of coach who coached more than football, who cared about more than just the scoreboard," said late Arkansas football coach Frank Broyles, whose Razorbacks had a 22-game winning streak snapped when they lost 14–7 to McClendon's Tigers in the 1966 Cotton Bowl. "He prepared his players for life."

McClendon was a Lewisville, Arkansas, native who didn't play a snap of football until he was 21 years old and eventually was invited to walk on at Kentucky, where he played for the legendary Bear Bryant. He never considered coaching as work. "I loved it; it was my life," he said. McClendon became an LSU assistant in 1953 after being an assistant at Vanderbilt for a year. It was the start of McClendon's remarkable 27-year relationship with LSU: nine years as an assistant (two with Gaynell Tinsley and seven with Paul Dietzel, with whom he had coached as a grad assistant on Bear Bryant's Kentucky staff) and his almost two-decade run as head coach.

When Dietzel bolted for Army after the 1961 season, McClendon signed on to lead the Tigers at $13,000 per year. He made it clear he was going to be his own man after constantly being asked if his coaching style was more like his mentor Bear Bryant's or Dietzel's. "I'm going to coach like Charles McClendon," he said at the time. "I don't know what that's going to be. Whatever you see is what you're going to get. Whatever I did yesterday, I'll do it tomorrow. I'm going to be consistent with it."

Such as his two-quarterback system, which he developed after losing his starting QB four times in his first four seasons. He wanted to have two QBs ready to play at all times, and he would adjust the offense to their strengths. He stayed with the two-QB system for most seasons of his career, even when the Tigers had a strong-armed future College Football Hall of Fame quarterback and future NFL MVP named Bert Jones from 1971 to 1973. "I probably threw more third-down passes than any man in history but never a first-down pass," Jones once lamented.

McClendon's team recorded many significant wins through the years, such as the aforementioned Cotton Bowl upset of Arkansas, his 1969 and 1970 wins over Bryant-coached Alabama (the first times Bryant lost to one of his former assistants), and a 28–8 win over No. 7 Notre Dame in 1971 on the Fighting Irish's first-ever trip to Tiger Stadium. But no game meant more to McClendon personally than his 1966 season-opening 28–12 win over Dietzel-coached South Carolina. "I've worked under that man's shadow for four years now, and honestly, it's beginning to frighten me," McClendon said the Wednesday before playing South Carolina. "It doesn't seem to matter that we've won 75 percent of the time since I've been head coach and that we've gone to a bowl every year and won all but one. Regardless of what I do, I'm always compared to what he did or would have done. . . . I keep thinking that maybe if I can just whip his britches this Saturday night, it will clear the air around here. . . . I'll probably never get a chance like this again. And if I blow it now . . ."

He didn't. At game's end, McClendon was carried to midfield, where he reached down to shake Dietzel's hand. A few minutes later in the locker room, team captain Mike Pharis gave McClendon the game ball and said, "This is from us, Coach Mac, and it means that we've forgotten all about Paul Dietzel. You're our coach."

Three straight subpar seasons from 1974 to 1976 started a Help Mac Pack campaign to get McClendon ousted as coach, but he maintained his sense of humor. A week or so after he coached LSU to a Tangerine Bowl win over Wake Forest in his final game, McClendon was in his office packing his career mementos when a reporter dropped by. "I need to know one thing," McClendon said with a laugh. "Where are those people who wanted to Help Mac Pack when you need them?"

To the very end of his life, McClendon never quit loving the game of football or his players. Two months after his final LSU game in the Tangerine Bowl, he became the bowl's executive director. He delivered back-to-back sellouts and then became executive director of the American Football Coaches Association from February 1982 to February 1994. In his final years, he headed his Charles McClendon Scholarship Foundation, which gives scholarships to the children of former LSU players.

LSU All-American Jerry Stovall—who played under McClendon, coached on his staff, and eventually became the Tigers' head coach—summed up McClendon's life perfectly. "He worked with a passion, he lived with a passion, and he coached with a passion," Stovall said.

7 Skip

It was 1984, Skip Bertman's first season as LSU's baseball coach. While laying the foundation for what would be one of the greatest dynasties in college baseball history, Bertman's job extended to educating football-crazed fans in the game of stickball. "Someone yelled down, 'Hey, Bertram!' (I was 'Bertram' for three or four years.) 'We're one point down!'" Bertman recalled in 2019. "I vowed to myself that you just [teach them] one person at a time. I turned and yelled up, 'They're called runs! And we'll get some more.'" Two years later, Bertman took his third LSU team to the College World Series, and five years after that, the Tigers won their first of five national championships between 1991 and 2000, an unrivaled title-winning stretch in modern college baseball history.

The Miami native transformed Baton Rouge into a college baseball town, creating the country's most raucous home environment in the sport through the most humbling of starts. He used to have to walk around the city in his uniform to sell baseball tickets, and his very first team alternated between practicing and painting a dilapidated Alex Box Stadium.

He's arguably the biggest influencer in modern LSU athletics history. He was not only the leader of a winning baseball club, but he served as athletic director from 2001 to 2008, a stretch that includes two significant decisions: the creation of a new fundraising effort through football seat licensing and the hiring of football coach Les Miles, eventually the second-winningest coach in program history.

Bertman has been inducted into five coaching halls of fame: University of Miami, Louisiana Sports, LSU Athletics, American Baseball Coaches Association, and College Baseball. In a *Baseball*

America poll published in 1999, Bertman was voted the second-greatest college baseball coach of the 20th century behind Rod Dedeaux of USC.

In September 2019 LSU erected a statue outside of Alex Box Stadium and dedicated it in an outdoor ceremony where Bertman delivered an emotional 15-minute speech to hundreds in attendance. "What I learned most of all is I could get whatever I wanted if I helped enough people get what they wanted," Bertman said. "If you vividly imagine, heartily desire, sincerely believe, and enthusiastically act upon it every day, it will come to pass."

Bertman's ascension in the baseball world began at Miami Beach High School, where he coached the Hi-Tides to a Florida state championship and two runner-up finishes. He then joined Ron Fraser's staff at Miami, eventually becoming his top lieutenant and helping the Hurricanes win the 1982 national championship. He learned about more than baseball during his eight years at Miami. Fraser taught Bertman how to build a program and rally a fan base, components he took to Baton Rouge in 1984. "Ron Fraser helped me off the field and on the field," Bertman recalled. "He helped me with fund-raising and he helped me with people skills and in many other ways."

LSU athletic director Bob Brodhead, aware of Bertman's success in Miami, convinced the coach to move his family to south Louisiana to take over a program that had been to the College World Series only once—a place where home games drew about 500 fans.

Bertman's success in Baton Rouge extended well beyond the play on the diamond. He wore multiple hats: marketer, fund-raiser, and more. He sold baseball to the people, and they eventually bought it up. By his second season, hundreds of fans became a thousand or more. In 1985 LSU won the SEC Western Division title by beating out the vaunted Mississippi State team led by All-Americans and soon-to-be major leaguers Will Clark, Rafael

Palmeiro, and Jeff Brantley; it was a pinnacle moment for a young program.

He grew the sport of baseball across a state more obsessed with football than anything else. After a weekend series during his first five springs in Baton Rouge, Bertman gave the players off on Monday; then he and maybe one assistant coach took to the road. There was a coaching clinic in all corners of the state for 10 straight Mondays, according to a 2013 story in the *Advocate*. Years later, many of those kids from the clinics sprouted into championship-winning players for Bertman's 1990s dynasty: national titles in 1991, 1993, 1996, 1997, and 2000. "Those 5 championships in the span of 10 years is phenomenal," former Auburn coach Hal Baird said. "It was amazing how Skip kept sending great pitching staffs out there every year."

Bertman was on the field for the College World Series's two most memorable plays: 1) Warren Morris's two-out, two-run homer that beat Miami 9–8 for the 1996 national championship. 2) The 1982 play known as the Grand Illusion, when Bertman—then a Miami assistant—masterminded a phantom pickoff play at first base that nailed an unsuspecting Phil Stephenson at second to eventually lead to the Hurricanes title. "Everybody chased the imaginary ball," Bertman laughed about the play years later. "The [LSU] catcher came back laughing. I asked why. He told me the umpire said to him, 'Tell me what just happened.'"

Bertman's success transitioned to Team USA, with a gold medal in the 1988 Olympics and a bronze four years later. His on-field achievements at LSU included those five national titles, seven SEC championships, 11 College World Series trips, six SEC tournament titles, and nine 50-win seasons. There's another stat too. Beginning in Bertman's 13th season, in 1996, LSU baseball led all programs in attendance for the next 20-plus years, now normally averaging more than 10,000 tickets sold per game.

LSU's biographical page on Bertman aptly sums up his time as baseball coach: "Bertman's unyielding desire to succeed drove him to the pinnacle of his profession, and his astute knowledge of the game—obtained from over 40 years of coaching—combined with his steadfast determination and irrepressible enthusiasm transformed LSU Baseball into the nation's premier program."

As athletic director, Bertman presided over a department that boomed with cash. He saw the start of the golden age of LSU football. Coach Nick Saban, hired in 1999, transformed a middling program into a perennial juggernaut, resurrecting a sleeping giant by leading the Tigers to two SEC titles and the first national championship—2003—in more than 40 years.

Bertman and school administrators took advantage, operating from behind the scenes to spearhead a movement to connect seating priority in Tiger Stadium with financial donations to the Tiger Athletic Foundation. Administrators toured the state to convince LSU's fan base that the plan would benefit the university in the long run. Seat prices for many longtime season ticket holders jumped significantly. Emotions were high. Tempers flared. Bertman thought he might get fired, recalled Herb Vincent, then an LSU administrator on Bertman's staff. "I remember meeting with Skip and [deputy AD] Dan [Radakovich] in Skip's office, and he was showing us the diagrams for all the facility improvements that would come from this money," Vincent said in a *Sports Illustrated* story in 2020. "They start talking about the price increase on the tickets through donations, and he says, 'I'm going to do all this and they're going to fire me.'"

In the end, it all worked out, just like it often did with Bertman. One of his defining legacies was hiring the man who replaced Saban in 2005. He chose Les Miles from a list of candidates he interviewed, including then–LSU assistants Bobby Williams and Jimbo Fisher, then–Arkansas coach Houston Nutt, and then–Louisville coach Bobby Petrino. There were five candidates, but a sixth emerged amid the search. In the middle of the night, Bertman and his wife, Sandy, were awakened when their hotel room phone rang. The caller encouraged Bertman to at least grant an interview to former Texas A&M coach R.C. Slocum. Who was the caller? Former U.S. president George H.W. Bush. "OK, Mr. President," Bertman said he responded.

"Dan [Radakovich] and the staff had conversations with Skip," recalled Verge Ausberry, then an LSU administrator. "We said, 'We can't mess this up. This is a career killer for us.' It got to the point where we said, 'All the championships you've won, all of that goes down the drain if you don't hire the right one.'" They made the right choice. Miles won 112 games in his nearly 12-year tenure, led the Tigers to a national title in 2007, a runner-up finish in 2011, and two SEC crowns.

Miles's success solidified Bertman's legacy at LSU as one of the school's greats decades after some fans mispronounced his name. "I'd hear, 'Bertram, the referees stink!'" he recalled. "And I'd say, 'They're not referees. They're called umpires, and yeah, they're pretty bad!'"

8 The Rematch

LSU's 2011 football season is one of the most successful not only in program history but in college football lore. The Tigers completed a perfect regular season (12–0) for the first time since 1958, reached the 13–0 mark for the first time ever, and spent 11 consecutive weeks as the nation's No. 1 team—another first for the school.

They won 12 of their first 13 games by double digits, the most in school history, and set an NCAA record with eight victories over ranked teams in a single season. They even had a cornerback, Tyrann Mathieu, bolt up the Heisman Trophy favorite list. They crushed No. 3 Oregon in the season opener; claimed top 25 road wins at Mississippi State, West Virginia, and Alabama; and clobbered No. 12 Georgia in the SEC Championship Game.

Then came January 9, 2012: the rematch with the Crimson Tide in the BCS National Championship Game and a result—Alabama 21, LSU 0—that to this day lives as one of the most depressing, humiliating, and baffling affairs in Tigers football history. In a 700-plus-word story about the 2011 season in the school's 2017 media guide, the game is not referenced even once—a sign of the deep wound that lingers.

TIGER DRAG, read the front page of the *New Orleans Times-Picayune* a day after the game, a play off one of the school's fight songs, "Tiger Rag." STUNNED! read another Louisiana newspaper. ZERO DOUBT! read the *Tuscaloosa News* in Alabama. National football pundits called it a beatdown and a blowout, an all-around whipping at the hands of LSU's former coach, Nick Saban, in its own backyard, the Louisiana Superdome, and two months after winning 9–6 in overtime in Tuscaloosa.

The Tigers crossed midfield just one, and that came in the fourth quarter. They were outgained 384–92 in total yards, 21–5 in first downs, and 35–24 in minutes of possession. After missing four field goals during the first meeting on November 5, 2011, Alabama made five in the Superdome that night. Jeremy Shelley hit kicks of 23, 34, 41, 35, and 44 yards, and Trent Richardson put an exclamation point on the win with a 34-yard touchdown jaunt in the waning minutes. It was the first touchdown in 115 minutes, 34 seconds played between the teams that season.

The Tide took full advantage of a rematch that drew a paltry TV rating and one that many across college football disapproved of. Via the BCS computer formula, Alabama snuck into the title game just ahead of Oklahoma State. The Tide needed OSU, Oklahoma,

Stanford, and Oregon all to lose a game in the final month of the regular season. The most unlikely of those came on November 18, when four-touchdown underdog Iowa State beat No. 2 Oklahoma State 37–31 in double overtime.

"When we learned that we were playing LSU again, there was no doubt in our minds we were going to beat the hell out of them," Alabama defensive tackle Damion Square told *Bleacher Report* for a story published in 2016. "They had escaped death once before, and it wasn't going to happen again. I had never been so ready to put my hand in the dirt and destroy whatever was in front of me."

The Tigers felt the opposite. "When we found out we had to play Alabama again, I was pissed," LSU safety Eric Reid said. "We had already beat[en] them. Alabama didn't even make it to the conference championship game, and now they get to play us again for the national title? I'll be upset about that forever."

Alabama racked up 10 tackles for a loss during the game, harassing LSU dual-threat quarterback Jordan Jefferson. Jefferson completed 11 of 17 attempts for just 52 yards. Coach Les Miles's decision not to insert Jarrett Lee, even during the final minutes, is one of the more contentious coaching moves in LSU football history. Lee began the 2011 season as the starter, starting the first eight games—four of them while Jefferson was serving a suspension for his involvement in a bar fight. Lee later claimed he could have helped if inserted, and he said in an interview with the *Advocate* that he did not understand why LSU coaches didn't give him a crack.

Rumors swirled after the game that a locker room altercation or argument had led to Lee's benching, but all parties involved denied such. "We felt like with Jefferson's feet and the ability to get out of the rush that it was fair that he finished," Miles said after the game. "He certainly had a tremendously strong year in any regard."

Some claim the loss began the decline of LSU football from a yearly championship contender to a team that struggles to reach the 10-win mark. Alabama's seven-game winning streak over LSU began that night, something that had a significant part in the 2016 firing of Miles.

9 Paul Dietzel

It's safe to say LSU has never had a head football coach with the magnetism of Paul Dietzel. When the West Point assistant was hired on February 15, 1955, and signed to a three-year contract at $13,000 per year to lead the Tigers, he was a tall, blond, and handsome 29-year-old charmer with a gleaming smile that earned him the nickname Pepsodent Paul. Dietzel, who flew World War II bombing missions in a B-29 Superfortress over Japan in the Army Air Corps, had the looks and charisma that played well in recruiting.

But Dietzel was more than a pretty face. "One of his great strengths as a coach was he knew what we were going to do," said Charles McClendon, who was retained as an assistant by Dietzel from the previous staff, and who eventually succeeded Dietzel as head coach. "He did an excellent job drawing up game plans."

Dietzel coached the Tigers for seven seasons, producing a 46–24–3 record. His first three seasons—a combined 11–17–2 record—were vastly different from his last four, which produced LSU's first national title in 1958, two SEC championships, three bowls, finishes in the nation's top four three times, and a combined record of 35–7–1.

He was also a master psychologist and motivator. "He'd come by and get us at the athletic dorm and we'd walk over to Tiger Stadium, and we'd watch a movie he picked out in the film room," Lynn LeBlanc, a former lineman under Dietzel, told *USA Today's*

Glenn Guilbeau. "It was always a war movie. People fighting, always a lot of action. Then he'd stop under this big oak tree on the way back to the dorm and talk to us about the game the next day. He was a great motivator. He knew how to talk to you."

Dietzel's job was in jeopardy in his third season in 1957, when a 4–1 start dissipated into a four-game losing streak. He said he felt he was playing for his job in the Tigers' 25–6 regular-season finale win over Tulane. In the 1958 preseason, SEC coaches picked LSU to finish eighth in the 10-team league. The Tigers received just five points in the AP preseason poll.

What the Tigers' naysayers didn't know was LSU was changing its offense from a single wing to a Wing T full of counters, reverses, and men in motion. The deception was designed to help LSU's lack of size on the offensive line. Also, Dietzel realized to create depth he needed to play platoon football. So he placed his 11 best athletes regardless of position on the first team, his 11 best offensive players on the second team, and his 11 best defensive players on the third team. He called the first team the White Team because they wore white jerseys in practice and the second team the Gold Team (later shortened to the Go Team) because they wore gold jerseys in practice, and Dietzel called the third team the Chinese Bandits, a name he took from the comic *Terry and the Pirates*. "The Chinese Bandits were the meanest, most vicious people in the world," Dietzel said.

In practice, the White Team spent 50 percent of the time on offense and 50 percent on defense. The Go Team went 75 percent on offense and 25 on defense. The Chinese Bandits went 75 percent on defense and 25 on offense. The platoon system worked wonderfully. The Tigers went 11–0, producing four shutouts and three one-possession victories, including the season-ending 7–0 Sugar Bowl victory over Clemson.

The 1958 season was the bulk of an 18-game winning streak that ended in 1959 with a 14–13 loss at Tennessee. It came a week after Billy Cannon's historic 89-yard TD punt return on Halloween night provided the No. 1 ranked Tigers with a 7–3 win over No. 3 Ole Miss. At year's end, LSU agreed to a rematch with the Rebels in the Sugar Bowl. The No. 2 Rebs trounced the No. 3 Tigers 21–0.

Two years later, in what was Dietzel's final season, LSU was 10–1 after losing the opener to Rice and getting 10 straight wins, including a 25–7 Orange Bowl victory over Colorado. Before the Orange Bowl, Dietzel began pursuing the Army head coaching vacancy after Coach Dale Hall was fired. At a heated post–Orange Bowl LSU Board of Supervisors meeting, Tigers athletic director Jim Corbett asked the board to release Dietzel from his contract so he could accept the Army job. Dietzel was freed, but only after a board vote not to release him from his contract failed 8–5.

Eventually Dietzel and LSU crossed paths again. He returned to Tiger Stadium as South Carolina's head coach in the 1966 season opener for both teams. LSU won 28–12. Then, in 1978, Dietzel replaced the retiring Carl Maddox as LSU's athletic director. He lasted five years before he was fired by the school's Board of Supervisors in 1982.

But he never let his termination get in the way of his love of LSU. After Dietzel eventually retired from college athletics, he and his wife, Anne, lived in Baton Rouge until he died at age 89 in September 2013, a day before their 69th wedding anniversary.

10 An Improbable Title

The photo is somewhat iconic: Nick Saban, clad in purple and gold, his finger pointing toward the roof of the Georgia Dome, mouth agape and eyes on LSU's traveling fan section, all of them celebrating an improbable Southeastern Conference title. How Saban and the Tigers arrived here—a 31–20 win over No. 2 Tennessee for the 2001 SEC championship—is something that borders on implausible. Two years before this moment, this program completed the season at 3–8. Six weeks before this moment, LSU dropped a home game to Ole Miss to fall to 4–3 overall and 2–3 in the conference.

That's not all. In the second quarter of this tussle with Tennessee, LSU lost its starting quarterback, Rohan Davey, and its starting running back, LaBrandon Toefield, to injury. The Tigers fell behind by 10 in the second quarter and went into halftime losing 17–7. A 22-year-old redshirt freshman who played four years of minor league baseball before arriving at LSU stopped that losing momentum.

At the time, even Tigers fans knew little about Matt Mauck. Tennessee played like it knew much less. Using a QB run package LSU had implemented that very week in practice, the dual-threat Mauck ran for 43 crucial yards. Many of them came on quarterback draws on critical downs: 8 and 9 yards on a pair of second-and-10s, 2 yards on a second-and-1, and a 13-yard game-winning touchdown run. The Tigers stormed back from that 17–7 first-half deficit, with Mauck and backup running back Domanick Davis leading the way. They spoiled what many believed to be a coronation of sorts to Tennessee's meeting with Miami for the national title.

"After the game I remember seeing how dejected the Tennessee fans were," Mauck said in a 2014 interview with OutkicktheCoverage .com. "They were in disbelief. It seemed a forgone conclusion that they'd win. 'There's a backup QB and second-string RB and we still can't win.' It was a shock for most Tennessee fans."

For the LSU Tigers, it was a massive moment in Saban's second season, the foundation to an eventual national championship in 2003. The victory served as LSU's first SEC title since 1988, and a month later, the Tigers got their first trip to a Sugar Bowl since 1986. The key to it all? Mauck's feet. Coming into that game, LSU's staff installed a scheme for Mauck "on a whim," as he puts it.

"As it happens before that Tennessee game we were worried because they had such a good defensive line and Rohan Davey wasn't the most mobile guy in the world," the quarterback said. "They actually put a package in that we hadn't done all year that was a series of QB draws out of an empty backfield and some other plays out of that. We put it in with me in mind a little bit, but I think I only got three reps of that throughout the week because Rohan did most of it. That was kind of the crucial piece for us to be able to win that game. It was something we kind of threw in on a whim."

This wasn't all LSU, of course. The Volunteers stubbed their toe. Two lost fumbles in the second half led to 11 LSU points, something former coach Phillip Fulmer hasn't soon forgotten. "The problem was turnovers in the ballgame that we had . . . which usually is at least an equalizer, and can get you beat," he said in 2014 to OutkicktheCoverage.com. "I think we had a third-and-short and we turned the ball over, and we turned it over at the end of the game when we had a chance to win the game."

Most believed Tennessee would win well before the game began. QB Casey Clausen led a unit with talents such as Donté Stallworth, Jason Witten, and Travis Stephens. Earlier in the season, the Volunteers had beaten LSU 26–18 in Knoxville, a game in which UT receiver Kelley Washington rolled up a then-record 256 yards receiving. Tennessee entered the rematch knowing a victory would send it to the Rose Bowl to meet Miami for the national title. Ahead of the game, newspapers in Tennessee were already advertising for Rose Bowl travel packages, and some fans—and media—admitted to purchasing plane tickets and booking hotel rooms in California before the game with LSU. "We were all so sure Tennessee was going to roll LSU. It was a foregone conclusion so much so that we had already bought airline tickets to Pasadena through the station," said Tony Basilio, then a sports radio host in Knoxville. "The GM was really happy with me after the LSU game."

The UT crowd at the Georgia Dome tripled that of LSU, and many Volunteers fans arrived to the game clutching orange roses. "It is my most difficult loss," Stephens said. "It still hurts to this day. I still think about it."

11 Golden Band from Tigerland

It might be mere coincidence that the birth of LSU's band in 1893 came several months before the school played its first football game. Or not. Because as football slowly progressed, the band's growth and burst of popularity mirrored the football program's. Even now, as the football team and the Golden Band from Tigerland begin their 127th season in 2020, they continue to march in perfect lockstep with each other. The 325-member band creates a second-to-none game day atmosphere, especially at home in Tiger Stadium, that the football team feeds from on Saturdays in the fall.

LSU started its first band thanks to student cadets Wylie M. Barrow and Ruffin G. Pleasant. Barrow was named captain, and Pleasant—a future governor of the state—served as director of that first 11-member band. Twenty-four years later, with the LSU cadet band firmly established after playing in such events as Mardi Gras several times and the St. Louis World's Fair, it led the inaugural parade for Louisiana's new governor in May 1916. That governor was Pleasant, co-organizer of the band.

The year before, in 1915, LSU established its first music department, with all music class participants required to perform in the military band. The band performed its first halftime show at an LSU football game in 1924.

Four years later, in 1928, when Huey Long was elected governor, he changed the entire dynamic of the university—especially the band, which needed an overhaul. It had just 53 members wearing old uniforms, and they played a limited range of instruments. The band director also was the school's superintendent of grounds. In 1930 Long hired a new band director. He chose Alfred Wickboldt, an accomplished New Orleans trombonist, and promised him unlimited funding to revamp the band to make it more of a show band.

Long was a man of his word. He bought the band snazzy purple-and-gold show uniforms, dumping the military look. He got the money for additional instruments to be added, such as bassoons and oboes, which Frank Wickes, the late LSU director of bands emeritus, once noted Long erroneously called "baboons" and "hobos."

In 1934 Long took it up notch. He fired Wickboldt and hired Castro Carazo, the orchestra leader at the Roosevelt Hotel in New Orleans. Carazo gave Long full access. They cowrote songs, such as "Touchdown for LSU," which is still played today in the Tigers' pregame show. Also, Carazo allowed Long to periodically conduct band rehearsals and to march on its front line during performances. It was Long's dream that the band would grow to 250 members, yet he never got to see it through. He was assassinated in 1935. Carazo carried on Long's legacy for five more years until the LSU administration fired him in 1940.

For the next 30 years, under various directors, the band made advancements such as:

1) Adding female members: When World War II started, LSU band numbers dipped as male students went off to war. Tigers band director J.S. Fisher supplemented the all-male band with female members, which opened the door for LSU coeds to become regular members of the marching band.

2) The creation of Golden Girls: Just months after LSU won the 1958 national championship, Thomas Tyra became band

director in July 1959. His innovation was creating an all-female dance team called the Ballet Corps. The team, with some jazzy new costumes, eventually morphed into LSU's iconic Golden Girls dance team, which is featured front and center at every LSU pregame and halftime show and parade.

3) The introduction of the Twirling Corps and the LSU Color Guard: LSU band director William Swor started a group of baton-twirling majorettes in 1965 who were eventually named the Tigerettes. Then in 1971 Swor added the LSU Colorguard, a flag-twirling unit.

Aside from Carazo, Tyra might be the most influential band director in LSU history, though he was originally not a big fan of the school's new fight song "Hey Fighting Tigers," which in 1962 LSU adapted from the Broadway show *Wildcat* as a fight song.

Swor's biggest contribution was arranging the band's iconic pregame show, starting with four notes of the song "Hold That Tiger" as the band plays it slowly four times as it turns to salute every side of the stadium. The band then transitions into the more up-tempo "Touchdown for LSU," the 1935 Carazo-Long composition. Swor's arrangement debuted in 1964.

Over the years, the band has won numerous national awards and has played in parades all over the world, including a St. Patrick's Day Parade in Dublin, Ireland, in March 2014, before a crowd of 500,000. The Golden Girls also performed in Hong Kong in 2011 as part of the Chinese New Year celebration.

LSU band members must audition every year to win or retain a spot. They practice 90 minutes four days per week and for up to two hours before Saturday night home games. About 20 to 24 percent of music majors comprise the band. The band is the equivalent of a class, and students receive course credit.

On LSU home game days, the band marches from its band hall to Tiger Stadium, taking one last turn at Victory Hill before it marches down to play the pregame show. LSU plays a new halftime show for every home game, and all the shows are designed by a student group of bandleaders.

Weekly meetings to brainstorm music and theme ideas start in February. The list, with some themes containing combinations of multiple ideas, is cut to 10. The committee shares the list with band members, who vote for their top picks. Then the directors decide the final shows to be performed the following fall.

The band is currently capped at 325 members for such reasons as seating availability in Tiger Stadium, costs for buses and meals on road trips, and the $1,000 stipend each student receives annually.

12 Mike the Tiger, Tiger Habitat

Through the generations, Mike the Tiger has been the enduring symbol of LSU. "I'll be talking to grown men who went to LSU, and I can't have a conversation with them without them tearing up because Mike means so much to the community," said David Baker, an LSU School of Veterinary Medicine professor who has been the personal veterinarian for and supervised the daily care of the Mikes since 1994. Baker said, "Mike reminds people of everything good they remember about LSU, and there's a lot of good to remember."

Since 1936 a succession of Bengal and Bengal-Siberian Tigers has graced the LSU campus, where, through the decades, Mike has been visited daily at his now-magnificent $3.7 million, 15,105-square-foot habitat that includes a waterfall, a stream, a huge pool, lush greenery, a live oak tree, a rocky formation with plants and trees, and a 1,000-foot night house where he sleeps.

The latest Mike is Mike VII, a Bengal-Siberian tiger donated to LSU from the Wild at Heart Wildlife Center in Okeechobee, Florida. Mike VII is the fourth Mike donated to LSU from rescue facilities. Mikes IV, V, and VI were also donated to LSU from rescue facilities because LSU doesn't support the for-profit breeding of tigers.

After Mike V died in 2007, People for the Ethical Treatment of Animals (PETA) urged LSU not to replace him with a new Mike, but then-chancellor Sean O'Keefe said the school would indeed obtain a new tiger. He noted that four of the previous five Mikes had lived to be at least 17 years old, nearly twice the normal 8- to 10-year life span of tigers in the wild. He also said that tigers were a critically endangered species in the wild, and any attempt to preserve them as a species would require some level of raising them in captivity, such as at LSU's veterinary school.

LSU's tiger habitat and Mike's care plan are licensed by the USDA. The facility, tiger, and animal-care programs are inspected annually to ensure that they comply with the Animal Welfare Act and other USDA policies and guidelines. Baker oversees the daily care, which includes two veterinary students who are his twice-daily caretakers. They make sure Mike is fed and his habitat is maintained. In the beginning, the first few Mikes didn't live in such luxury and didn't have a personal on-campus vet.

LSU was given its mascot nickname by Charles Coates Jr., the school's first football coach in 1893, who lost the only game he ever coached. It wasn't until 1934 that LSU trainer Mike Chambers, athletic director T.P. Heard, school swimming pool manager and intramural swimming coach Hickey Higginbotham, and LSU law student Ed Laborde decided to bring a real tiger to campus. By collecting 25 cents from each student, they eventually raised $750 to purchase a 200-pound one-year-old tiger named Sheik from the Little Rock Zoo. Sheik's name was changed to Mike in honor of Chambers, who spearheaded the drive for a live tiger.

Mike I arrived by train on October 21, 1936, and LSU students skipped class to welcome him. He reigned as mascot for 20 years before dying of kidney disease. Not all the Mikes have lived such sedate lives, though. There have been a couple instances of unanticipated excitement:

Mike I Gets Kidnapped: On the night before the 1950 LSU-Tulane game in New Orleans, where Mike was to appear, he and his caretaker visited Ye Old College Inn on Carrollton Avenue around 1:00 AM. Already inside were four Tulane students named Norbert James, Oscar Riess, Joe Miller, and Tex Powell, who had stopped in for a midnight snack after a few hours of coon hunting.

When they left, they noticed a trailer in the parking lot with a long cage on it. Inside was Mike I, so they thought it would be a hoot to catnap him. "We thought there would be some security, but the wheels were not locked," an 84-year-old Norbert told the *Macon Telegraph* newspaper in January 2012. "So I undid the trailer and hooked it up to Oscar's car. He didn't have a trailer hitch, so we used a chain."

They drove Mike I to the Tulane campus in Riess's 1942 Plymouth. At one point, the chain came loose and the cage kept rolling. Then a police officer stopped them, but they convinced him they were escorting the tiger from the LSU campus to Tulane's stadium.

The plan was to hold Mike I captive until halftime of the game the next day. But when John Stibbs—Tulane's dean of students—was summoned to see Mike I, who had been hidden by his kidnappers behind some barracks on campus, he told them Mike I should be taken to a safe place off campus.

James and Riess drove to Riess's house, parked the cage in the garage, and went to bed. Riess's father woke up at 2:00 AM and asked his son to go outside and see why the dogs were barking. "Because there is a tiger in the garage," his son explained.

"Have you been drinking?" asked his dad before the entire Riess family rushed out of bed to see the tiger.

Several hours later, the police showed up at Riess's house and took in James and Riess for questioning. They weren't arrested and went to eat breakfast before the game, which ended in a 14–14 tie.

Mike IV Takes a Short Campus Stroll: In the early morning hours before LSU's 1981 game at Tulane, someone cut the locks of Mike IV's habitat, which was and still is located in front of the Pete Maravich Assembly Center next to the Bernie Moore Track Stadium.

Legend has it Mike IV went through the track stadium and was wandering around on Nicholson Drive when a partying passerby saw the big cat and immediately went to campus security. "I know I've been drinking," he told the LSU police, "but I just saw Mike the Tiger walking around in the track stadium." The police had a good laugh while going around the corner to check it out. But they stopped dead in their tracks when they saw Mike's midnight stroll.

The late Everett Besch, the founding dean of LSU's School of Veterinary Medicine, recalled the incident. "The campus police called about 2:00 in the morning," Besch said, "and said, 'You know that Tiger is walking down Nicholson Drive.'

"A couple of their cops got the tiger back into Bernie Moore Stadium. We called Dr. Sheldon Bivin, who was our laboratory animal veterinarian. He walked into Bernie Moore Stadium with a [tranquilizer] gun, darted that tiger, and got him back in the cage."

For years, LSU used Mike the Tiger as part of its home-field advantage. Before the LSU cheerleaders would climb on top of Mike's portable cage and he was wheeled into Tiger Stadium around the perimeter of the field, the cage was always parked by the visiting team's entrance to the field. "We'd sit in our locker room at Tiger Stadium and hear that tiger roar over the loudspeaker, because the LSU cheerleaders would beat on his cage," said Jan

Gwin, an offensive lineman at Mississippi State in the late 1960s. "Then they'd park the cage next to where the visiting team ran out, and the tiger would still be growling."

Starting with Mike VII, Baker began cutting out the Tiger Stadium pregame visits to preserve Mike's mental well-being. "Imagine having a large party in your backyard with lots of people and music," Baker said. "You won't see your cat for a week. That was Mike on the field."

13 Alex Box Stadium

Alex Box Stadium, the home of the six-time College World Series champions LSU, has lived two remarkable lives linked by one unforgettable war hero. The original Alex Box Stadium—then called the LSU Diamond—was a 2,500-seat facility, a concrete-and-steel grandstand completed in 1938. Its funding came from the Works Progress Administration, a federally sponsored New Deal agency that carried out public works projects, including the construction of public athletic facilities.

In its first two years, the LSU Diamond was the site of spring training for baseball's New York Giants. Such legendary figures as Mel Ott, Carl Hubbell, Bill Terry and Dick Bartell trained there.

It wasn't until May 1943 that the LSU Board of Supervisors voted unanimously to rename the stadium in honor of former Tigers football and baseball player Alex Box, who was a U.S. Army tank commander killed in action in February 1943, at the age of 22. The *Daily Reveille*, LSU's student newspaper, applauded the naming of the stadium. An editorial read, "For the first time in the school's history, the service and memory of the military hero came to be esteemed so highly that a structure on the campus was named in his honor."

During the 1991 season, the Box family made a special presentation of Alex's personal memorabilia to LSU. It is now permanently housed in a specially constructed glass case in the Wally Pontiff Jr. Baseball Hall of Fame inside the new Alex Box Stadium.

The original Alex Box Stadium stood for 70 years, through 2008. After Skip Bertman took over as LSU's coach in 1984 and built LSU into a national powerhouse, Alex Box expanded with 4,522 bleacher seats down both foul lines. By 1991, when Bertman won his first of five national titles, LSU had climbed to No. 5 in college baseball attendance. In 1996 LSU started its remarkable run of 25 straight years as college baseball's attendance leader.

The largest actual attendance figure in the original Alex Box Stadium was 8,173, for the NCAA Super Regional Championship Game against UC Irvine on June 9, 2008, the final game in stadium history. LSU won 21–7 to advance to the College World Series.

Bertman retired as LSU's coach at the end of the 2001 season, became the school's athletic director, and made it one of his goals to build one of the best college baseball stadiums in the nation. On February 20, 2009, LSU beat Villanova 12–3 in the first game in the new Alex Box Stadium, a gleaming 10,326-seat structure with open concourses, great sightlines, and suites.

Since then, the Box has been outfitted with even more bells and whistles, in 2019 adding the largest video board in college baseball and in 2020 adding an auxiliary scoreboard in right field as well as extending safety netting down the line to the beginning of the outfield grass.

In May 2019 the Marucci Performance Center, which is connected to the hitting facility behind the right-field wall of the stadium, was dedicated. It is a 4,300-square-foot structure that features a 3,500-square-foot weight room and has a locker room that

Major League Baseball players who attended LSU can use if they care to work out in Baton Rouge in the off-season.

Yet it's the fans who have created an atmosphere that opposing teams want to experience. Florida State coach Mike Martin, who ended his 45-year career in 2019 with one last trip to the College World Series, punched his CWS ticket by beating LSU in the Super Regionals in Alex Box Stadium. He was absolutely dazzled. "It's just the way that we were treated when we got off the bus," said Martin, who was greeted by LSU fans seeking autographs. "It was like you were coming into an environment in which people really understand we're dealing with young men and treat everybody with respect."

He continued, "Those people were as classy and represented their families and this great university of LSU to the utmost degree. And I just couldn't stop telling people the way I felt. Because that shows they get it. . . . Alex Box Stadium is as good as it gets. They have the loudest fans I have ever played in front of in 45 years of coaching baseball."

Which is what Bertman hoped for. His contributions to the program and the facilities have never been forgotten. In May 2013, during a pregame ceremony that also celebrated the 20th anniversary of Bertman's 1993 national championship team, the field at Alex Box was officially dedicated as Skip Bertman Field. Then, in September 2019, a statue of Bertman was unveiled in front of the stadium. "If you really want to see a monument to a coach, to somebody who has built a program, just look behind you," LSU president F. King Alexander said. "The best college baseball facility in the United States [with] 13,000 [fans per] game. Coach, that is all you. That is what you created at this university. That is a tribute few will ever have."

Bertman said he was "truly humbled." "This statue represents a lot of people," he said.

14 2007 Championship

According to Les Miles, his 2007 LSU football team was perfect. "I look at a team that hasn't lost a game in regulation," Miles most famously said at the end of that regular season. His team's only two losses came in triple overtime.

His Tigers, at that point 10–2 and ranked No. 7 in the BCS, entered the 2007 SEC Championship Game needing several results to happen in order to advance to the national title game. The odds were such that even the usually optimistic Miles proclaimed in the same news conference that he wouldn't "bet [his] house" on it.

First, LSU—its starting QB, Matt Flynn, sidelined with injury—had to beat 9–3 Tennessee with its backup quarterback (they did). Second, the Tigers needed No. 2 West Virginia, 28.5-point favorites, to lose at home to Pitt (they did). Then they needed No. 1 Missouri to lose to Oklahoma in the Big 12 championship (they did). Finally, in the final BCS rankings, LSU needed to be ahead of two other 11–2 Power 5 conference champions, Oklahoma and Virginia Tech (they were).

Boosted by their "undefeated in regulation" campaign, Miles and the Tigers surged to No. 2 in the BCS poll and then whipped Ohio State in New Orleans to win it all—champions of what is widely regarded as the craziest season in the modern history of college football. But 2007's wackiness extended well past that final week. You might know 2007 by its nicknames—Year of the Upset and Curse of No. 2. Unranked teams that year beat top 5–ranked teams an AP poll–record 13 times, and teams ranked No. 2 lost seven times in the final nine weeks of the regular season, a whopping six of those to unranked foes. LSU was involved in two of those games, losing in triple overtime while ranked No. 1 both times: first at Kentucky and then at home against Arkansas in the final regular-season game.

In fact, in 2007 LSU was the first two-loss team to win the AP title since 1960 and the only championship squad to do it having lost both games in overtime. Chalk at least some of it up to that "undefeated in regulation" PR campaign the school used late that season. As a way to influence the human voters who factored into the BCS formula, the university's athletic department started the public movement, which was hatched from the brain of Miles's wife, Kathy. "You know, Les, you're undefeated in regulation," Kathy told her husband one night. The coach shared the message with the school's longtime sports information director, Michael Bonnette, and off went the campaign. From emails to poll voters and media to Miles's comments in press availabilities, the "undefeated in regulation" campaign marched on. "We sold it," Bonnette said in an interview in 2008 with Yahoo! Sports. "We did the best we could to get it out there."

On the field, meanwhile, the Tigers leaned on an efficient quarterback in Flynn; a hard-running fullback in Jacob Hester; some timely, electric plays from receiver / track star Trindon Holliday; and an opportunistic defense led by safety Craig Steltz and his six interceptions. Don't forget about their gambling coach either.

The 2007 season went a long way in developing Miles's reputation as an unpredictable and downright confounding in-game decision maker. Of course, those decisions all worked out in 2007, but that didn't make them any less bizarre. In wins over Auburn, Florida, and South Carolina, the Mad Hatter did his thing.

Down by one point and in field goal range in the closing seconds against Auburn, Flynn inexplicably threw to the end zone, finding receiver Demetrius Byrd for a game-winning touchdown with one second on the clock, a somewhat maddening play that could have ended with an LSU loss in a number of ways: interception, clock expiration, or sack.

Earlier in the season against Florida, the Tigers came back from two separate 10-point deficits, converting a whopping five fourth-down attempts, two of them for touchdowns and two of them on a game-winning 15-play, 60-yard touchdown march. The boldest from Miles came when he passed on what would have been a game-tying 24-yard field goal in the final two minutes, instead handing off to Hester on fourth-and-1 from the Florida 7, a play that eventually resulted in the winning touchdown—a Hester run on third-and-goal.

In a game against South Carolina that year, Miles called a fake field goal on fourth-and-4 with his team up 14–7. Flynn, the snapper, flipped the ball blindly over his shoulder to kicker Colt David, who raced 15 yards for a touchdown.

"It was something Les felt comfortable with because Matt Flynn was honestly automatic with it," Hester explained later in a story in the *Daily Reveille*. "We had a unique situation where Colt David could really run pretty fast. We had an athletic kicker and a quarterback holder that was first-rate doing the flip."

Off the field, 2007 featured one of the most bizarre impromptu news conferences ever. Miles called the media gathered before the SEC Championship Game to refute an ESPN report that he planned to leave for Michigan, describing his team as "damn strong" and ending the event by smirking into cameras and saying, "Have a great day."

Hours later, LSU beat Tennessee 21–14, getting the winning points via a fourth-quarter interception cornerback Jonathan Zenon returned for a touchdown. The other shoes dropped that day—Pitt stunned the Mountaineers 13–9 and Oklahoma waxed Missouri 38–17—and then the BCS crunched its numbers and spit out No. 1 Ohio State vs. No. 2 LSU, the ending of the wildest season college football's maybe ever seen.

15 Geaux to Hell, Ole Miss

On the Friday before LSU and Ole Miss played their football game each year, the *Daily Reveille*, the on-campus LSU student newspaper, used to print at the top of its front page five words in jumbo type: GEAUX TO HELL, OLE MISS. That short-lived tradition has since stopped, but the sizzling rivalry between the two Southeastern Conference Western Division programs rages on, rooted in historic moments, heated battles, and legendary figures.

The two teams have played every year since 1945 and have met a total of 107 times as of 2019. Ingrained in this annual showdown are their meetings as SEC powers in the 1950s and 1960s, where they slugged it out in typically defensive battles with conference and national title implications on the line.

Starting in 1958, the Rebels and Tigers met five times in a five-year stretch while both ranked inside the top 6. They accounted for five SEC championships in an eight-year span beginning in 1954. "The rivalry was crazy in those days," said Baton Rouge radio personality Jim Engster, an LSU freshman in 1977 and a lifelong Tigers fan. "The intensity of those rivalries exceeded the LSU-Alabama stuff of a few years ago by a good margin."

With LSU's Paul Dietzel and Ole Miss's Johnny Vaught roaming the sidelines—the two met eight times—championships were normally at stake in these big bouts. The top-ranked Tigers toppled No. 6 Ole Miss 14–0 on the way to winning the 1958 national championship. The Rebels and Tigers tied 6–6 in 1960, the only blemish on Ole Miss's season that year and something that likely stopped most wire services from crowning Ole Miss outright champions. The Rebels claim the 1960 national title via the Football Writers Association of America.

"There was a time when the Ole Miss game meant more than any other to the LSU people," Bud Johnson, former LSU sports information director, said in an ESPN story published in 2014. "You could get more [money for] the LSU–Ole Miss ticket than any other if you were in that business."

The rivalry is one between two of the most revered college football fan bases for their tailgating and partying ways. LSU's campus is sprinkled with beer kegs, boiling gumbo pots, massive white tents, and colorful recreational vehicles. Ole Miss's famous Grove is a more luxurious setting on a lush, tree-lined area, scattered about with liquor-stocked bars and smoking barbecue grills. The hate between them runs deep on and off the field. Who's got the better team? Who's got the better party? No matter the game, "Go to hell, LSU!" is still shouted during the anthem at Ole Miss.

There's a lengthy list of heroic moments in notable games during this series. Billy Cannon's Halloween Run is first among them. Cannon's 89-yard punt return for a touchdown served as the only touchdown in LSU's 7–3 victory over the Rebels and all but secured him the Heisman Trophy. (The Rebels got sweet revenge two months later, pounding the Tigers 21–0 in the Sugar Bowl.) In 1964 Doug Moreau caught a two-point conversion for a victory. Then there's the controversial 1972 game dubbed When Time Stood Still. The Tigers and quarterback Bert Jones ran two plays in the final four seconds, scoring the game-winning touchdown as time expired.

The border war died off somewhat during Ole Miss's post-Vaught slump in the 1970s and '80s, and then LSU's post-McClendon slide in the 1990s. It returned with a vengeance in 2003, one of the more notable affairs in this yearly matchup. With the SEC West championship on the line, Nick Saban and his Tigers beat Ole Miss 17–14 in Oxford in a No. 3 vs. No. 15 clash that unfolded in front of the most fans ever to see a college football game in the state of Mississippi.

Then there was the Spike Game in 2009, when time ran out on LSU and coach Les Miles as he mystifyingly signaled for his quarterback to spike the ball with one second left deep in Ole Miss territory. And there was the 2014 affair during which the Tigers, 6–2, knocked off No. 3 undefeated Ole Miss, a result that spawned the first field storming at Tiger Stadium in more than a decade.

"I remember the first time I played against LSU in 1968," Archie Manning said in a story published in 2014 at Nola.com. "The Monday before the game, I hopped in [Ole Miss] coach [Johnny] Vaught's El Camino to ride over to the football office for our quarterbacks meeting. He looks at me and says, 'Archie, this is it. Tiger Stadium. Saturday night. Ole Miss–LSU. This is what college football is all about.'"

The rivalry's magic turned into a trophy in 2008, when the student body from both schools elected to designate the yearly bout as the Magnolia Bowl. The trophy is a giant portrayal of a magnolia—the state flower of both Louisiana and Mississippi—and sits atop a wooden base. It resides with the winning team.

The Tigers lead the all-time series 61–41–2, but the Rebels had the upper hand in the Vaught days. He was 15–8–3 against LSU during a stretch when the "Go to hell, Ole Miss" and "Go to hell, LSU" chants first began. Legend has it that before the 1959 clash with Ole Miss, Dietzel—a military man who served during World War II—used a plane to litter the LSU campus with flyers that said "Got to hell, LSU" as a way to motivate fans, students, and players.

The story remains the stuff of legend. "They say he sent down leaflets. I don't recall that," said Smiley Anders, a columnist for the *Advocate* and a student at LSU from 1955 to 1959. He added, "But I remember a banner on the assembly center that read, Go to hell, Ole Miss."

16 Bob Pettit

This is how the athletic career of former LSU forward Bob Pettit—one of the 50 greatest players in NBA history and a Naismith Memorial Basketball Hall of Famer—started in the late 1940s at Baton Rouge High School.

Ninth-grade football: lasted one day after a running back ran 65 yards for a touchdown through the hole at right tackle that Pettit was supposedly defending.

Ninth-grade basketball: saw action in only three games, scored zero points.

Ninth-grade baseball: first player cut from the squad.

Then, to boost his son's sagging confidence, Pettit's father erected a basketball goal in the backyard of the family home. "My parents gave me encouragement, kept telling me not to quit, to keep working," Pettit said. So he shot for hours and hours, day and night.

He sprouted from 5'10" at age 14 to 6'7" when he led Baton Rouge High School to the state championship in 1950, which Pettit always has called "one of the two greatest moments in [his] basketball career."

Pettit's recruitment process by LSU coach Harry Rabenhorst was to the point. "He took me to dinner at the old Bob and Jake's and said, 'Bob, we've got a scholarship if you want it,'" Pettit said. "I said, 'I do want it, Coach.' He said, 'Okay.' That was it."

At LSU, after playing on the freshman team (because freshmen weren't eligible to play on the varsity squad), the 6'8" Pettit averaged 27.4 points during his three-year varsity career. "As a young player in college, Bob reminded me of a wobbly colt, always getting bumped around and knocked down," former LSU teammate

Benny McArdle once said. "But he got on a good weight program and he was stronger by his junior year."

As a junior in 1952–53, Pettit averaged 24.9 points and 12.7 rebounds as the Tigers went 22–3, advancing to their first-ever Final Four. A year later, as a senior in 1953–54, he averaged 31.4 points and 17.3 rebounds, boosting the 20–5 Tigers to their second straight SEC championship. LSU immediately retired his No. 50 number, the first in school history.

Pettit said college teammates such as Joe Dean, who later became LSU's athletic director, helped him immensely. "When I was a sophomore," Pettit said, "Joe looked at me through those horn-rimmed glasses and said, 'Boy, let me tell you something. When you walk out on that court, you've got to think you are the greatest thing out there. You have to believe you are the greatest. There's nobody as good as you are. You understand?' I said, 'Yessir, I understand.' From then on, the rest of my career at LSU and the NBA, I'd wake up in the morning, shave, look in that mirror, and say, 'You're the greatest. Nobody can stop you.'"

He played with that quiet swagger throughout his stellar pro career. After he was picked overall No. 2 in the 1954 draft by the Milwaukee Hawks, who moved to St. Louis after his first season, Pettit was named first-team All-NBA 10 times in his 11-year pro career and won an NBA title in 1958.

One of the first things Hawks coach Red Holzman did was move Pettit from center to forward. He felt Pettit's 205 pounds put him at a disadvantage in the pivot but gave him an advantage on the wing, where he crashed the boards as a relentless offensive rebounder. "Pettit knew what he could do and what he couldn't do," said Naismith Memorial Basketball Hall of Fame guard Oscar "Big O" Robertson. "And what he could do, he could do expertly."

Pettit would often jump-start his games with put-backs off missed shots and go from there. "Offensive rebounds accounted for 8 to 10 of my points, as well as 8 to 10 free throws [30 percent of

Pettit's 20,080 career points were free throws]," he said. "I'd be off and running when my jump shots fell."

Injuries finally caught up with Pettit. In his final season in the NBA in 1964–65, he sustained a torn abdomen, a torn knee ligament, and four broken bones in his back. He didn't have to be convinced to retire at the age of 32, especially when he had a job offer from a Baton Rouge bank where he had worked in the off-season.

When it was over, the kid who was a walking disaster as a ninth-grade athlete had left one of the greatest legacies in NBA history. Not only was Pettit a two-time league MVP and four-time All-Star Game MVP, he was also the first NBA player to eclipse the 20,000-point career mark (20,880 for a 26.4 average). He also remains one of three players ever to average more than 20 points and 20 rebounds in a season (Wilt Chamberlain and Jerry Lucas are the others), as he was good for 27.9 points and 20.1 rebounds in 1960–61. "I'm very comfortable with the career I had. I maximized all my abilities and I played as hard as I could every night," Pettit said. "I've had as much enjoyment after basketball as I had playing, and I don't think a lot of guys can say that."

In February 2016, 62 years after his jersey retirement, LSU erected a statue of Pettit. After thanking sculptor Brian Hanlon—"I asked him to give me hair and muscles, and Brian has done that," Pettit said—he put the honor in perspective. "I've found in my life that when you start something, you set a goal for yourself," Pettit said. "When you reach that goal, you ratchet up that goal to another level, and when you reach that, you ratchet it up again.

"But when you start down here, you never realize where you were going. My ambition in high school after I got cut as a sophomore was to win a letter by the time I was a senior. That's all I wanted. Here I am, all these years later, next to [the statue of] Shaquille O'Neal. I never dreamed this. I've had quite a few honors over the years, but nothing compares to this."

17 Night Games: An LSU Tradition

It doesn't matter if kickoff starts after sunset in Tiger Stadium or before sunset. When the sun does set and public address announcer Dan Borne says, "Ladies and gentlemen, the sun has found its home in the western sky. It is *now Saturday night* in Death Valley!" it is on. It's like someone reached over and jacked the volume up to jet engine level for the rest of the night. Tiger Stadium night games are heaven for the Tigers and hell for opponents.

Maybe it's because the hard-partying LSU fans have a complete day or more to get fully prepared to scream their lungs out for three or more hours, 100,000-plus fans strong, unleashing a wall of sound that can be impossible for the opposition to handle, particularly regarding offensive signals.

Before playing in Tiger Stadium night games, opposing coaches always say they've piped in loud crowd noise for their team's practices during the week of preparation for a trip to Baton Rouge. But the coaches can't simulate LSU fans beating on the sides of an opposing team bus as it pulls next to its dressing room shortly before sunset, with little kids, middle-aged dads, and fired-up grandmas welcoming the visitors by screaming "Tiger Bait! Tiger Bait! Tiger Bait!" "Baton Rouge happens to be the worst place in the world for a visiting team," legendary Alabama coach Bear Bryant once said. "It's like being inside a drum."

That's one of the tamer observations about a stadium where night games were first played in 1931. LSU athletic director Skipper Heard began scheduling home games at night because he wanted to avoid the Louisiana heat and humidity of day games. Also, since Tulane and Loyola also played day home games in New Orleans, Heard wanted the night slot so more fans could see the Tigers play.

It was a strategic move that suddenly accelerated in the mid-1950s when Jim Corbett became LSU's athletic director. He was the first to market Tiger Stadium Saturday nights as a true happening, and LSU players, coaches, and fans bought into his vision. Through the 2019 season, LSU has played 76.7 percent of its home games (460 of 600) at night and has won 75.1 percent (339–108–13) of those games after dark.

Naturally, Tiger Stadium night games have produced plenty of testimonies through the years, such as:

- "Dracula and LSU football are at their best after the sun goes down."—Beano Cook, ESPN
- "From Bourbon Street to Baton Rouge, the freaks come out at night in Louisiana. And nowhere are they more raucous and unnerving than at Tiger Stadium"—Pat Forde, Yahoo! Sports
- "When it gets rocking at night, it's a different animal. I've played there in the daytime as well, and it's just a different animal at nighttime."—1997 Florida quarterback Doug Johnson
- "When LSU plays on Saturday night and the band takes the field and plays the first four notes of 'Hold That Tiger,' it will make the hair stand up on a dead man's chest."—Ed Hinton, *Atlanta Journal-Constitution*
- "When they announce that it's Saturday night in Death Valley, when the band plays, when that crowd stands and cheers for the Tigers, there is no place like it in America."—Former LSU head coach Les Miles
- "For three hours on Saturday night, I don't know that there has ever been an atmosphere in sports that I've been a part of that was as memorable to me. . . . I was told it was going to be awesome. It was better than I was told it was. . . . There is nothing I would put ahead of that, that I've *ever* seen in any sport. When you're there, you don't want to miss anything."—Scott Van Pelt, ESPN Radio, on the 2012 LSU-Alabama game

- "It was so loud I could barely read the signals. My eyes were vibrating."—South Carolina receiver Bruce Ellington
- "LSU's Tiger Stadium at night is the toughest place on the planet to play. You've heard it. I've heard it. The person in the cubicle next to you has heard it. It's pointless to argue against it: give fans in Baton Rouge a full day to prepare, and they'll bring in the noise and the funk. LSU players and coaches will attest to it. So will opponents. Shoot, even the seismograph in the university's Howe-Russell Geoscience Complex proves it. No other stadium, no other crowd, can put that on a résumé."—Ken Bradley, the *Sporting News*
- "Tiger Stadium is the best place in the world to watch a sporting event. I'm not sure what it was like to walk into the Colosseum, but I bet it was something like this."—Wright Thompson, *ESPN the Magazine*
- "There's no place like Tiger Stadium. I swear it shakes. How could you not want to play football for a school like this?"—Former LSU cornerback Patrick Peterson

18 Halloween Run

"A white-shirted ghost wearing jersey No. 20." That's how Baton Rouge sports editor Dan Hardesty described Billy Cannon during the most famous 17 seconds in LSU history. Cannon's 89-yard punt return against Ole Miss on Halloween night in 1959 is as integral to the program as the colors purple and gold, as storied as Tiger Stadium itself, as noteworthy as that national championship the year before.

It is *the* play in LSU football history. All others—the Bluegrass Miracle, the Earthquake Game touchdown pass, the Jacob Hester fourth downs against Florida—kneel at its feet. Nothing tops Cannon's Halloween Run, as the school's media guide describes it. "I still get goose bumps watching it, and I *played* in the doggone game," LSU All-SEC tackle Lynn LeBlanc said in a story by Marty Mulé published on LSUSports.net in 2009.

Cannon's tackle-breaking punt return—at least seven Rebels got a hand on him—served as LSU's only touchdown that night, October 31, 1959. It was enough, with a final goal-line stand from the Tigers' defense in the waning seconds, to lift LSU to a 7–3 victory in a clash of football powerhouses. No higher-ranked teams—LSU No. 1, Ole Miss No. 3—ever met in Tiger Stadium before or after (as of 2019). These were two football juggernauts then, the cream of the crop in the Southeastern Conference. The schools claimed five SEC titles during an eight-year stretch that began in 1954.

They entered Tiger Stadium on that hot, humid, foggy night with identical 6–0 records and indestructible defenses. A combined 13 points had been scored on them in their previous six games. The squads had pitched nine shutouts in a cumulative 12 contests.

Cannon's performance on such a grand stage helped him secure the 1959 Heisman Trophy. He was the game's leading rusher (48 yards on 12 carries, a 4.0 average), returned three punts for 102 yards, punted four times for a 42-yard average, and was in on a half dozen tackles. But it wasn't all good. In fact, it was Cannon's lost fumble in the first quarter that resulted in Ole Miss's only points.

He more than made up for it. With just more than 10 minutes left in the game, Ole Miss punter and quarterback Jake Gibbs boomed a 47-yard punt to a waiting Cannon, standing just inside his 10-yard line. He defied one of LSU coach Paul Dietzel's cardinal rules: don't field a punt inside the 15. "If I get a chance on this one, I'm going to try to take it back,'" Cannon said he told himself before the ball arrived.

"I was trying to kick out of bounds, expecting the ball to come down and roll out. Instead it took a high bounce—right to Billy," Gibbs said in Mulé's piece from 2009.

Cannon's goal was to reach the wide side of the field, to his left, but an Ole Miss defender blocked that path. He faked a dash to his left and went back inside to his right at the 19-yard line. The fake was enough to elude the defender, but it also left him just a few feet from the sideline. "Now I'm trapped inside," Cannon said, retelling the story in 2015 at a banquet in Baton Rouge videotaped by *Tiger Rag* magazine. "It ends up you're running to colors—they're blue and red and I'm running toward those whites."

He received a block as he crossed the 20, opening a lane that quickly closed. Three Rebels descended on him around the 25, almost encasing him in their arms. That's when he got the most crucial block of the return. "Some guy got his hand on me and I went down to one hand on the ground," Cannon recalled. "Emile Fournet comes in and takes him and two others right off my butt. I come out of that running as fast as I could."

He dragged one would-be tackler about three yards, bursting out of the pile of bodies before sidestepping another defender. It left one man to beat: the punter. "Jake thinks I'm going back to the wide side of the field. I gave him . . . I thought it was a great fake. On the film, it looks like my head leaned over and came back," Cannon said. "I went to the sideline and Jake missed the tackle. Only tackle in four years at Ole Miss he missed. Only one he ever attempted."

Cannon dashed to the end zone to a crescendo from the more than 67,000 in Tiger Stadium. "I round into the end zone," he said. "I guess I should have had some dance to do or something, but I hand the ball to the referee, hands on my knees, trying to breathe. And here come my teammates. I think they're going to beat me to death."

Minutes later, Cannon breathed from an oxygen tank on the sideline, a moment caught on camera. The photograph is now an iconic moment in LSU football history—Cannon in his dirtied white jersey, completely exhausted and seated on a bench, eyes closed and a team staff member affixing an oxygen mask around his nose and mouth.

But Cannon's night was not done. He played safety on LSU's second-team defense. Cannon watched from the sideline as Ole Miss's offense marched down the field against the Tigers' first-string unit, nicknamed the Chinese Bandits. Sophomore Doug Elmore—a new quarterback that Rebels coach John Vaught employed—and his fresh legs moved Ole Miss inside the 20 before Dietzel inserted Cannon and the second string. The Rebels pressed inside the 5 and called three consecutive fullback dives. None found the end zone.

At this point, so close to the goal line, Cannon crept from his safety position to play middle linebacker. "It's fourth down," Cannon recalled. "I go, you know, 'They're not going to go over the top again. Coach Vaught wouldn't. He's going to bootleg.' But what if I go to the bootleg and [the fullback] falls over the top? I'm a goat. I had to wait to make sure [the fullback] didn't get the ball."

Cannon continued, "[Elmore] rolled out. Warren Rabb comes up to make as beautiful stop as anybody. I'm two steps back and I jump over top of the pile. We pushed him back. I got all the credit for it. Warren made the stop."

That wasn't the end of LSU–Ole Miss in 1959. They met about two months later in the Sugar Bowl, with LSU ranked No. 3 and Ole Miss ranked No. 2. The Rebels smothered the Tigers 21–0 and finished second nationally behind Syracuse, the AP's national champion.

19 The Mad Hatter

He eats grass and acts in movies. He botches the English language and ruins syntax. He scales high-rises and kisses pigs. He's a hat-wearing, odd-clapping man who left Baton Rouge with a better winning percentage than any LSU coach in modern history. He's Les Miles.

"He did an awful lot, and he did it with a personality that's quirky, and I mean that in a nice way," said Skip Bertman, the former LSU athletic director and baseball coach who hired Miles after the 2004 season. "He wasn't just like any coach. His legacy is he came in and he gave us what we asked for."

What was that? Victories and championships. During his near-12-year tenure as LSU's head coach, Miles extended one of college football's dynasties, the golden years of LSU football that spanned three coaches—Nick Saban, Miles, and Ed Orgeron. From 2005 to 2016, Miles amassed a 112–32 record, winning a national championship (2007), playing for another (2011), and claiming two SEC titles (2007 and 2011). His winning percentage (.767) is tops among LSU coaches since the school joined the Southeastern Conference in 1933. He went 63–30 in SEC games, a mark of .677, and led the Tigers to a bowl game in each of his first 11 seasons, going 7–4 in those contests. From 2006 to 2016, he produced more NFL Draft selections (69) than any other SEC team, including 13 first-rounders.

A former Michigan offensive lineman under Bo Schembechler, Miles built his teams on a foundation of toughness and physicality. His squads usually leaned heavily on a hard-hitting defense and a controlled, traditional offense that battered an opponent black and blue. At times, his Tigers won games both because of and despite his mystifying late-game decisions, the outcomes often unfurling only after wild, heart-pounding events in the final seconds.

Miles didn't necessarily take his conservative offensive approach to other areas of football. He was known for elaborate fake field goals, many of them including lateral passes, and he didn't shy away from the occasional fourth-down attempt, notably attempting five fourth downs—converting them all—in an eventual win over Florida in 2007.

He even developed a nickname, the Mad Hatter, for his on-field approach and the peculiar way in which he wore his hat—high atop his head. He embraced his quirky nature—a loveable character who endeared himself to college football fans across the nation with on-field mannerisms and off-field quotes. He admitted to eating stadium grass after television cameras caught him chewing on the green stuff during one game. He once scaled a downtown Baton Rouge building, rappelling from its side while smiling for a camera. At a student-led event each year on campus, Miles smooched a live pig.

His news conferences were an event to behold—oftentimes altogether confusing, with bizarre twists and turns and his baffling vernacular as a backdrop. Miles once called an impromptu media gathering before the 2007 SEC Championship Game to refute an ESPN report that he planned to leave for Michigan, describing his team as "damn strong" and ending the event by smirking into cameras and saying, "Have a great day." He used multiple news conferences to express his affection for certain holidays, including Columbus Day, telling media members, "All those of you that know Italians and like Italians or the people that might venture onto a ship and travel to explore and find new lands, this is your day." He then ended the rant, "So it's not St. Patty's Day. That's a different day entirely."

Miles once said his team played "like a son of a bitch," and after one rainy home game, he described the precipitation as a "very stiff dew" because, as the saying goes, it doesn't rain in Tiger Stadium.

In 2012 he said a recruit who decommitted from LSU's signing class didn't have "the chest" to play for the Tigers, and he once characterized his running ability as being in the "upper quadrant of speed."

"We'd joke with each other that you'd better have your Les Miles dictionary [for a team meeting]," former LSU defensive back Patrick Peterson told ESPN in a 2013 story. "He'd make up these mysterious words, and we'd all lean over and say, 'What in the world did coach just say? Is that even a word?'"

After a 2012 victory over South Carolina in Tiger Stadium, Miles coined a phrase many use to describe Tiger Stadium to this day. He said it is a place "where opponents' dreams come to die." Over Miles's first eight seasons at LSU, his teams were sensational in Saturday night home games, losing only 2 out of 43.

"There was never a dull moment with Les," Miles's lifelong friend John Wangler said of the coach. "He's always had that goofy sense of humor about him, and he's not afraid to let his hair down and enjoy life. You can see that in the way his teams play. They play extremely hard for him."

Miles's old-school mentality and archaic offense, while in the end his undoing, led LSU to key victories. In 2014 his Tigers knocked off No. 3, undefeated Ole Miss 10–7, a slobber-knocker of a game in which LSU's game-winning 95-yard touchdown drive in the fourth quarter spanned 13 plays—12 of them runs. In 2007 LSU beat Florida 28–24 in a top 10 showdown at Tiger Stadium in which the Tigers scored the game-winning touchdown on a fourth-quarter drive that stretched 60 yards on 15 plays—13 of them runs.

In the end, his stubbornness to evolve his offense into a more spread-centric scheme led to poor performances and mounting losses. He survived a coup attempt to oust him in 2015 before the school fired him four games into his 12th season in 2016. Ranked No. 5 in the preseason, his 2016 LSU team started 2–2 with dreadful offensive showings in losses to Wisconsin and Auburn. At the time of his dismissal, Miles's teams had declined. He was 12–10 in his last 22 games as coach against Power 5 teams and 4–5 overall in his last 9.

After promises of a nearly $9 million contract buyout, the school later settled with Miles for a total of $4 million, and he didn't coach for two years until his hiring at Kansas in November 2018.

While out, Miles dabbled in acting on the big screen, an unusual move for any football coach—if his name wasn't Les Miles. A huge movie buff who has befriended Tom Cruise, Miles has appeared in at least four films, most notably playing a NASA engineer in the 2019 drama *The Challenger Disaster*. "I don't know that anybody ever doesn't dream at one point in time, 'I'm going to be in a movie,'" Miles said in a 2016 interview with the *Advocate*. "I don't know how you don't think that way. As a child, I wanted to be the president of the United States, wanted to be a head football coach, and wanted to be an actor in a movie. We only get one go-around at this thing called life. There's no do-overs."

20 Buck Fama

Bear Bryant coached his very first game at Alabama against a team whose fan base he would eventually cause great anguish. In Game 1 of the Bryant era in Tuscaloosa, halfback Billy Cannon and LSU cruised to a 13–3 win over the Tide on September 27, 1958, in Mobile's Ladd Memorial Stadium.

Bryant wouldn't lose to the Tigers again for another 10 years (five games), as the Alabama coach began his incredible dominance over his SEC rival from Louisiana. After that first game, the Tide went 16–2–1 against LSU over Bryant's tenure. Bama went unde-feated in Tiger Stadium from 1970 to 1999, a span of 15 games in which the Tide registered 14 victories and a tie. "Bear Bryant seemed to own the Tigers and was not the least bit intimidated by Tiger Stadium," a 2017 story on TheSportsHistorian.com read. "He had a pre-game ritual that would enrage Tiger fans and calm his players."

And thus began LSU's deep-seated vitriol for Alabama, the program that for so many years prevented the Tigers from bigger postseason prizes. Through the 2019 season, the Tide holds a 53–26–5 edge in the series, one of the more lopsided of any of LSU's regular opponents.

The title of this chapter—"Buck Fama," a slogan printed on LSU-carried signs and LSU-worn shirts—is a vulgar example of the hate the LSU fan base has for the Crimson Tide. In fact, a 2009 poll of SEC fans found that more than 60 percent of them picked the Tide as their most bitter rival.

The immediate post-Bryant days of the rivalry were one-sided too. Bama won 9 of 11 games starting in 1989. That stretch ended with a 2000 loss in Baton Rouge to a coach who is a central figure in the latest chapter of this series: Nick Saban. Saban helped shift the tide in his five years as LSU's coach, from 2000 to 2004, going 4–1 against Bama. He led the Tigers in 2003 when they claimed a national championship and began a five-game winning streak against the Tide. He ended the streak too—as Alabama's coach in 2008.

Saban's role in the latest chapter of this rivalry cannot be under-stated. He revived Bryant's sleeping giant, returned the Crimson Tide to its stranglehold position in this series, and replaced Bryant in the crosshairs of the LSU fan base's hate. Saban's teams won seven straight in the series, starting with a victory in the 2011 BCS National Championship Game in, of all places, New Orleans.

He plucked some of the best talents in Louisiana to build his dynasty in Tuscaloosa, winning five national championships from 2009 to 2017. "Both programs have zealous fan bases," Nola.com's Jeff Duncan wrote in a column published in 2017. "Both enjoy massive eight-figure operating budgets. Both attract the bluest of blue chip recruits. And both annually dominate the NFL Draft. But Alabama has Saban. And therein lies the difference."

Saban and his replacement at LSU, Les Miles, waged some of the most intense and highly billed matchups of the entire 82-game history of the series. These were yearly must-see games between two SEC juggernauts, the winner all but guaranteed a trip to the league title game.

They were each ranked in the top 10 in meetings in 2009, 2011 (twice), 2012, and 2013. None were bigger than the pair of No. 1 vs. No. 2 duels in 2011. The regular-season bout in Tuscaloosa that season—a 9–6 LSU win in overtime—is still heralded as one of the greatest slugfests in college football history.

The Tide got revenge two months later, downing the Tigers 21–0 in the BCS National Championship Game to start that seven-game winning streak—a skid that eventually resulted in the firing of Miles in 2016. The streak is the longest since Bear Bryant directed Alabama to 11 straight in the 1970s—which, some say, resulted in the ultimate firing of LSU longtime coach Charles McClendon in 1979. McClendon was 2–14 against Alabama.

Jerry Stovall, a former LSU quarterback and McClendon's replacement as head coach, ended the streak in 1982 with a 20–10 win in Birmingham. He delivered a postgame quote that offers a window into this lopsided annual clash. "You don't understand how it feels to get hit in the mouth for 11 years," Stovall said in a *New York Times* story published after that game. "This is going to feel pretty good when it soaks in."

21 The Walk-Off

A week rarely goes by without Warren Morris hearing from an LSU fan about an event that many refer to as the single greatest moment in Tigers athletics history. "I've heard lot of stories over the years," Morris said in a story published in the *Advocate* in 2016. "It amazes me how much detail they have—where they were, what they were doing, how they celebrated."

Some were late for weddings. Others were caught in bathrooms. Many were driving, eventually pulling over their vehicles for an impromptu roadside party. At least one fell off his lawnmower. Another man stripped naked while at a South Beach pool bar in Miami, and a woman watching from the stands in Omaha literally peed herself. One man leaped so high during a watch party at a Baton Rouge bar that his head broke ceiling tiles. So many others injured themselves too. "Forty or 50 percent of the stories involve somebody jumping up and hitting their hands or head on a ceiling fan," Morris said.

Morris's two-run, two-out bottom-of-the-ninth blast sent LSU to the national championship in 1996, where they toppled Miami 9–8. As of 2020, it remains the only walk-off two-out dinger in the ninth inning of a title game in College World Series or Major League Baseball history. It is *the* shot, a screeching blast heard around the college baseball world, a smoking line drive that shot through the LSU community. "Since 1876, you got to think somebody else would have done that," former LSU coach Skip Bertman said.

The 1996 home run delivered to Bertman the third national championship of his dominant reign over the sport—five College World Series titles from 1991 to 2000. For many, it is the most memorable, eliciting some of the wildest "Where were you when . . .?" stories attached to LSU sports. Where was Morris? Racing to first base with hopes of turning his line drive to right field off relief pitcher Robbie Morrison into a double. "I wasn't thinking it was a home run," Morris said. "I knew when it came off my bat that it was hit well and low. I was running hard trying to hit second base."

He only realized the length of his shot when he saw Daniel Tomlin, LSU's first base coach, leap off the ground. Running between first and second, Morris saw Miami infielders splayed on the ground, scattered on the dirt like dropped flies. That's when he knew he'd won the College World Series.

What made Morris's homer so unfathomable wasn't only its timing or place. It came off the bat of a man who hadn't hit a home run all year and who had missed two-thirds of the season because of injury. Is it the most legendary moment in LSU sports? Plenty believe so. "The Warren Morris home run is the Jack Ruby shooting Lee Harvey Oswald of LSU sports," said Derek Ponamsky, a radio host on WNXX 104.5 FM. "Everybody remembers exactly what they were doing and where they were."

Morris's shot nearly brought down a Baton Rouge bar, images of broken barstools and shattered tables still stuck in the owner's mind two decades later. Cars on Nicholson Drive in Baton Rouge honked in celebration, some of them completely stopping in a wild scene just blocks away from Alex Box Stadium. Some weddings were missed, and others were barely made. During his ceremony, one groomsman received updates on the game from a friend sitting in the church pews. They had worked out a signaling system, a 2016 *Advocate* story noted.

Several people missed Morris's home run completely, having given up on the Tigers after Tim Lanier struck out for the second out. One man walked outside to water his grass, rushing into the house seconds later after hearing bloodcurdling screams from his wife. Fans at summer baseball games in Louisiana huddled around portable televisions and radios. Officials at one softball tournament in Bunkie completely stopped the game, pumping the radio broadcast into the stadium's speakers for all to hear.

One of the biggest parties came at Ivar's, a cozy sports dive in Baton Rouge nestled under an interstate overpass and known for its LSU watch parties. Pat Quigley, then the bar's owner, never saw a celebration like he did that Saturday, June 8, 1996, when Morris slammed Morrison's low curveball out of Omaha's Rosenblatt Stadium. Quigley restocked beer three times that day, and the bar didn't close until after 4:00 AM. (By law the legal closing time was 2:00 AM.)

That night, LSU athletic administrator Herb Vincent showed up at the bar after flying back from Omaha on athletic director Joe Dean's private plane. Vincent drove straight to Ivar's, carrying with him quite the hardware: the national championship trophy the Tigers had won hours earlier. "One of my friends, John Haefner—we called him Beef—walked in with it and held it over his head," Vincent said. "The place went crazy. They put it behind the bar the rest of the night."

Jason Williams was on the field for the shot. He stood in the on-deck circle as the team's starting shortstop and leadoff hitter. Morris batted ninth in that game. "I knew Robbie Morrison was one of the top closers in the nation that year. I was trying to get my timing down. I was trying to get ready," Williams said. "It happened so fast because it was the first pitch. Everybody rushed out of the dugout. I was bombarded by everybody. I was standing there living the moment, watching Warren run the bases and the Miami guys collapse. I had the shortest walk, but I kind of stood back and just watched the moment."

Rudy Gomez—the Hurricanes' second baseman—wasn't one of those collapsed Miami players. He slowly walked to the dugout as Morris rounded the bases. He got a perfect view of Robbie Morrison's breaking ball—a low curveball that Morris golfed into the air. "Robbie had the best breaking ball on the staff that year. It was down. I see it over and over in my head," he said. "[Catcher Jim] Gargiulo went down to his knees to block it. He got the head of the bat out and made contact."

Seconds later, it landed in the hands of Richard Dawson—the actor and game show host—who was seated in the third row of the right-field bleachers. Then a 38-year-old Omaha resident, Dawson traded the ball to Morris for another baseball Morris had autographed. Morris still has the ball, tucked away in his Alexandria, Louisiana, home. "I remember the ball inching its way over," Morris recalled. "That's what you play sports for. I wasn't really in it for personal statistics. It was to help the team win. To have that exclamation mark was special to me. I was as shocked as anybody to see the ball go across the fence."

22 Pistol Pete

It is a record that will never be broken. That's a crazy statement to make, but do you really think it's possible for anyone to average 44.2 points per game in a three-year career as did LSU's "Pistol" Pete Maravich, college basketball's all-time scoring leader? Maravich's critics argue that since his father, Press, coached him at LSU, he had carte blanche to shoot as much as he pleased in college; therefore he could post the gaudy scoring totals.

True, Maravich averaged 38.2 field goal attempts in his 83-game varsity career, during which LSU was just 49–35. The Tigers' only postseason appearance was in the National Invitation Tournament in Pete's senior season. But you have to consider Maravich was almost a 44 percent career field goal shooter. Even more impressive is he scored all those points—3,667—in only three seasons because freshmen were ineligible for varsity competition. Also, Maravich didn't benefit from playing with a three-point line. Former LSU coach Dale Brown once looked at Maravich's LSU game film and determined Pistol would have averaged 57 points per game had there been a three-point line in college when he was firing away.

Ask any coach who had to try and stop him, such as the late C.M. Newton, and he'll tell you 6'5" Pete Maravich—with his sagging lucky socks flopping and his mop-top haircut almost covering his eyes—was way more than just a scoring machine. "He'd get his 44 points, but he was such a great passer that he made everybody else on his team better," said Newton, who was Alabama's coach when he had to face Maravich. "Not only was he a complete player, but he had unbelievable mental toughness."

Teams that defended Pistol Pete had to make a decision: whether to guard him with more than one defender or let him get his points and try to cut off everybody else. Newton tried the latter when Maravich was a senior, and Maravich ran up a career-high 69 points in a 106–104 loss to the Crimson Tide. "We played him straight up with one man. I never dreamed he'd get 69," Newton recalled.

While Maravich's scoring managed to get the attention of the national media, it was his passing and ball handling that packed gyms wherever he played. Standing-room-only crowds for basketball was something the SEC had not seen much of before.

Maravich turned heads in his first days playing pickup games on the LSU campus as a rail-thin 6'4" freshman. "I remember when I was a senior and our assistant coach Jay McCreary told me that the new kid Maravich was a hell of a player," said Brad Brian, who was LSU's radio analyst during the Maravich era. "And when I saw this terrible, skinny-looking kid walk on the floor, I started chuckling.

"After we played for an hour and he threw passes I'd never seen before, I went straight to a phone to call my brother. I told him,

'Come out to LSU tomorrow and buy all the season tickets you can. I just played against the finest basketball player I've played in my life.'"

Maravich rarely threw a pass that didn't require a degree of difficulty. Every fast break was an adventure as he fired passes between the legs, behind the back, behind the neck, and the no-looks. Nothing was beyond his imagination.

"I recognized early that basketball, more than any other team game, gives a guy the opportunity to be a showman," Maravich once said in a *Sports Illustrated* story during his senior season in 1969–70. "Sure, I come out to win the game. That's always No. 1. But I also want to put on a performance that the fans will enjoy. The people at LSU and in Baton Rouge, where I play, and all over the Southeastern Conference know that when Pete Maravich comes out on the court, it's showtime."

Maravich relished personal challenges issued to him by opponents. When he played in the Loyola University Field House in New Orleans—which was also the home court of the American Basketball Association Buccaneers—he scored 52 points on 22 of 34 shooting attempts, with more than half of his baskets coming from behind the ABA three-point line. One time a University of Wyoming guard named Harry Hall issued a pregame challenge that he would "jam the Pistol." The Pistol went for 45 points, fouled out Hall, and said afterward, "That was stupid of him to say that. . . . If I have to stick the ball in my pants and jump through the hoop myself to win, I'll do it."

And there was his legendary 35-foot hook shot for his 57th and 58th points at Georgia in the final game of his junior year, when he dribbled like a Harlem Globetrotter through the entire Bulldogs team trying to run out the last seconds in a double-overtime win. "I got the ball and was feeling so great I decided to start a dribbling exhibition," Maravich recalled. "Between the legs, around my back, through defenders' legs, everything. I went outside, sideline, all over. Finally, I dribbled underneath, then went all the way back out again without putting the ball up.

"By this time 14,000 people were berserk. This was on the road. But now the Georgia players were mad. They had fire in their eyes. They all came after me, and I thought they were going to kill me. I started dribbling to midcourt, then to my bench. I wanted out. About two feet from the bench I looked up and there were four seconds to go, so I threw a hook shot from about 35 feet. Just as the buzzer sounded, the ball went in, my 58th point. It didn't touch anything, just oxygen.

"Well, 14,000 just sat there stunned. I was stunned too. I had walked over to sit down when I looked back and saw the shot. Damn, it went in. Then the place exploded. It was like we had won the national championship. I'll tell you one thing: They didn't take any films of that game, but I don't mind. When I'm 70 years old and telling my grandchildren about the shot, I imagine the distance will match my age."

Maravich averaged 24.2 points per game in a 10-year pro career with the Hawks, the Jazz, and the Celtics, showing his same breathtaking ball-handling skills and a more refined shot selection in the NBA. In 1986 he was enshrined in the Naismith Memorial Basketball Hall of Fame. In 1996 he was named one of the NBA's 50 greatest players of all time. That came eight years after his death, when he died playing a pickup game at age 40 in January 1988. An autopsy revealed Maravich's cause of death to be a rare congenital defect. He had been born without a left coronary artery.

His greatness and style transcended the decades, as noted by former NBA guard Isiah Thomas, a member of the 2000 Naismith Memorial Basketball Hall of Fame induction class. "Players in the NBA today still can't do the things with a basketball that Pete did," Thomas said when the NBA staged its 2014 All-Star Game in New Orleans.

23 Jim Hawthorne

If not for the persistence of his mother, Jim Hawthorne isn't sure he would have been a radio broadcaster at all, let alone the Voice of the Tigers for 35 years. As a teenager calling his first game—the Leesville Wampus Cats—he hated his voice the very first time he listened back to it. "I sounded like a cross between Gomer Pyle and Daffy Duck," Hawthorne said in a 2015 story published in the *Advocate*. "I was embarrassed to tears." Planning to quit, his mother urged him to continue his craft, and so he did—for roughly half a century, a large portion of that as LSU's play-by-play broadcaster.

Hawthorne called 393 consecutive football games from 1984 to his retirement after the 2015 season. He broadcast all of the Tigers' games in the College World Series during his stint, a whopping 60, and he was on the mic for three of the basketball team's four trips to the Final Four. He called nine national championship games, eight of them LSU wins.

His career included a host of memorable moments, none greater than his call of Warren Morris's game-winning two-run home run in the College World Series championship game in 1996: "That's way back there, way back there . . . home run! The Tigers win! The Tigers win! It's a two-run home run, and the Tigers are the national champs! I don't believe it!"

"That was the most thrilling and exciting single moment," Hawthorne said. "You can hear [sports information director] Bill Franques sobbing, actually crying. He was standing next to me. I had never experienced anything else like that. That one moment will always stand out."

Known for his crisp, nasally pitch and trademark "Holy cow!" Hawthorne saw the rise of LSU's three major sports under coaches

Dale Brown (basketball), Skip Bertman (baseball), and Nick Saban (football). He called elite performances from some of the school's best players, such as running backs Leonard Fournette and Kevin Faulk, quarterbacks JaMarcus Russell and Tommy Hodson, hoops legends Shaquille O'Neal and Ricky Blanton, and baseball stars Alex Bregman and Ben McDonald.

Hawthorne, 73 when he retired, began with the LSU men's basketball team in 1979–80. He moved into the football booth in 1983 and started calling baseball games the next year. His broadcasting journey started in Leesville, a small town on the western edge of the state that sits just south of Hawthorne's hometown of Anacoco. His broadcasting run continued as a DJ and commercial radio broadcaster for KNOC in Natchitoches while he attended school at Northwestern State. He then moved on to Shreveport's KWKH, where he wrote commercials. The sports part of his career took off when he began broadcasting games for the Shreveport Steamer, a World Football League squad that had moved from Houston to north Louisiana. "They were going to be big time," he said. "They lasted two years."

That work led to a gig broadcasting Centenary College sports. He spent 10 years doing that before joining LSU, a school close to his heart. He used to listen intently to LSU football games on the radio with his mother on Saturday nights. Hawthorne said his mom was a "huge" sports fan who always had on a game—mostly the Houston Astros—or *Louisiana Hayride*, a country music show.

His mom encouraged him—her oldest child of three—to pursue his passion of broadcasting. She helped during those early years when he struggled as a young broadcaster, when he was embarrassed by his voice. Hawthorne polished his delivery, in part from listening to other broadcasters, and he soon picked up catchphrases. "I stole 'Holy cow' from Harry Caray," he said. "I thought, *What the heck?*"

A little-known fact about Hawthorne: During his years as LSU's play-by-play man, he moonlighted as a country music singer.

He used to regularly perform at local country music shows and has even sung at the famed Nashville Palace, a rustic honky-tonk. "I have been, a whole lot more than most anybody knows, involved in music all my life," Hawthorne told the *Advocate* in a 2019 story. "It was my passion outside of doing sports."

But at LSU Hawthorne will be remembered as the Voice of the Tigers. And that's OK with him.

24 The Cajun Coach

Ed Orgeron used to sack oysters, shovel shrimp, and guzzle beers on the bayou. His grandfather operated a bayou ferry, and his mother grew up trapping and skinning muskrats. He comes from a long line of hunters and fishers, tugboat operators and oil field workers, gumbo makers and jambalaya cookers. If you need more proof of his heritage, take his nickname, Bébé, a French word meaning "baby," by which he's known back home in south LaFourche Parish. "You can't get more Louisiana than him," said his old friend Bobby Hebert.

Louisiana wrapped its collective arms around this barrel-chested, gravelly-voiced Cajun, but only after he led the Tigers to the 2019 national championship. Roundly criticized when hired in November 2016 to replace Les Miles, Orgeron defied a country of naysayers by completing one of the greatest comeback stories in college football history. A former bar-brawling alcoholic jettisoned from Miami and then dismissed years later as head coach at Ole Miss, Orgeron marched his home-state Tigers to a national championship in his third season, a magical year in which Heisman

Trophy–winning quarterback Joe Burrow captained a record-setting offense.

While operating mostly hands-off from schematics, Orgeron asserted himself as the CEO of the LSU football program. An expert motivator and tireless recruiter, he made a handful of bold decisions that proved significant for the Tigers' title run. He hired little-known New Orleans Saints assistant Joe Brady, then 29, to overhaul the Tigers' traditional offense into a spread unit. He also helped land Burrow, rolling out the proverbial red carpet for the quarterback and his family during a recruiting visit to Baton Rouge in the spring of 2018.

All of it led to a somewhat magical moment: a Cajun-bred man holding up the national title trophy in, of all places, the Superdome in New Orleans. "It's unbelievable," Cody Orgeron, Ed Orgeron's son, told *Sports Illustrated* for a story published in 2020. "God's story. No man can write this besides God. So proud of my dad. He's the man on the top of the mountain now."

For so long, he was beneath it, at one point ostracized from the coaching industry for off-the-field transgressions. In 1992 Orgeron headbutted the manager of a bar in Baton Rouge and was arrested. The charges were dropped, but the incident, and perhaps others, resulted in his resignation as the defensive line coach at the University of Miami. He spent the next 18 months out of coaching and back home in Larose, Louisiana, where he began a treatment for alcoholism that lasted through the 1990s (as of 2020, he's been sober for 20 years). It was a low point in his coaching career, followed by another one 15 years later when Ole Miss fired him after he won only 10 games in three seasons.

Six years later, despite going 6–2 as interim head coach at USC, Orgeron was passed over for the full-time job—something his wife, Kelly, claims was one of the most difficult blows of his life. "It was devastating," Kelly Orgeron said in a 2016 story in the *Advocate*. "That was a hurt that goes deep."

Despite some bad breaks along the way, the Orgerons are replete with inspirational tales. For instance, Kelly—born with scoliosis—lives with a metal rod down her spine, nearly died during a neck operation in 2017, and experienced the death of her father in college when he was the victim of a collision with a train. "We've got plenty of stories," Kelly said.

Like any coach, Ed Orgeron needed some lucky breaks. For example, he landed on Jimmy Johnson's staff at Miami in 1987 through a single phone call to the UM football offices. A secretary sent the call to a then–UM assistant by the name of Tommy Tuberville, who scribbled Orgeron's name onto a sheet of paper. "We just happened to go into a staff meeting an hour later," Tuberville recalled in 2007. "Jimmy asked, 'Does anyone know of a defensive line type of guy to come in as a graduate assistant?'" A few weeks later, Orgeron moved into Tuberville's two-bedroom apartment.

In 1993, while considering leaving the industry after his arrest and ouster at UM, Orgeron landed an assistant job at Nicholls State, only after his friends pleaded with Colonels coach Rick Rhoades to give the troubled youth a second shot. "He'd basically lost his career," Rhoades recalled in a 2020 interview. "I like to think we were able to crack the door and get his career back. He's taken it and run with it."

In 2000 Pete Carroll retained Orgeron as his defensive line coach and recruiting coordinator at USC, doing it only after bumping into the coach at a California high school state championship game. The two immediately hit it off. "It was a couple of days before I got the [USC] job," Carroll said. "Since he didn't have a job and I didn't have a job, we were able to get down there and watch the game up close. I was trying to figure out who the players were that I was going to be recruiting if I got the job."

Carroll continued, "We spent the night watching a high school football game. I just realized how connected he was and how much he loved USC at the time and how instrumental he would be. I couldn't hire him fast enough."

Orgeron's final big break happened in Baton Rouge. Elevated to replace Miles in an interim role, Orgeron was one of two finalists for the permanent coaching position. The favorite, then–Houston coach Tom Herman, ultimately spurned LSU's interests and accepted the job at Texas, leaving the Tigers with their Louisiana man.

On November 26, then–athletic director Joe Alleva informed Orgeron of the news outside the football operations building. "I was rolling, baby, playing 'Born on the Bayou,' windows open," Orgeron said of his drive into campus that day. "I get there at 7:29. Joe is sitting in front of the Tiger [statue], right there. He says, 'Well, you want the job or not?' I took him and bear-hugged him, and he said, 'Put me down, you big son of a gun!'"

The rest, of course, is history. A little more than three years later, Orgeron and the Tigers became national champs. "He's proof that dreams come true," Coco Orgeron, Ed's mother, said. "He has brought the state of Louisiana happiness. I'm telling you, you don't know how happy these people are. We did it! They always said, 'No, he's not going to do it.' I always said, 'Oh, yeah he will.'"

25 Game of the Century

For Josh Chapman, the short bus ride to the stadium signaled the significance of the impending game between No. 1 LSU and No. 2 Alabama. "None of us could get cell service," Chapman, the Tide's nose guard in that game, told *Bleacher Report*. "That was the first and only time in Tuscaloosa that ever happened. The cell towers were overwhelmed."

In a physical grudge match that included nearly 60 future NFL players, the Tigers beat the Tide 9–6 in overtime on November 5, 2011, in a match with more pregame hype than maybe any regular-season duel in college football history.

The game included zero touchdowns, four missed field goals by Alabama, and some nifty punting by LSU's Brad Wing. All of it happened in front of a sold-out Bryant-Denny Stadium (101,821 capacity) with a host of celebrities on hand: NBA star LeBron James, former secretary of state Condoleezza Rice, and Patriots owner Robert Kraft, to name a few. About 18 million more watched on television, glued to CBS's primetime affair of what was billed as the Game of the Century—the first-ever regular-season match between two undefeated Southeastern Conference squads ranked No. 1 and No. 2.

More than 600 media were credentialed, nearly doubling Alabama's usual count for a game, and the average price for tickets on the secondary market was $600. The star-studded cast of players included LSU's Tyrann Mathieu, Eric Reid, Odell Beckham Jr., and Morris Claiborne and Alabama's A.J. McCarron, Trent Richardson, Mark Barron, and Dont'a Hightower. "People had been talking about the game for weeks on ESPN," Wing said. "When we got off the bus, it was just a crazy, electric atmosphere around Bryant-Denny Stadium. There were so many people, and you knew thousands wouldn't even make it inside. You couldn't be on a bigger stage in college football."

Special teams played a key role in a game that included only 534 combined yards and a whopping four turnovers. LSU kicker Drew Alleman made all three of his field goals, including a 25-yard game-winning boot in overtime. Alabama kickers Jeremy Shelley and Cade Foster made two out of their six attempts, with Foster missing a 52-yard field goal in overtime. "Everyone was telling me that it might come down to a field goal, and I let that get to me. I overtrained that week," Foster said. "I must have kicked 200 to 300 balls instead of my normal 50. So by the time the game started, my legs were almost dead."

Players, coaches, and others involved in the game described it as an old-school slobber-knocker—a "human tug-of-war," said Alabama radio color analyst Phil Savage. Les Miles, LSU's coach for the game, described it as "maybe the most physical game I ever saw." Former LSU linebacker Kevin Minter, during a 2016 interview, heaped more praise on the battle. "I've been in the NFL for four years, and I still haven't played in a game that was this big," he said. "I think the only way to top it would be to play in the Super Bowl. That's it."

In a way, this wasn't even the biggest game the two teams played that season. They met again two months later in the BCS national title game. Oklahoma State's stunning loss to Iowa State in late November pushed the Tide to the championship match in New Orleans against SEC champion LSU. The Tide whipped the Tigers, making five field goals en route to a 21–0 spanking in the Superdome. Coach Nick Saban denied his former team a third national championship in nine seasons starting with his 2003 crown in Baton Rouge.

That rematch served as a sort of final blow to the BCS system, spawning the College Football Playoff in 2014. "I think us playing again for the national title was the straw that broke the camel's back of the BCS system," Minter said. "It wasn't fair that they got another shot at us, and I think the rest of the country knew that."

26 The Jersey

It is a jersey—white with purple numbers and lettering and purple-and-gold shoulder stripes—so beloved by its fan base that an LSU head football coach once swayed an NCAA rules committee to change a rule that allowed the Tigers to return to the tradition of wearing them at home. It is a jersey that ranked No. 5 on ESPN's 2019 list of all-time college uniforms. Sports247.com selected LSU's uniform as college football's best in 2019 and said, "Royalty. That's the word that always comes to mind when LSU's recognizable purple and gold graces the field."

There are a couple stories of how LSU got its colors. The first is that in the spring of 1893, when LSU beat Tulane in baseball—which was the first intercollegiate contest played by any LSU sports team—LSU team captain E.B. Young handpicked those colors for his squad.

The second version is that shortly before LSU's first football game in history against Tulane, on November 25, 1893, Dr. Charles Coates—LSU's first football coach—quarterback Ruff Pleasant, and a couple other men shopped for colored ribbons at Reymond's, a store in downtown Baton Rouge. "We told them we wanted quite a lot of ribbon for colors, but no one knew what our colors were," Coates said. "It happened that the store was stocking ribbon for the coming Carnival [Mardi Gras] season and had a large supply of purple and gold. The green had not yet come in. So we adopted the purple and old gold, bought out the stock, and made it into rosettes and badges. Purple and old gold made a good combination, and we have stuck to it ever since."

Two years later, Coates was an LSU professor when he decided the football team needed a nickname. "It was the custom at that time, for some occult reason, to call football teams by the names of vicious animals; the Yale Bulldogs and the Princeton Tigers, for example," Coates recalled before his death in 1939 at age 73. "It struck me that purple and gold looked Tigerish enough, and I suggested that we choose 'Louisiana Tigers,' all in conference with the boys. The Louisiana Tigers had represented the state in the Civil War and had been known for their hard fighting. So 'Louisiana Tigers' went into the New Orleans papers and became our permanent possession.

"A few years later when Col. David F. Boyd, who had been president of the university from 1865 to 1880 and again from 1884 to 1886, returned to the university, he was rather surprised to find purple and gold as the colors. He told me they were not the colors, that white and blue had been chosen by him many years ago. But purple and gold had by that time established itself and nothing was ever done about it. Colonel Dave also liked the name 'Tigers.' I think he was one of them himself during the Civil War."

LSU jerseys eventually advanced in the 1930s to an old gold color with purple numbers and purple stripes on the sleeves above the elbow. By the 1940s the Tigers also had a purple jersey in the same design as the gold ones.

In 1952 LSU coach Gus Tinsley and sports information director Jim Corbett devised a unique letter and number system for the Tigers' jerseys. Ends, guards, and tackles wore the letters *E*, *G*, and *T* followed by a single number—even for the right side of the line and odd for the left. Centers, quarterbacks, left and right halfbacks, and fullbacks wore *C*, *Q*, *L*, *R*, and *F*. It was as confusing as the way the Tigers played that season as they limped to 3–7. The one-year experiment died.

In 1957, under third-year coach Paul Dietzel, LSU debuted its iconic white jerseys. The next year in 1958, when the Tigers won the national championship, they wore white jerseys for every home game. Dietzel, a superstitious sort, never changed the uniform again. It stayed that for the most part until Jerry Stovall became head coach in 1980 when he decided to occasionally wear purple jerseys at home so fans could see a different color.

But the NCAA changed its rule requiring home teams to wear dark-colored jerseys. The rule lasted 12 years, from 1983 to 1994. In the last six years of the rule, when LSU had losing records, including an 18–24 home record, Tigers fans were convinced wearing purple jerseys at home was bad luck. In 1993 Coach Curley Hallman asked the NCAA if LSU could start wearing the white jerseys at home again during LSU football's centennial. He was denied.

When Gerry DiNardo replaced Hallman in 1995, at his introductory press conference in November 1994, DiNardo vowed he would get the NCAA to change the rule. DiNardo pleaded his case in person with the rules committee in February 1995. He brought each committee member a white LSU jersey with his or her name on the back. "I knew I had them as soon as they accepted the graft," said DiNardo of the committee that altered the rule so state home teams may wear white jerseys if the visiting team agrees. Almost all visiting teams have gone with the flow, allowing LSU to don white uniforms for home games. Under coach Nick Saban, starting in 2001, the Tigers began the policy of wearing purple jerseys for nonconference home games.

Starting in the late 1950s, each gold LSU helmet began featuring the number on it that corresponded to the wearer's jersey number. In 1972 a Tiger logo was added that included LSU within the logo. In 1977 LSU advanced to its current look with LSU spelled out over a Tiger logo. The one constant has been the helmet's front-to-back centered purple/white/purple stripes.

The Tigers have occasionally worn a white version of the helmet. For its 2018 homecoming, LSU wore a special Nike uniform that featured a helmet that changed colors from purple to gold depending on the light.

There have been minor tweaks to the helmet, jersey, and pants in the last few decades. But the biggest change in the uniform in the last 60 years is the shoulder stripes, which used to go all around the arm. Now they basically are crescent-shaped.

27 NFL Leader

When Will Clapp arrived at LSU with the rest of the 2014 signing class, he heard the chatter from some of his fellow freshmen: "Three years and I'm out of here." "We hadn't hit the field yet, and we got guys thinking three years and out," the former Tigers offensive lineman said in a 2018 story in the *Advocate*.

LSU sends so many players to the NFL that some of them plan to leave early for the pros before they even take a snap. The wave of junior departures from 2013 to 2018—a nation-leading 32 under-classmen—illustrates the school's production of pro players, even if the losses negatively affect the team. The university churns out an astonishing amount of NFL talent each year, so much so that it often leads the nation in active players in the league at any given time. There were 47 former Tigers in the NFL in the 2019 season.

The NFL Draft is annually peppered with purple and gold. From 2006 to 2017, no college program had more players drafted. LSU's 77 led Southern Cal (76), Ohio State and Alabama (73), Florida (66), Florida State (61), Georgia and Oklahoma (60), and Clemson and Miami (58). LSU had a run of 13 consecutive drafts with at least four players selected, hitting its peak with a record nine players picked in 2014, the most of any college that year. From 2006 to 2018, the Tigers' 16 first-round selections ranked fourth among college football teams, trailing only Alabama, Ohio

State, and Florida. They've had two overall No. 1 selections (Billy Cannon in 1960 and JaMarcus Russell in 2007) and a whopping 41 first-round picks all-time.

Players succeed after being drafted too. Forty LSU players have won at least one Super Bowl ring. As of 2019 the school had a streak of at least 17 consecutive years with an ex-player competing in a Super Bowl, the longest such run of any SEC team. The program's success at the next level turned into a recruiting tool for coaches to woo high school prospects to campus. Under Coach Les Miles, coaches pitched to prospects a three-years-and-out model, promising to have them NFL-ready after year three—a strategy that, in a way, backfired. Miles lost a combined 18 underclassmen to the NFL in 2013 and 2014, a blow to the program's roster from which it never fully recovered under the coach. (He was fired in 2016.)

"It hurts you. There are some guys who made some terrible mistakes about going, but when you play on a team drafted regularly and leads the NFL in the number of players that are in the NFL, here's what happens," Miles explained in the *Advocate* story. "Guys that shouldn't really go are going. There were guys that felt like 'Just because I played with some of the best players, I can play in the NFL.' Some did it. Some did not."

Clapp, an all-conference guard and center, left for the NFL with a year of eligibility remaining, but his situation was different from that of most of the early departures. He redshirted as a true freshman, attending school for four years and graduating. He would have been a fifth-year senior in 2018. Clapp was selected by the Saints in the final round of the 2018 draft, and he made the team, even drawing some significant playing time as a replacement for injured starters late during his rookie season—yet another LSU player succeeding at the highest level of the sport.

28 Bernie Moore

Bernie Moore was a man of firsts: The first LSU head football coach ever hired by a United States senator. The first and only coach at LSU to win a national track-and-field championship and have a football squad finish as the nation's No. 2 team in the Associated Press poll. The first LSU coach to take the Tigers to a bowl game and the only Tigers field boss to guide LSU to three Sugar Bowl appearances. The first head coach, and one of only two in Southeastern Conference history, to win the league championship in his first season. The first LSU coach ever to have a former player elected to the Pro Football Hall of Fame, remaining the only Tigers coach ever to have two Pro Football Hall of Fame inductees. The first and only man to retire from coaching to immediately become commissioner of the Southeastern Conference; his 19 years as commissioner are easily longest in league history.

His 13-year stint as the Tigers' head coach from 1935 to 1947—during which the team record was 83–39–6 (.671)—remains the second-longest in LSU history behind Charles McClendon. Moore's tenure was highlighted by two SEC titles, four nine-win seasons, and the first five bowl trips in school history. But his tenure as the top Tiger was also marked by other historical notables in the LSU football program, such as Tiger Stadium adding 24,000 seats by enclosing the north end to raise the capacity to 45,000 and the debut of LSU's live Bengal tiger mascot, Mike I.

With the sport taking a jump in popularity in Baton Rouge, Moore also may have been the first LSU head coach to experience pressure from the Tigers' growing fan base. "There are wolves the nation over," said Moore, who died at age 72 in 1967, a year after he retired as SEC commissioner. "And there are all species of 'em.

Elsewhere the wolves howl all night long. In Baton Rouge they howl all night and all day."

Moore was a Tennessee native, one of 14 children born to a missionary Baptist preacher. He played football and ran track at Carson-Newman University in Jefferson City, Tennessee, before being called into military service, where he fought in combat in World War I.

When he returned, his student loan debt forced him to abandon his dreams of going to medical school. He went into coaching at Winchester (Tennessee) High School, where he coached all sports and was an English teacher. Well, that's what his title indicated. "May the Lord forgive me for what I did to the language," Moore once said jokingly.

He eventually got into college coaching at Mercer University and then Sewanee before LSU coach Russ Cohen hired him as an assistant in 1929. He quickly impressed Cohen with his handling of the freshman team and his scouting. But Moore's name became known on a national scale when, in his third year as LSU's track coach, the Tigers won the 1933 NCAA championship with only five athletes scoring all the points. His track teams won the 1932 Southern Conference championship and 12 of the first of 15 SEC titles after the formation of the league in 1933. His track athletes set five world records, won eight NCAA titles, collected 29 All-America honors in 18 seasons, and won Olympic gold and silver medals.

But the national championship track team is what got him named head football coach, a hire that Louisiana senator Huey Long had to sign off on early in 1935. Long had begun sticking his nose in LSU's business when he was Louisiana's governor from 1929 to 1932. "Winning that track meet showed me he could handle men," said Long, who decided to hire Moore after he got a recommendation from Vanderbilt head football coach Dan McGugin. Twenty days before Moore's debut as LSU's head coach,

Long was assassinated at the Louisiana State Capitol Building. LSU lost its season opener and then went on a 23-game regular-season streak without losing a game.

Through the years, Moore's teams were powered by a succession of stars. He had first-team All-American ends Gus Tinsley and Ken Kavanaugh; center Moose Stewart; and future Pro Football Hall of Famers quarterback Y.A. Tittle and running back Steve Van Buren, who was used as a blocking back by Moore until the final year of Van Buren's LSU career. "He was probably the greatest back in SEC history and I used him as a blocking back until his last year," Moore said. "Folks down in Baton Rouge will never quite get over it."

They eventually did. In 1971, two years after its construction, LSU's track stadium was named in Moore's honor.

29 Cotton Bowl Stunner

Like no other athletic director in LSU history, Jim Corbett was a master salesman. Here are a few examples: When he hurt his leg and could no longer play football as a scholarship athlete for Southeastern Louisiana University, he convinced school officials to allow him to remain on scholarship as the school's first sports publicity director. (In 1954 he became LSU's athletic director, a position he kept until his death in 1967.)

After a business trip to New York City—inspired by the Broadway show tune "Hey, Look Me Over!"—he put the wheels in motion to create a new LSU fight song, "Hey Fighting Tigers," for the start of the 1962 season.

And at the end of an injury-riddled 1965 LSU season, he convinced Cotton Bowl officials to match a 7–3 Tigers team that had gone 2–2 in its last four games against unbeaten Arkansas, ranked No. 1 by the Associated Press and owners of a 22-game winning streak.

The Razorbacks placed 10 players on the 23-man All–Southwest Conference team. Behind quarterback Jon Brittenum, All-American receiver Bobby Crockett, and running backs Bobby Burnett and Harry Jones, Arkansas was averaging a nation-leading 32.4 points.

LSU had ended the regular season with some significant injuries, but coach Charles McClendon knew the time off between the regular season and the bowl would heal many of them. Quarterback Pat Screen, a onetime starter who replaced Nelson Stokley in the seventh game of the 1965 season when Stokley sustained a season-ending knee injury, used bowl practice to continue to knock the rust off his game.

It wasn't lost on McClendon that Arkansas had allowed more than 400 yards in edging Texas 27–24 after the Longhorns compiled some healthy rushing totals.

In LSU's pre-bowl practices in Baton Rouge—to remind his players of Arkansas's 22-game winning streak with the Tigers as the possible 23rd victim—McClendon had all the defensive players wear red jerseys with the white No. 22 and all the offensive players wear white jerseys with a red No. 23.

Once in Dallas, McClendon didn't have to create motivation for his team. It was all around them. Arkansas fans asked loudly "L-S-Who?" whenever they crossed paths with the LSU team and Tigers fans. One reporter asked LSU split end/place-kicker Doug Moreau, "How bad do you expect your team to lose?" Then, as LSU exited the lobby of its team hotel on the way to the game, they came across a group of Arkansas fans. One lady, wearing a Razorbacks porker hat, exclaimed, "Look, they're actually going to show up."

On its second possession of the game, Arkansas drove 80 yards with Brittenum throwing a 16-yard touchdown pass to Crockett over LSU defensive back Jerry Joseph for a quick 7–0 lead. It looked like the rout was on for the 10-point underdog Tigers, but quite the contrary. LSU secondary coach Bill Beall adjusted the coverage to give Joseph help from speedy safety Sammy Grezaffi.

After Arkansas missed a field goal, LSU's offense began pounding away at the Razorbacks just as Texas had done in the regular-season finale. LSU adjusted its offense in a different look than Arkansas had seen on film. Tailback "Lighting" Joe Labruzzo lined up deeper than usual so he could have more time to decide on his cuts.

The Tigers drove 80 yards in 16 plays for Labruzzo's game-tying TD. Then Brittenum sustained a separated shoulder that was numbed the rest of the game with painkillers. Two plays later, LSU recovered a fumble and cashed it in with Labruzzo carrying five straight times over left tackle and scoring on a one-yard TD for a 14–7 lead with 18 seconds left in the half.

The Tigers were so fired up they didn't even want to go to the dressing room at the half. They were so eager to get back out for the second half that McClendon had to hold them back four times when they were headed for the door while bands were still on the field. They impatiently scraped their metal cleats on the concrete floor, ready to close the book on an upset win.

Which is exactly what they did. The Tigers' defense kept the Hogs off the scoreboard. Arkansas missed a 32-yard field goal, and then Joseph got revenge for being burned for the first-quarter TD by intercepting Brittenum at the LSU 20 with 4:38 left in the game. "When [Crockett, the intended receiver] turned, I turned," Joseph once told author Marty Mule. "It was like a dart. All of a sudden, there was a ball and I caught it."

Arkansas's last threat ended with Crockett catching a pass and getting tackled at the LSU 24 as time expired.

"I knew we were ready to play," said McClendon, who embraced Corbett in a hug at midfield moments after the game ended. Standing on an equipment trunk in the middle of LSU's postgame dressing room celebration, McClendon told his team, "The rest of your lives you won't ever forget what you did today."

McClendon thought his players would want the No. 22 and No. 23 practice jerseys as keepsakes. "As soon as they got to the locker room after the game," McClendon later recalled, "they tore those jerseys to pieces. Nothing was left but shreds."

It was a loss that legendary Arkansas coach Frank Broyles, who later became the school's athletic director, never forgot. "That's the sickest I've ever been in coaching," Broyles said.

30 Billy Cannon

There's no debate about who's the greatest LSU football player in the program's storied history. It's Dr. Billy Cannon, the school's only Heisman Trophy winner, in his senior season of 1959. "Billy Cannon was LSU football through and through," said current LSU head football coach Ed Orgeron after Cannon died at age 80 in May 2018. "He was a legend."

There's also no argument that Cannon's 89-yard TD punt return on Halloween night 1959 in Tiger Stadium to provide No. 1 LSU with a 7–3 victory over No. 3 Ole Miss is the most memorable play ever by anyone wearing the Purple and Gold. "It was one of the greatest efforts in the history of college football," said LSU coach Paul Dietzel, who combined the talents of Cannon and others to guide the Tigers to their first national championship in 1958.

Cannon took Rebels punter Jake Gibbs' punt off a high bounce on the muddy field at the Ole Miss 11. Seven Rebels had a shot at him. He shook off some of the tacklers and dodged others, such as Gibbs, who was the last man standing between Cannon and the goal line. "As I approached him, there wasn't any doubt in his mind that I was gonna cut back to the middle of the field," Cannon said. "When I made the little weave to the inside and took the sideline, well, he like to have died. And that's when he missed the tackle, and Jake was a fantastic tackler. That's probably the only one he missed his entire career. I knew then if I stood up and made it to the end zone, we'd go ahead."

Through the years, Cannon became friends with Gibbs and many of the Ole Miss players from that era. "Billy would always say, 'I gave you the hip and took it away,'" Gibbs said. "I'd say, 'Billy, you were a straight-line runner.' And then we'd laugh and laugh."

The 6'1", 210-pound Cannon, who played running back and defensive back, was a physical freak. He consistently ran 9.4 seconds in the 100-yard dash, bench-pressed 270 pounds, and threw a 16-pound college shot put almost 55 feet. "Billy was a special person and unique athlete," said former Ole Miss athletic director Warner Alford, who was a lineman who faced Cannon in the heated Tigers-Rebels rivalry. "Who was faster than him? Who was stronger than him?"

In his three-year LSU career from 1957 to 1959, Cannon rushed for 1,867 yards on 359 carries and scored 24 rushing touchdowns. He also caught 31 passes for 522 yards and two touchdowns. An all-purpose player, Cannon returned 31 punts for 349 yards and 21 kickoffs for 616 yards in his career, punted 111 times for an average of 36.7 yards, and intercepted seven passes. He also completed 12 of 26 pass attempts for 121 yards and threw the game-winning TD in a 7–0 Sugar Bowl win over Clemson that clinched the 1958 national title.

Cannon was born in Philadelphia, Mississippi. His family moved to Baton Rouge when he was five. He would often sneak from home to watch football practice at Istrouma High School. When he attended the school himself, he grew from a scrawny 168-pound kid to a 187-pound All-State back and track star by the time he graduated.

He embraced weightlifting, training under Alvin Roy, coach of the 1952 U.S. gold medal–winning Olympic weightlifting team. Roy, a Baton Rouge native who was an LSU basketball walk-on and a World War II veteran, opened a health club just off Nicholson Drive a couple miles from the LSU campus.

There was never a doubt that Cannon, who once sold soft drinks at LSU home games in Tiger Stadium, would sign with LSU. It's where his dad, Harvey Sr., was employed and where Billy's brother, Harvey Jr., had run track.

Cannon was the first LSU football player to have his uniform number (No. 20) retired and was the only Tiger so honored until 2009, when Tommy Casanova joined him. He was the No. 1 draft pick in 1960 of the AFL's Houston Oilers and the NFL's Los Angeles Rams. He chose the Oilers, which led to an 11-year career for three teams before he became an orthodontist after graduating from the University of Tennessee's dental school.

Cannon established a successful Baton Rouge orthodontic practice that went awry. He overextended himself on real estate investments on condos and apartment complexes and undeveloped land in New Orleans and Baton Rouge. He hatched a scheme to eliminate his debt by investing $10,000 in a counterfeiting operation run by former LSU boxer John Stiglets, a previously convicted counterfeiter who was an employee at a Baton Rouge T-shirt printing company Cannon owed.

The two men had initially joked about printing money, but it became more serious when Cannon believed rising interest rates would financially squeeze him dry. "It's funny, the more you talk about something, the easier it becomes," Cannon wrote in his 2015 autobiography. "Why it changed from something I wouldn't normally do, I can't answer that."

On July 9, 1983, while Cannon was at the Fair Grounds horse track in New Orleans, the FBI raided his house. He was arrested, pleaded guilty, and was sentenced to five years in prison and fined $10,000. Fewer than two months after his arrest, he went to prison until he was released to a halfway house in Baton Rouge on August 4, 1986. He declared bankruptcy and sold his Heisman Trophy to Baton Rouge restaurant owner Tom Moran because he was short on cash.

Cannon regained his orthodontist license but had difficulty reestablishing his practice. He was hired as a dentist on a contract basis at the Louisiana State Penitentiary at Angola. In 1997 Cannon was named the prison's hospital director by warden Burl Cain. Cain said when Cannon was hired, he immediately connected with inmates. He quelled a possible inmates' lawsuit against the prison for inadequate healthcare. "When [the inmates] knew Billy was in charge, everybody settled down and everything got perfect," Cain said.

Inmates, relating to the fact Cannon had once been in prison, called him Legend. He was so beloved by staff and inmates that when he died, inmates built his coffin after paying for the construction materials themselves.

Through former athletic director Joe Dean, Cannon was gradually welcomed back into the LSU fold. He received a rousing Tiger Stadium ovation in 2009 when the school celebrated the 50th anniversary of his memorable punt return vs. Ole Miss.

He was later honored as LSU's 2010 Alumnus of the Year by the LSU Alumni Association. Former LSU quarterback Jimmy Field, who called Cannon "a man of love," told him that night, "You're redeemed, you're accepted, you're forgiven and loved."

Cannon told the crowd, "The people of Louisiana are quick to love and quick to forgive."

The College Football Hall of Fame selection committee wasn't as eager to make amends with Cannon, however. His 1983 election into the HOF was rescinded before his induction when he pled guilty to counterfeiting. The Hall reinstated him in 2008 and he was finally inducted. Cannon told an Associated Press reporter after the ceremony, "You heard all [that at the ceremony] about guidance, leadership, doing the right thing, and here's a convicted felon sitting in the middle of them. One of the reasons I'm here today: I did the crime, I did the time, and I haven't had a problem since, not even a speeding ticket."

Cannon died before he had a chance to see his statue, which was revealed on the west side of Tiger Stadium in September 2018. Current LSU president Dr. F. King Alexander succinctly assessed Cannon's place in school history. "To say that Billy Cannon was legendary is an understatement," Alexander said. "His talent catapulted LSU athletics into the national limelight, but more than that, he had unwavering commitment to his alma mater. He will forever remain a part of the LSU legacy throughout the nation."

31 The Kingfish

Say what you will about the legend of the late Louisiana governor and U.S. senator Huey Long—a flamboyant, self-serving, power-hungry force of nature—his love and development of LSU in every area grew the university immensely.

When Long was elected Louisiana's 40th governor in 1928, LSU was labeled a "third-rate" institution by the Association of State

Universities. It had only 1,800 students, 168 faculty members, and an annual operating budget of $800,000. LSU didn't draw much attention in-state; most people viewed it as a small country school. But by 1936 LSU had risen in size from 88th in the nation to 20th, and it was the 11th-largest state university in the nation. How? Huey Long, nicknamed the Kingfish.

In 1930 he began a huge building program to expand the physical plant on campus and add departments. Six years later, in 1936, LSU had the finest facilities in the South, a faculty of 394 professors, more than 6,000 students, a new medical school, and a winning football team. He ensured every person had a shot at getting a college education by reducing tuition and awarding needs-based scholarships. Long financed these improvements by arranging for the state to purchase acreage from the former site of the LSU campus, which adjoined the grounds of the new State Capitol Building. He essentially diverted $9 million for LSU's expansion and increased the annual operating budget to $2.8 million. His critics didn't care for his method of financing.

It didn't take Long much time to entrench himself into decisions at LSU that university administrators would normally make, especially when it came to creating the pomp and circumstance he loved. He made LSU football a spectacle through coaching hires to bolster the program and by vastly improving the LSU band. "He loved music and he wanted to expand the credibility of LSU," Frank Wickes, LSU's band director from 1980 to 2010, said several years ago. "He wanted LSU to be a great university, and he felt that by having the band be really great, that it was the right kind of representation to show to the public all over the country."

Long hired accomplished New Orleans trombonist Alfred Wickboldt as the new band director in 1930. He replaced him in 1934 with Castro Carazo, the orchestra leader at the Roosevelt Hotel in New Orleans. Both Wickboldt and Carazo did their best to appease Long, since he gave their programs unlimited funding.

Carazo allowed Long to occasionally conduct band rehearsals as well as march on its front line at performances. Also, Carazo cowrote songs with Long, including "Touchdown for LSU," which is still played today during pregame festivities.

Long made sure students got involved with supporting football and the band. In 1934 he announced he had arranged for several trains to carry the entire student body to the Tigers' away game at Vanderbilt University in Nashville to boost the team's morale. Long gave seven dollars to each student needing to go to the game.

He had already negotiated a $6 train fare for students for the game by threatening to reassess the value of the railroads. Trains were taxed at $100,000, and Long said it would have been a shame if he had to tax them at their true value of $4 million. The Illinois Central got the point and lowered the fares. Five thousand LSU students made the trip to watch a 29–0 Tigers win. Long and the LSU band marched through the streets of Nashville.

That same year, LSU promised a $10,000 guarantee for Dallas-based SMU to play in the home season opener in Tiger Stadium. But ticket sales lagged because the Ringling Bros. and Barnum & Bailey Circus was also scheduled in Baton Rouge on the same night. Enter Long. He called the circus advance man and told him he had to dip all the animals to prevent disease before crossing the Louisiana state line. "You know we have laws in this state, mister," said Long, who discovered a little-known animal-dipping law in Louisiana's sanitary code. The circus canceled. Ticket sales for the game took off, and more than 20,000 were in Tiger Stadium to watch LSU rally for a 14–14 tie.

Long finally overstepped his bounds at the end of the 1934 season when the Tigers went on a losing streak. LSU was trailing Oregon 13–0 at halftime when Long went to the dressing room and asked head coach Biff Jones if he could speak to the team. Jones refused, igniting a dialogue both men would regret.

"I'm sick and tired of losing and tying games," Long said. "You'd better win this one."

"Well, Senator, get this," Jones replied. "Win, lose, or draw, I quit!"

"That's a bargain," Long replied as Jones closed the door in his face.

Jones quit as football coach but stayed on as a military professor. Long hired Bernie Moore, one of Jones's assistants, as the next head coach, but Long never got a chance to see his debut. On September 8, 1935, he was shot at the state capitol by Baton Rouge physician Carl Weiss. Weiss was immediately killed by more than 60 shots from Long's bodyguards. Long died two days later, along with one of the most interesting periods in LSU history.

32 Hurricane Katrina

Les Miles says he suffered from some sort of post-traumatic stress after Hurricane Katrina. "Those helicopters got me, the thump-thump-thump-thump," the former LSU head coach said in a story published in 2015 at Nola.com. "That got me. Helicopters transporting refugees from storm-battered New Orleans whizzed over many of LSU's camp scrimmages and practices ahead of the 2005 season, a stark reminder of what football really is—a sport.

Katrina affected LSU football in a variety of ways when it slammed into southeast Louisiana on August 29, 2005. The third-most-intense tropical cyclone to make landfall on U.S. soil, the hurricane flooded 80 percent of New Orleans, forcing families of football players, among so many others, to Baton Rouge. Receiver Skyler Green, for instance, housed 17 family members at his apartment, and quarterback JaMarcus Russell served as host to at least 20 people, including the late Fats Domino, the famous New Orleans pianist and singer-songwriter.

LSU was designated as an evacuee center, with its basketball arena, the Pete Maravich Assembly Center (PMAC), serving as a triage center. The gym's basement acted as a morgue, the outdoor track a helipad, and the Carl Maddox Field House a center for uninjured evacuees.

Players were heavily involved in the relief effort. They visited area shelters, stopped by the triage unit at the PMAC to cheer up the sick and injured and help unload trucks. Some players packed an 18-foot trailer full of clothes and other items that players were willing to donate, according to an ESPN.com story published then.

All the while Miles was preparing the preseason No. 5–ranked Tigers for his inaugural season as coach. "It was a very difficult time and it was a great time," Miles said in an interview with reporters in 2015 on the 10th anniversary of Katrina. "I think it was one of the strongest moments of Louisiana history, and I was really fortunate to be here to witness it."

School officials postponed the season opener against North Texas, originally scheduled for five days after the date of Katrina's landfall. They moved a scheduled home game against Arizona State the next week to Tempe, Arizona, before another hurricane wreaked havoc. Rita slammed into southwest Louisiana just 23 days after Katrina. School officials were forced to shift the Southeastern Conference opener in Baton Rouge against No. 10 Tennessee to a Monday night.

The two games—against the Sun Devils and Volunteers—were emotional affairs for an exhausted squad so affected by a catastrophic event. "I think there's no way we can say that we're not going out there with this on our minds and this being an inspiration for us, to have a chance to make this state proud of something," LSU offensive tackle Andrew Whitworth told ESPN for a story that ran the week of the game against ASU. "From all of the people I've talked to that have been through this, they can't wait for some sense of normalcy, some sense of something to be happy about [to] take their mind off of it for a little while. I think a lot of people want this. A lot of people support this, and we're going to do our best to make this state proud."

Against the Sun Devils, LSU stormed back from a fourth-quarter 17–7 deficit, scoring 28 in the final quarter and winning 35–31 in wild fashion. JaMarcus Russell, on a fourth-and-10, completed a 39-yard touchdown pass to Early Doucet for the game winner with 1:13 left. The play landed the Tigers on the cover of *Sports Illustrated.*

The Tennessee game finished much differently. LSU blew leads of 21–0 at halftime and 24–7 early in the fourth quarter, eventually losing 30–27 in overtime to Phillip Fulmer's Volunteers.

Despite the circumstances in south Louisiana, Miles's Tigers won their next nine games in nine weeks, claiming the SEC West championship. It is still viewed in Baton Rouge as one of the most arduous and taxing football seasons in LSU history. Why? Miles answered that. "I walked into the [PMAC] and saw doctors and nurses, our players and coaches with volunteer badges just busting it to do what they could," Miles said. "I remember one girl had a severed Achilles' tendon because something had hit her underwater. Families were connecting. It was the first time I met Big Baby [LSU basketball player Glen Davis]. He was holding up an IV bottle. It was special."

33 No. 18

The now–LSU tradition started out as "kind of a joke," said Matt Mauck—the original No. 18—who wore the number as the starting quarterback of LSU's 2003 national championship team. Now it is a jersey number that every LSU football player would like to have on his résumé when trying to enter the NFL. "Scouts always have questions about players," LSU football trainer Jack Marucci said. "But when you tell them one of guys wore No. 18, suddenly there are no questions [about that player]."

Just before the start of the 2020 season, and for the 17th straight year, Marucci and his unofficial committee of equipment manager Greg Stringfellow, sports information director Michael Bonnette, Mauck, and Jacob Hester—the first No. 18 honoree after Mauck's departure—will consult. The goal is simple: recommend awarding No. 18 to an LSU player or players who demonstrate exemplary skill, work ethic, and character on and off the field. The committee recommends a name or names to the Tigers' head coach, and he almost always rubber-stamps the selection(s).

Hester was a unique choice. He was given No. 18 as a lightly recruited two-star freshman running back. He had the number for four years, longer than any other No. 18. That was because he proved he merited the number. In LSU's 2007 national championship season, he ran for 1,103 yards and 12 touchdowns. He was at his best in the biggest games, such as when he ran for 106 yards and scored the game-winning TD against defending national champion Florida. On that scoring drive, he converted two fourth-and-1s.

If there was anybody who clearly defined the criteria for all the No. 18s who would follow, it was Hester. "The ultimate Tiger wears No. 18," Hester said. "He's not going to get in trouble off the field, he's going to class, he's going to do the right thing. He's going to be a leader on the team, a guy everybody can count on. You don't have to worry about ever seeing his name in the newspaper for the wrong reasons. He'll be the first player in the football complex and the last one to leave."

The Tigers have a tradition during one of their bowl practices in which teammates swap jersey numbers. In Hester's final bowl practice jersey exchange of his career, he swapped with tight end Richard Dickson. As it turned out, Dickson was chosen to succeed Hester as No. 18 and wore it for two seasons. He ended up as the best tight end in LSU history, catching 52 passes for 481 yards in his last two years.

Many times No. 18 has been awarded to players battling back from injuries, such as outside linebacker K'Lavon Chaisson. He and Lloyd Cushenberry were the No. 18s on the Tigers' 15–0 2019 national championship team. Chaisson underwent season-ending knee surgery after tearing ligaments in the 2018 season opener. But he didn't feel sorry for himself. "I'm a part of the roster, so I feel it's my job to help in some way whether it's physically or mentally," Chaisson said. "I wanted to help Coach [Ed Orgeron] make sure everyone was on the same page, one team one heartbeat, man down, man up."

Chaisson and Cushenberry are the latest in the proud Tigers tradition to chase their NFL dreams. Here is the complete list of No. 18s, starting with Mauck; 9 of the 12 No. 18 recipients prior to the two 2019 No. 18 honorees have played in a regular-season NFL game.

QB Matt Mauck 2001–03: Mauck was 18–2 as a starter and led LSU to the 2003 national title. His career stats include completing 310 of 529 passes for 3,831 passing yards with 37 touchdowns and only 18 interceptions.

RB Jacob Hester (2004–07): Hester started 27 straight games at running back during his final two years with the Tigers. He ran for

1,103 yards and 12 touchdowns in 2007, when the Tigers won the national championship.

TE Richard Dickson (2008–09): Dickson was a four-year starter at tight end, playing in 50 games with 35 starts. He is regarded as the school's all-time most productive tight end with 90 receptions for 952 yards and 10 touchdowns.

RB Richard Murphy (2010): Murphy suffered a torn ACL in high school and again in 2009 at LSU but still managed to run 527 career yards for two TDs, catch 29 passes for 214 yards, and record 15 tackles on special teams.

S Brandon Taylor (2011): Taylor had 33 starts in his LSU career, finishing with 160 tackles, 11.5 tackles for loss, 15 pass break-ups, and 4 interceptions.

DT Bennie Logan (2012): After redshirting as a true freshman, Logan took over as a starter as a sophomore in 2011. He finished his career with 107 tackles with 12.5 for loss, including 5 sacks.

LB Lamin Barrow (2013): Barrow played in 51 games with 28 starts. He had career totals of 230 tackles with 14.5 tackles for loss, 7 pass breakups, 7 QB hurries, and 4 fumble recoveries.

RB Terrence Magee (2014): A former high school quarterback, Magee split time as a running back and wide receiver early in his LSU career before settling in at running back as a junior and senior. He capped his career with 1,330 yards rushing and 12 rushing TDs.

CB Tre'Davious White (2015-16): White was LSU's first (and currently only) NFL first-round draft choice to wear No. 18. He played all four seasons and bypassed the 2016 NFL Draft to return to LSU for his senior season when he was named first-team All-American. He registered 167 career tackles, 11 tackles for loss, 34 pass breakups, and 6 interceptions, and he scored 4 TDs (3 punt returns, 1 interception return).

DE Christian LaCouture and FB/TE John David Moore (2017): LaCouture missed all of 2016 with an injury, then had his best college season as a senior in 2017, wearing No. 18 when he had a career-high 66 tackles with 8.5 tackles for loss, including 6 sacks, 8 pass breakups, and 5 QB hurries. Moore spent most of his college career as a selfless fullback clearing paths for LSU running back greats Leonard Fournette and Derrius Guice.

TE Foster Moreau (2018): Moreau had 52 career receptions for 629 yards and 6 touchdowns. As a senior, he caught 22 passes for 272 yards and 2 TDs.

OLB K'Lavon Chaisson and C Lloyd Cushenberry (2019): First-team All-SEC choice Chaisson, battling back from knee surgery that caused him to miss most of the 2018 season, had 60 tackles, including 4.5 of his season-total 6.5 sacks, in the Tigers' last four games pushing to the national title. Cushenberry started 28 straight games at center, and the Tigers went 25–3 during that two-year span. He was leader of an LSU line that was named the Joe Moore Award winner as the top offensive line in the nation.

34 LSU and the Sugar Bowl

LSU is 6–7 in the 13 Sugar Bowls in which it has played. After LSU lost its first four Sugar Bowl appearances by a combined 65–16, the Tigers rallied for three Sugar Bowl wins in their next four appearances. Following a pair of Sugar Bowl losses to Nebraska, LSU has won its last three. Here is a brief summary of all 13 LSU Sugar Bowl appearances:

1936: TCU 3, LSU 2

The Setup: There was the anticipation of plenty of offense in this matchup between No. 4 TCU and its quarterback, "Slingin'" Sammy Baugh, and SEC champions LSU, led by QB Abe Mickal.

Hard rain the last three days of 1935 turned Tulane Stadium into a swamp. The game turned into a defensive battle.

How It Played Out: TCU's defense stopped the Tigers' offense on three series inside the 2-yard line, including once six inches from the goal line. LSU's offense didn't allow TCU to get closer than the LSU 16.

The game's points were scored within two minutes of each other in the second quarter. LSU scored a safety when Baugh fumbled while passing on a fake punt. A 36-yard field goal by TCU's Taldon Manton on a placekick held by Baugh followed.

Quote to Note: "I guess you could say I had a hand in all the scoring." —TCU's Baugh, who fumbled for LSU's safety and held for the Horned Frogs' field goal

1937: Santa Clara 21, LSU 14

The Setup: LSU, repeating as SEC champ, was ranked No. 1 by Williamson and No. 2 in the first year of the AP poll. The Rose Bowl bypassed LSU for Pittsburgh, so the Tigers settled on a second straight trip to the Sugar Bowl to play one-loss West Coast powerhouse Santa Clara.

How It Played Out: The Tigers, playing for a second straight year on a rain-soaked field, had an incredible 10 turnovers with 6 lost fumbles and 4 interceptions. Santa Clara also had 6 turnovers, but the Broncos' defense held LSU without a first down in a 25-minute stretch of playing time. Santa Clara led 14–0 and 21–7, and the Tigers never made enough plays to catch the visitors from California.

Quote to Note: "We had heard of the Sugar Bowl. The West Coast papers concentrated on the Rose Bowl, but we felt we were good enough to play in a bowl against a really good team." —Santa Clara tackle Al Wolff

1938: Santa Clara 6, LSU 0

The Setup: LSU ended up back in the Sugar Bowl for a third consecutive year, again meeting the Broncos.

How It Played Out: LSU did everything but win. It outgained Santa Clara 201 to 101 and held a 10 to 4 first-down advantage. The Broncos even lost three fumbles, but the Tigers just couldn't score. Santa Clara's first-quarter four-yard TD pass stood up as the game-winning points.

Quote to Note: "We were the better team. Our feeling was LSU would have to play over their heads to stay close to us." — Santa Clara tackle Al Wolff

1950: Oklahoma 35, LSU 0

The Setup: Second-ranked Oklahoma hadn't lost in 20 games. LSU was 8–2 with wins over conference champions Rice, North Carolina, and Tulane. At an Oklahoma pre-bowl practice in Biloxi, Sooners coach Bud Wilkinson accused former LSU lineman Piggy Barnes and LSU fan Goober Morse of spying on them.

How It Played Out: Oklahoma's passing game worked with several new plays the Sooners hadn't even practiced. Trailing 14–0 at halftime, LSU held out hope until Oklahoma fullback Leon Heath ran 86 yards for a touchdown.

Quote to Note: "If we played LSU a dozen times, we'd never played that well against them ever again. They're too good a team." —Oklahoma's Wilkinson

1959: LSU 7, Clemson 0

The Setup: Unbeaten and No. 1 LSU, already named national champions by the AP and UPI polls, was a 14-point favorite over 8–2 ACC champion Clemson. Clemson coach Frank Howard said before the game, "You can tell [LSU] from me that they're gonna have to be No. 1 to beat us."

How It Played Out: LSU starting QB Warren Rabb broke his hand in the second quarter and the Tigers blew three first-half scoring opportunities. A bad Clemson punt snap set up the game's only score, a nine-yard TD pass from halfback Billy Cannon to end Mickey Mangham.

Quote to Note: "I wasn't sure it would get to him until he grabbed it." —Cannon on his game-winning TD pass

1960: Ole Miss 21, LSU 0

The Setup: This was a rematch of LSU's dramatic 7–3 Halloween night win over Ole Miss from a few months earlier. The Tigers didn't want to play the Rebels again. LSU had a long list of injuries. It took three rounds of votes by the Tigers players to accept a Sugar Bowl invitation.

How It Played Out: LSU played like it didn't care to be in the game. Ole Miss, a seven-point favorite, shut down Heisman Trophy winner Billy Cannon. He gained only eight yards on six attempts while Ole Miss QB Bobby Franklin won game MVP honors after throwing for 148 yards and two TDs.

Quote to Note: "I don't think there is any question the [Ole Miss] touchdown pass before the half broke our backs." —LSU coach Paul Dietzel

1965: LSU 13, Syracuse 10

The Setup: LSU and Syracuse accepted Sugar Bowl bids, and then both teams lost their last regular-season game, setting up a Sugar Bowl matchup with teams combining for the most losses (five) since 1945.

How It Played Out: Syracuse running backs Floyd Little and Jim Nance, the first African Americans to appear on Sugar Bowl rosters since Pittsburgh's Bobby Grier in 1956, combined for 116 yards on 23 carries but no TDs. After trailing 10–2 at halftime, LSU rallied with split end/place-kicker Doug Moreau catching a

57-yard TD pass, kicking the extra point, and drilling a game-winning 28-yard field goal.

LSU's Charles McClendon became the first former Sugar Bowl player to come back and coach a team to victory.

Quote to Note: "The kick felt good when it left my shoe." —LSU's Moreau, the game MVP, on his game-deciding field goal

1968: LSU 20, Wyoming 13

The Setup: Unbeaten Wyoming, owning a 14-game winning streak and sporting the nation's best defense and rushing defense, took on six-win LSU, a team that had a tie and lost three games by a combined six points.

How It Played Out: Wyoming dominated the first half, leading 13–0 and allowing LSU one first down and 38 yards of total offense. On LSU's first offensive series of the second half, the Tigers inserted third-string tailback Glenn Smith, who excelled at cutback running. The eventual game MVP ran for 74 yards and one TD on 16 carries, caught a 39-yard pass, and jump-started LSU's comeback featuring two Nelson Stokley TD passes to Tommy Morel.

Quote to Note: "If Wyoming had beaten us, I wouldn't have been able to go home." —LSU's Smith, a New Orleans native

1985: Nebraska 28, LSU 10

The Setup: Eleventh-ranked LSU (8–2–1), the second-place team in the SEC, got its shot at playing No. 5 Nebraska (9–2) when the SEC banned league champ Florida, which was under NCAA investigation.

How It Played Out: Against the nation's No. 1 defense, Bill Arnsparger–coached LSU gained 291 yards in the first half and led 10–7. The Cornhuskers dominated after halftime, throwing a 21–0 shutout by outgaining the Tigers 282 to 113. Nebraska switched to a three-man defensive front with an eight-man secondary, and it intercepted five LSU QB Jeff Wickersham passes.

Quote to Note: "We picked . . . up [the second half defensive scheme] from the Miami Dolphins a few years ago, and I think [defensive coordinator] Bill [Arnsparger] is responsible for that." —Nebraska coach Tom Osborne

1987: Nebraska 30, LSU 15

The Setup: Fifth-ranked LSU—0–4–1 lifetime against No. 6 Nebraska—badly wanted to win. But two late LSU distractions— head coach Bill Arnsparger announcing he would be resigning after the game to become Florida's athletic director and LSU lineman Roland Barbay being banned from postseason play for a positive drug test—hurt the Tigers.

How It Played Out: LSU scored on its first drive for a 7–0 lead then fell apart, committing 12 penalties for 130 yards as Nebraska scored 30 consecutive points.

Quote to Note: "The thing I'll always wonder is that you don't know if they were really that good or if the penalties made us that bad." —LSU center Nacho Albergamo

2002: LSU 47, Illinois 34

The Setup: Nick Saban's second LSU team turned a 4–3 start into five straight victories including an SEC Championship Game win over Tennessee that got the Tigers a Sugar Bowl date with Big Ten champion Illinois.

How It Played Out: LSU had a stretch in which it scored on five of six possessions, including a Sugar Bowl–record 27 points in the second quarter. LSU quarterback Rohan Davey threw for 444 yards and three TDs, running back Domanick Davis ran for 129 yards and four TDs, and wide receiver Josh Reed had 14 catches for 239 yards and two TDs.

Quote to Note: "There came a point in the second quarter when Coach [Saban] told me to settle down. I was trying to hit a home run on every play. It was just pitch-and-catch." —LSU's Davey

2004: LSU 21, Oklahoma 14

The Setup: The Sugar Bowl hosted this BCS National Championship Game between a pair of 12–1 teams—No. 1 Oklahoma and No. 2 LSU, ranked according to the BCS formula.

How It Played Out: Oklahoma entered the game averaging 461 yards and 45 points. The Tigers held the Sooners to 152 yards on 70 plays and two TDs. OU Heisman Trophy–winning QB Jason White threw for only 102 yards and had two passes intercepted, including a 20-yard pick-six TD by defensive end Marcus Spears. LSU's Justin Vincent ran for 117 yards and a TD.

Quote to Note: "I dropped back and it was a gift." —LSU's Spears on his interception TD return

2007: LSU 41, Notre Dame 14

The Setup: After a 4–2 start, LSU won six straight games to earn an invitation to the first Sugar Bowl played in the Superdome since Hurricane Katrina ravaged the city of New Orleans and the Dome in August 2005.

How It Played Out: LSU gained 577 yards (including a 333–30 second-half domination) and scored the most points ever allowed by Notre Dame in a bowl game. After the Fighting Irish tied it up at 14–14 with 2:25 left in the first half, LSU scored 27 unanswered points. The game MVP, LSU QB JaMarcus Russell, threw for 332 yards and two TDs.

Quote to Note: "The fact that we're here, I think it's right. I can't imagine it any other way." —LSU coach Les Miles on his team playing in the first Sugar Bowl in the Superdome after Hurricane Katrina

35 Dale Brown

Few head coaches in the history of college basketball stubbornly and relentlessly led with their chin and heart more than former LSU head coach Dale Brown. He's the third-winningest coach (by victories) in SEC history with 448 wins in 25 seasons from 1973 to 1997, including two Final Four appearances (1981 and 1986) and three SEC championships.

It wasn't just about pursuing victory for Brown. It was about fighting the good fight, whether it was on or off the court. "The game was bigger than the court to me," Brown said. "Basketball was part of the mission. I felt basketball restricted me, but I stayed with it as long as I did because it gave me the visibility to help the down-and-outers."

His grit came from his childhood. Growing up in Minot, North Dakota, he was the son of a single mother whose husband walked out on her two days before Brown was born on Halloween 1935. He never forgot he was once a kid who lined his worn-out shoes with popcorn boxes he picked up in theaters. It eventually gave him the passion to succeed, especially when the odds were against him, and the compassion to serve others.

While most coaches talked about X's and O's, Brown talked about everything from world hunger to the blight of communism. He quoted everyone from Nelson Mandela to Martin Luther King Jr. He traveled every summer, seeking such ultimate experiences as climbing the Matterhorn, searching for Noah's Ark, pheasant hunting in Canada, riding camels in Baghdad, and traversing the length of the Mississippi River in a speedboat. He often invited foreign coaches to Baton Rouge for extended visits. Sometimes the end of the LSU bench during games consisted of a trainer and what appeared to be United Nations representatives.

Brown earned the reputation that he was more of a character than a coach, something that the late Joe Dean, who was LSU's athletic director when Brown finally retired, once said just wasn't true or fair. "Just because a guy doesn't like to go to the coaches' convention at the Final Four and sit around and diagram plays on napkins doesn't mean he's not a good coach," Dean said. "Dale came to LSU when the program was nothing and he made it something special."

Brown was a little-known 36-year-old Washington State University assistant when he was hired by then–LSU athletic director Carl Maddox in 1972. Maddox, a former LSU assistant football coach, had no clue who to pursue after he fired Press Maravich following the 1971–72 season. It was Dean, then a former LSU All-SEC guard turned Converse Rubber Company rep, who suggested Brown to Maddox. Maddox, knowing Dean was probably one of the most well-connected men in college basketball, took Dean at his word.

Once hired, Brown took a program that was as dead as dead can be and breathed life into it, doing anything that popped into his head to promote it. He drove around the state of Louisiana, stopping whenever he saw a bare basketball goal, just so he could hang a purple and gold net on it.

He called his first LSU team the Hustlers, promoting them by sticking the team picture on replicas of the old Wild West wanted posters. His promise was his team would always play hard, diving for every loose ball and taking every charge. "The Hustlers just grabbed me," Brown said. "They gave every ounce of energy almost every night."

Just like Brown did when he coached. Because of his warp-speed personality, because he never met an opinion he didn't like, because he usually spoke from his heart and not his head, because he wanted to fight every injustice he came across, it's astounding he didn't burn out after 10 years. And in doing so, Brown earned the respect of coaching colleagues who sometimes made fun of his offbeat personality and motivation techniques. "Not long after Dale announced he was quitting, I sent him a letter," former Alabama coach Wimp Sanderson said. "I wrote, 'At first [Tennessee's] Don DeVoe left. Then [Auburn's] Sonny Smith. Then me. Then [Georgia's] Hugh Durham. You outlasted all of us.' He had a remarkable career."

It took seven years for the Tigers under Brown to reach their first NCAA tournament and win their first SEC title, dropping the banner before the end of the game in a title-clinching win over Alabama. For the next 14 years after the breakthrough in 1978–79, his teams were in postseason play with 10 straight NCAA appearances.

Brown put together some great teams. Some of his most talented squads, the ones with first-team All-Americans such as a skinny seven-foot center named Shaquille O'Neal and a sharpshooting guard named Chris Jackson, never made it to the Sweet 16.

Even after Brown finally got the Tigers to the Final Four for the first time in 1980–81, his ninth season at LSU, he realized anything can happen in the NCAA tournament, both bad and good. For instance, Brown's 1984–85 team won the SEC championship and entered the NCAA tourney as the No. 4 seed matched against No. 13 Navy. "I didn't know anything about Navy, and we didn't get films on them until the day before we left for the tournament," Brown said. "I look at the film. I see this guy scoring all over the place, blocking shots, rebounding. My coaches tell me, 'His name is David Robinson.' I say, 'Who's David Robinson?' But they had other good players."

Final score: Navy and its future Naismith Memorial Basketball Hall of Famer Robinson 78, LSU 55. It remains Brown's worst-ever NCAA tourney loss.

The next season, in 1985–86, Brown's Tigers made the greatest Final Four run of any Cinderella in NCAA tournament history, as a No. 11 seed that had to rally just to get a tournament bid. By the time LSU got to February, it had lost two seven-foot centers and a 6'8" center to a transfer, knee surgery, and academic ineligibility, respectively. And then there was an outbreak of chicken pox.

"I called Ricky Blanton in my office," Brown said of the 6'7" shooting guard from Miami, Florida, who had never played center in his career. "I said, 'Ricky, I've got nowhere to go, I've got to play you at center,'" Brown said. "I can still see his eyes widening. He says, 'Coach, are you kidding?' I said, 'I believe in you. You might have to put on a little weight.' Ricky went out and believed he was a center. It turned around the back half of our season enough to get in the NCAA tournament."

LSU got the enormous break of playing its first two NCAA tourney games on its home floor. This was back in the day before the NCAA insisted solely on neutral sites for tournament play. In Baton Rouge the 11th-seeded Tigers beat No. 6 seed Purdue 94–87 in double overtime in the first round, and then used a game-winning shot by Anthony Wilson after a scramble for a loose ball to beat No. 3 seed Memphis State 83–81. The Tigers got another break in that the Southeast Regional semifinals and finals were in Atlanta.

LSU handled No. 2 seed Georgia Tech 70–64 in the semis and then beat top seed and fellow SEC member Kentucky 59–57 in the finals after the Tigers had lost to the Wildcats three times during the season. Kentucky ended the year 32–4. Georgia Tech's entire starting five eventually played in the NBA.

In the Final Four semifinal against Louisville in Dallas's Reunion Arena, LSU led the Cardinals by nine points in the first half before losing 88–77. Louisville, led by freshman center "Never Nervous" Pervis Ellison, then beat Duke for the national championship two nights later. "We just simply ran out of gas. Our guys gave everything they had," Brown said. "That '86 team was disappointed, but it had a peace about it, because it gave everything."

When he retired, Brown had no regrets. Still living in Baton Rouge with his wife, Vonnie, he has continued to travel the world, always searching, always learning, always seeking new viewpoints and making new friends.

36 Perfect Tigers

Behind the talents of a Heisman Trophy–worthy quarterback operating from an innovative, fast-paced offense, LSU rolled to an undefeated season and a national title. Sounds a lot like 2019, right? Well, it was 1908.

LSU has produced many more perfect seasons than the widely known championship-winning years of 1958 and 2019. In all, the university has had seven perfect seasons, though four of those (1895, 1896, 1898, and 1905) were composed of a combined 13 games. In fact, the 1898 club played only one game—a 37–0 victory over Tulane—and the 1895 and 1905 teams each went 3–0. That 1905 club didn't allow a single point, and the 1895 team actually took down Alabama.

Still, of all those pre-SEC perfect teams, the 1908 squad is the most legitimate, as the Tigers went 10–0 with victories over Auburn, Mississippi State, Baylor, and Arkansas. That team outscored its opponents 442–11, eclipsing the 80-point barrier twice and shutting out seven opponents.

Their leader, tight end–turned-quarterback Doc Fenton, was recognized by the National Football Foundation as the retroactive Heisman winner. He captained an offense that second-year coach

Edgar Wingard had installed at the school the season before, a cutting-edge scheme for its quick play, deception, speed, and use of the newly invented forward pass.

The National Football Foundation crowned the Tigers its national champion that year, but the school does not recognize the title. The season was shrouded in scandal, according to a story on *SB Nation*. LSU, then a member of the Southern Intercollegiate Athletic Association (SIAA), was the focus of a conference investigation into allegations of cheating. Fellow conference member Auburn accused the Tigers of using ringers, professional players posing as college students.

LSU handed Auburn its only loss that season, 10–2, knocking off the preseason SIAA favorites. It was such a shocking result that during its postgame coverage, the Auburn local newspaper asked, "Who are these LSU people?" The SIAA eventually cleared LSU of wrongdoing, though there were two irregularities found, and the school fired Wingard.

The 1958 season came with less suspicion and marked the first perfect season for the Tigers since the inception of the SEC in 1933. Behind halfback Billy Cannon and Coach Paul Dietzel's platoon defense, the Tigers beat a pair of ranked teams—No. 12 Clemson in the Sugar Bowl and No. 6 Ole Miss in Tiger Stadium. They survived some close calls to remain perfect.

The first scare came against Florida in October. Cannon, a defensive back on defense, intercepted the Gators in the fourth quarter of a game tied at 7. LSU drove down after the pick and kicked a game-winning field goal. Against Mississippi State a few weeks later, the Tigers found themselves trailing 6–0 at halftime to the 3–6 Bulldogs on a muddy field in Jackson, Mississippi. LSU recovered a fumble and then completed a touchdown pass on fourth down at the 5-yard line, the eventual winning points. The Bulldogs missed three field goals that day, the last one a game-tying whiff from the 10-yard line in the fourth quarter.

The latest perfect season came in 2019, when Heisman winner Joe Burrow and the Tigers torched college football with their up-tempo, pass-heavy offense. They beat more top 10 ranked teams (7) than any other squad in history, led the nation in offense (568.4 yards a game), and crushed their three postseason opponents: Georgia in the SEC Championship Game (37–10), Oklahoma in the CFP semifinal (63–28), and Clemson in the CFP title game (42–25).

37 Bluegrass Miracle

Each Thursday during the 2002 season, the LSU football team practiced a Hail Mary play called Dash Right 93 Berlin—a pass that was supposed to come falling down like the Allied bombs on Berlin in World War II, according to a 2012 story in the *Advocate*. It never worked; the pass was normally intercepted or tipped, sent tumbling to the turf. But on November 9, 2002, in Lexington, Kentucky, Dash Right 93 Berlin became better known as the Bluegrass Miracle. Quarterback Marcus Randall connected with receiver Devery Henderson for a 75-yard game-winning completion to beat Kentucky 33–30 as time expired.

The pass sailed over intended receiver Michael Clayton's out-stretched fingers, was tipped by two Kentucky defensive backs, and fell into Henderson's waiting grasp at the 19-yard line. He raced into the end zone, raising both hands as Kentucky fans poured onto the field. The Wildcats' premature celebration spanned several more minutes. Fans flooded the field and leaped onto the goal posts, beginning to topple the structure in response to what they erroneously believed to be an upset of the heavy favorite—and defending SEC champions—LSU.

The Jefferson Pilot Sports broadcast of the game flashed the wrong score—Kentucky 30, LSU 27—on the screen as Henderson raced into the end zone. Kentucky coach Guy Morris, already bathed in a celebratory water cooler shower, glanced in disbelief at the stadium's Jumbotron.

"Don't know what to say," LSU coach Nick Saban said to a sideline reporter as he walked off the field. "Fans are up on the goal posts, and I don't know why."

LSU players rushed toward the end zone, creating a pile on top of Henderson that grew to eight feet high. Around them, bewildered Kentucky fans slowly realized the truth: they'd just lost on one of the most extraordinary plays in college football history.

"LSU fans throughout the world will never forget where they were that moment," Clayton said during an interview in 2012 with WAFB-TV in Baton Rouge. "That game was just as exciting as winning a national championship."

"There's a little bit of luck when you hit one," Saban said in a story published in 2012 in the *Advocate*. "The ball has to bounce right for you, and it did that day. It was fun to be part of a play that people remember this long."

Luck was indeed on LSU's side, but it went beyond that play. So many things needed to go right in the waning seconds, well after the Tigers coughed up 21–7 and 24–14 leads. Kentucky and thick-framed quarterback Jared Lorenzen could have milked the clock before their go-ahead 29-yard field goal with 11 seconds left, but a Wildcats player inadvertently signaled for timeout. Saban then attempted to use a timeout before Kentucky's field goal kick, a way to ice the kicker. Officials did not notice the coach, caught by TV cameras on the sideline gesturing for the timeout. It's a good thing. Saban needed the timeout. On the first play of the ensuing series, Randall hit Clayton for a 17-yard gain, and Clayton immediately bounced from the turf to use his team's final timeout with two seconds remaining.

It all set up Dash Right 93 Berlin. The pass was intended for Clayton, but he got caught up amid two Kentucky defensive backs—the same two who tipped the pass: Morris Lane and Earven Flowers. Henderson was supposed to be the short receiver on the play; he was wrongly positioned, he admitted. "Everything was kind of cluttered from where I was," Henderson said. "I knew for a fact I was out of position."

But this was one time when being out of position was a good thing. "[In practice] it never worked," Henderson told WAFB in 2012. "I just happened to be in the right place at the right time."

38 Kevin Faulk

In the fall of 1994, it seemed as if every big-time major college football coach found his way to the tiny south Louisiana town of Carencro outside Lafayette. They all wanted a glimpse of Kevin Faulk, a two-time state Class 5A MVP, a hell-on-wheels shotgun quarterback who helped Carencro High School deliver a state championship in 1992.

Though Faulk had 7,612 all-purpose yards and 89 touchdowns in his high school career, it was his running ability that had recruiters salivating over his potential as a five-star running back. Faulk averaged 8.1 yards per carry in his Carencro career—4,877 yards and 62 TDs on 603 attempts—and that is why the first thing Gerry DiNardo did after his introductory press conference as LSU's new football coach in December 1994 was visit Faulk. "It impressed me that he came to see me immediately," Faulk said.

DiNardo drove the 50 miles to Carencro from Baton Rouge to personally woo Faulk, who signed with the Tigers and remains the school's all-time rushing leader with 4,557 yards and 46 TDs. Faulk led LSU in rushing all four of his collegiate seasons and remains the fourth-leading rusher in SEC history. "Kevin was very smart on the field; he knew every position," DiNardo said. "He understood the game conceptually, not just his position. He was mature beyond his years academically. He took care of business."

Faulk took a leap of faith to join a Tigers program that was coming off six straight losing seasons. But his decision to attend LSU was more about location. "My parents came with me on an official recruiting visit to Notre Dame," Faulk said, "and I was still homesick. I'm not ashamed to admit I'm a mama's boy."

Faulk played with a quiet confidence that earned the respect of his teammates and opponents. "Kevin was a very quiet, loyal guy to his teammates," said former LSU defensive tackle Booger McFarland, now an ESPN studio analyst after two years on the *Monday Night Football* broadcast crew. "He flipped the switch when he got on the field. He had supreme confidence."

He was at his very best when his team needed him the most, such as in the Tigers' 1996 opener, when they trailed vast underdog Houston by a stunning 34–14 at the end of the third quarter. Faulk, then a sophomore, didn't even know if he was going to play. He was at the scene of an off-season bar fight in Carencro, got charged with four misdemeanors, and was suspended by DiNardo for the season opener. But two days before the game, the charges against Faulk were dropped ("I wasn't even part of the fight; I was just trying to stop it," he said), and DiNardo reinstated him. "I felt I had to do something special when Coach dropped my suspension," Faulk said.

Despite two of his fumbles that Houston converted into touchdowns, Faulk lived up to his silent promise. On the first play of the fourth quarter, he scored on a 78-yard punt return to jump-start a

21–0 LSU rally for a 35–34 victory. When the Tigers needed one last first down to run out the clock, Faulk jetted 43 yards. It was the mic drop on one of the best individual performances in school history. Faulk set school records for most rushing yards in a game (246 yards and two TDs on 21 carries) and for most all-purpose yards in a game (378).

As a junior, another vintage Faulk performance landed him on the cover of the October 27, 1997, issue of *Sports Illustrated* when the No. 14–ranked Tigers upset No. 1–ranked and defending national champion Florida 28–21. He earned it by rushing for 78 yards, returning a punt 30 yards to set up a touchdown, and returning three kickoffs for 76 yards.

The New England Patriots got the steal of the 1999 NFL Draft when they chose Faulk in the second round. He played all 13 of his pro seasons with the Pats, won three Super Bowl rings, and was such a valuable all-around back that quarterback Tom Brady said, "No one was more clutch than Kevin."

Faulk's pro career was a detour from his original career path of becoming a coach. He was one of the first LSU players to graduate in fewer than four years. Following his retirement from the NFL in October 2012, Faulk became an assistant coach at Carencro High School. In January 2018 he joined LSU's coaching staff as director of player development and was promoted to running backs coach in January 2020. "Coaching is one of the things I've always wanted to do," Faulk said. "Not too many freshmen know what they want to do when they get to college. I knew exactly what I wanted."

39 Dan Borné

Dan Borné is used to the question by now: "How did you become the Tiger Stadium public address announcer?" It's quite a funny and simple story, Borné says: No one else applied for the job.

In 1986, with the retirement of his friend Sid Crocker from PA duties, Borné wrote a letter to the LSU athletic department expressing interest in the position. Months passed and he heard nothing. Then one day he got a call from an LSU official requesting a meeting on campus. Borné interviewed for 30 minutes with school administrators and was hired. "We exchanged some small talk and didn't talk very much about the position," Borné recalled in a 2008 story published on *Bleacher Report.* "They then informed me that the job was mine if I still wanted it, because nobody else had asked for it. So a good life lesson is that if you want something, make sure you ask for it."

In 2020 Borné entered his 35th season as the Voice of Tiger Stadium, his baritone vocals and oratory staples rooted into LSU football just as much as some of the program's greatest stars. Not a home game passes without Borné's now-famous line about precipitation: "Chance of rain . . . never!"

How'd that start? That's a funny story too, he says. "I just saw [on the weather forecast during] one game, 'Chance of rain,' and I said 'Never,' just threw it out there. 'Never.' And then, hmm . . . hmm. . . . You could hear this kind of rumble," he said in a 2013 story in the *Daily Reveille.*

Nowadays, the line even appears in his pregame script, more a tradition now than an accurate weather prognostication. He has even boomed the line while rain fell on Tiger Stadium. The phrase has picked up steam among LSU fans, with those already in the venue normally screaming out the final word in unison: "Never!"

In 2018 he missed just his third LSU football game since 1986 while battling a bout of laryngitis. In 2006 he missed the Kentucky game because he was attending a retreat for his church. He was officiating a wedding when the 2015 South Carolina game had to be moved to Tiger Stadium on a few days' notice because of flooding in that state.

For his "real jobs," Borné—who turns 74 in 2020—is the president of the Louisiana Chemical Association and a Catholic deacon, but he began his career as a TV anchor for Baton Rouge Station WAFB. While in college, he did the play-by-play for Nicholls State baseball from 1964 to 1968.

He is a beloved figured at LSU. "His voice fits the sound system," said longtime sports information staff member Kent Lowe. "He has a style that people like, he gets the information across, and he gets it right, and that's probably three-quarters of it, to make sure what you say is accurate."

40 Leonard Fournette

The legend of Leonard Fournette began well before his arrival at LSU. It started in his hometown of New Orleans as a man-child playing youth football—a kid with receiver speed, lineman strength, and linebacker mentality.

Fournette once scored eight touchdowns in a youth league contest. He was so big and strong, so fast and agile, the parents of other children eventually signed a petition to have him banned. At age 13 he was outrunning college athletes, and as a high schooler he broke the leg of an opposing player during a collision on a toss sweep. "When he came out of his mama's womb," said Cyril Crutchfield, Fournette's high school coach at St. Augustine, "he was a lot better athlete than when others came out of their mama's womb."

The unanimous No. 1 recruit in the 2014 signing class, Fournette became arguably the most prized prospect to sign with LSU, snubbing coach Nick Saban and Alabama to join his home-state squad with a clear vision in mind: win Louisiana a national championship. He came up short, the same coach and team in his way each of his three seasons in Baton Rouge: Saban and the Crimson Tide.

While marked by his struggle against Alabama, Fournette's legacy is forever in LSU's annals. He produced the greatest string of rushing performances the school has ever seen, opening his sophomore season in 2015 with seven consecutive 100-yard games, including three straight 200-yard outings that set an SEC record. It was such an unbelievable streak that ESPN analyst Mel Kiper Jr. said that if he were eligible, Fournette would be the No. 1 pick in the 2016 NFL Draft.

Fournette's school-record 1,953 yards rushing that year led the nation and obliterated the school record. His 22 rushing scores in 2015 were a school record too, and his 284 yards against Ole Miss in 2016 broke the LSU single-game mark, only to be eclipsed weeks later by Derrius Guice's 285 at Texas A&M.

Fournette finished his career with 3,830 yards rushing in fewer than three full seasons. He may have caught the school's career leader, Faulk (4,557), if not for an ankle injury that lingered through much of his junior season. He missed roughly half the year with an injury he suffered during preseason camp, something that adversely affected the Tigers.

They entered the 2016 season ranked No. 5 in the preseason polls before struggling offensively in losses to Wisconsin and Auburn, the latter resulting in the midseason firing of coach Les

Miles. Fournette and the coach were close. The day of Miles's firing, he met with the coach in a one-on-one talk in his office before Miles exited the building. Fournette spoke to reporters afterward. "To me," he said, "he's one hell of a coach. It's shocking." Three months later, Fournette declared for the draft, was selected by Jacksonville with the fourth pick, and erupted as a rookie for more than 1,000 yards and nine touchdowns.

And to think, all that from a man who, as a five-year-old in New Orleans, quit football. Fournette stopped playing the sport because he didn't like the conditioning part of the training. After a year away, Fournette told his father, "I'm ready," said Leonard Sr. in a 2015 story in the *Advocate*. "I brought him out to the park, and the rest is history."

41 Throw It to Byrd

Demetrius Byrd refers to himself as Mr. Clutch. After what happened on October 20, 2007, in Tiger Stadium, no one is questioning that self-proclaimed moniker of LSU's former star receiver. What Byrd, quarterback Matt Flynn, and coach Les Miles did is still the stuff of legend in Baton Rouge.

With LSU down by one point to Auburn in the waning seconds and in field goal range, Miles elected to have Flynn throw to the end zone, a surprising and risky call with eight seconds left on a running clock. Flynn's fade pass floated short of Auburn cornerback Jerraud Powers, and a sliding Byrd made the catch for a 22-yard touchdown completion with one second remaining on the clock. The catch secured LSU's 30–24 victory in a critical game during a season that would end with a national title.

Before the play, Byrd waved toward the Tiger Stadium press box in hopes of signaling to LSU offensive coordinator Gary Crowton that he expected to be in one-on-one coverage on the outside. "Then I got in the huddle and that was the play call, and I knew I just had to go out there and make a play on it," Byrd said. "The stadium shook," Byrd said. "That's how crazy it was. I wish they had the earthquake monitor on because it would have registered. All Matt Flynn had to do was throw it up to Mr. Clutch, and Mr. Clutch did it. I can't thank him enough for giving me the opportunity."

What makes the play so legendary—aside from its game-winning result—is the situation from multiple perspectives: the season, the game, and the play call. LSU's title hopes were fading after losing at Kentucky the previous week. They looked even bleaker at halftime against Auburn. The out-of-town Tigers led 17–7. A second-half rally so synonymous with Miles's teams unfolded in a lively Tiger Stadium, but Auburn took a 24–23 lead with 3:21 left after an 83-yard touchdown march.

To avoid kicking off to LSU's electric kick returner Trindon Holliday, AU coach Tommy Tuberville called for a squib kick. LSU got possession at its own 42, roughly 30 yards from range for a game-winning field goal. Flynn scrambled for a combined 19 yards, and Jacob Hester had a 10-yard carry, putting the Tigers in striking range at Auburn's 22-yard line with a third-and-7. That's when craziness happened.

LSU players broke the huddle for the third-down play with 18 seconds left on a moving clock. They set up on the line with 11 ticks, and Flynn snapped the ball at 8 seconds. Surely this would be a rush toward the middle of the field, right? Surely they'd set up kicker Colt David for a field goal of no more than 40 yards, right? Wrong. Flynn dropped back into a clean pocket and lofted a fade pass to the end zone for Byrd. It left his hands with about six seconds left and arrived in Byrd's clutches at the three-second mark. He collapsed to the turf, and Tiger Stadium roared.

So many were shocked—even Will Muschamp, then Auburn's defensive coordinator. "I thought they were going to run the clock out," Muschamp said. "I called a run pressure thinking they were going to center the ball and was trying to give them a bad snap. They dropped back and threw. . . . If we tip the ball in the end zone, the game's over. . . . They made the play when they needed to make it, and Jerraud was in position to make the play."

Byrd's pre-snap signal to Crowton in the LSU press box was with good reason. "The whole drive, I guess Auburn didn't really pay me any attention," Byrd said. "They were really not respecting me at all. The whole drive I ran go routes on purpose just to see if they would double-team me. The whole drive it was just me and Jerraud Powers."

Ironically Powers excelled at the next level while Byrd never panned out. A third-round draft pick by the Colts in 2009, Powers played in the NFL for eight seasons, starting 88 games. A seventh-round selection by the Chargers in 2009, Byrd was released by San Diego 10 months later and never played again.

A week before the 2009 NFL Draft, Byrd was involved in a serious car accident that left him in critical condition and considering suicide. "I told myself I was going back to the league, I have to play football, and when I saw that door start to close, I went into a deep depression," he said. "If I wasn't so scared to use a gun to shoot myself, I don't know what would've happened. I was thinking about jumping off a bridge. I was really depressed because I wanted to play football. I think it took me a good six years to really get over it. It changed my life in a good way and it made me more humble now and thankful for the things that I do."

42

2019 Tigers and Offense

Nobody realized it at the time, but in the last week of June 2019, LSU issued storm warnings about the fury it was about to unleash on college football with its new spread/run-pass option–infused offense. Within days, at different events, first-year passing game coordinator Joe Brady and returning starting quarterback Joe Burrow basically inferred opposing defenses should move away from possible harm and seek shelter in their dressing rooms. "Get your popcorn ready," Brady said at an LSU alumni function. "That's what you're going to be doing when you see this offense this fall." Burrow went even bigger and bolder. "We're going to score a lot of points, and I don't think a lot of people are used to LSU scoring 40, 50, 60 points a game," he said on a muggy afternoon at the Manning Passing Academy, where he served as a counselor.

Given the fact LSU had averaged 30.7 points over the previous 19 seasons during arguably the best era in school history, including two national titles and four SEC championships, Brady and Burrow's ultra-optimistic declarations were met with polite smiles. But a little more than six and a half months later, the most prolific offense in Division 1-A history had scorched scoreboards from Austin to Atlanta as 15–0 LSU won the national championship and set NCAA single-season records for scoring offense (726 points, 48.4 points per game) and total offense (8,526 yards, 568.4 yards per game).

Burrow completed 76.2 percent of his passes, throwing for 5,671 yards and an NCAA season record 60 touchdowns. He won the Heisman Trophy and every national QB award, vaulting to a possible No. 1 overall pick in the NFL Draft. Brady leapfrogged from an unknown second-level New Orleans Saints assistant to winning the Broyles Award as college football's top assistant to landing a seven-year, $62 million contract as the new offensive coordinator of the NFL's Carolina Panthers.

How did all this happen? How did a historically good, but not consistently great, SEC football program finally dump its outdated offense and employ a system using its locker room full of NFL-caliber athletes to the fullest? Burrow likes to describe it as "the perfect storm."

It started when Burrow enrolled in LSU in June 2018 as a graduate transfer from Ohio State with two years of playing eligibility. He won the Tigers' starting job before he had a chance to learn all his teammates' names while playing in an unfamiliar offensive style. "I'd always played in offenses taking snaps in the spread," Burrow said. "My footwork wasn't great because I'd never been under center, so I'd never done that footwork play-action, turn-your-back, seven-step drop. I literally had never done that in my life. I had to learn that in about a month and a half."

Burrow did enough correctly, especially down the stretch, to guide LSU to a 10–3 record, a Fiesta Bowl win over UCF, and final rankings of No. 6 in the AP poll and No. 7 in the Coaches' poll.

But one of the losses, a 29–0 home blanking by then–No. 1 Alabama, stuck in LSU head coach Ed Orgeron's craw. "All the SEC teams, I knew that they were scoring points and we weren't," Orgeron said. "I knew that we had the athletes, I knew we had the coaches; we just had to change our system. I told [offensive coordinator] Steve [Ensminger] after the Alabama loss I was going to find somebody to help us install a spread passing offense the next season."

That somebody was Brady, recommended by Saints coach Sean Payton. Brady was 29 years old and Ensminger 61, but they immediately established a simpatico working relationship. "I've enjoyed him from the day he showed up," Ensminger said of Brady. "We brought him here to help us in the passing game, and I told Joe that. I said, 'Look, take it over. You present it. We'll discuss it. If

I think it fits, it goes.' He throws it up on the wall, [and] we agree with it or we throw it off. It has been that that type of relationship, a 'What do you think?'"

Brady loved the give-and-take. "Coach E. makes the final decision, but he listens to everybody's thoughts," Brady said. "So when you work for a guy that doesn't feel 'my way is the only way,' you enjoy that interaction every single day." Burrow, who was taking graduate courses online enabling him to plot offense daily with Ensminger and Brady, loved the old-school/new-school dynamic.

Brady also challenged LSU receivers, who had dropped too many passes in 2018, to catch 10,000 balls during the summer. He also created unique concentration drills in which receivers stood behind a closed door and had to catch a pass thrown to them as soon as the door opened.

While the offensive line, much maligned in 2018, was working on its footwork and drills, Burrow was an off-season taskmaster for the receivers, running backs, and tight ends. The team ran routes until he was satisfied with what he saw. He not only raised the level of expectation but created confidence and a connection with pass catchers that eventually allowed him to make accurate throws in tight windows once the season started.

As preseason practice began, Burrow and company grew eager for the August 31 season opener. "It's well-balanced and it's so unpredictable," running back Clyde Edwards-Helaire said of the new offense. "You can stand on the sideline and say, 'I wonder what play we're about to run.' It's pretty cool."

And they started sizzling hot, scoring touchdowns on their first five possessions in a Game 1 55–3 destruction of Georgia Southern. The fact Burrow, who passed for five touchdowns, was disappointed the Tigers didn't score 60 or more points spoke volumes about the relentless hunger the team would possess all season.

The offensive explosiveness was spellbinding. LSU scored in the 40s in five games, in the 50s in four games—including three consecutive November SEC Saturdays—and three times in the 60s. The points came in bunches. The Tigers scored 24 times on two or more consecutive touchdown drives and did it at least once in every game. That included LSU scoring four straight TD drives four times, with the most amazing display of all being TDs on seven consecutive possessions in the 63–28 Chick-fil-A Peach Bowl dismantling of No. 4 Oklahoma.

Was it the scheme that allowed LSU to have the first team in college history with a 5,000-yard passer (Burrow), two 1,000-yard receivers (Biletnikoff Award winner Ja'Marr Chase and Justin Jefferson), and a 1,000-yard rusher (Edwards-Helaire)? "This offense is built on triangles," Orgeron explained. "We're always going to form a triangle. Three receivers somewhere, somehow, are going to form a triangle. Joe is going to have a spot there; we go high to low [in progression], and we're making a decision based on the defense."

Burrow always had plenty of options while protected by an offensive line that won the Joe Moore Award as the college football's best O-line in 2019. "Everyone has to cover the entire field when they play us; we have too many weapons," Burrow said. "If you go back and watch the film, it's multiple places I can go with the football. The receivers always come back [after a play] and let me know 'I was open.' I say, 'That guy was open too, so he got the ball.'"

Or was it the way Ensminger, Brady, and Burrow worked together smoothly in the heat of battle? "When the offense comes off the field, Joe Brady talks to Joe Burrow and discusses what went on [during] that series," Ensminger said. "While they are doing that, I'm highlighting plays that I want to call in the next series. It's been perfect."

Or was it just an incredibly efficient offense that fed off its extremely prepared quarterback? "It's like having the answers to the test when you walk in there," Burrow told a roaring crowd at the Tigers' national championship parade and celebration. "That's truly how we felt when we were out there."

And it showed from the fast start to the glorious finish of Burrow throwing five TDs in the 42–25 CFP National Championship Game victory over Clemson. "This is a team for the ages, especially how prolific we were on offense, to have that type of quarterback that we have, to go 15–0 with a tremendous schedule, all the top teams that we played and beat," Orgeron said. "We answered the bell. These guys didn't blink. We didn't have a bad game. We played 15 good football games, and this is going to be hard to beat."

43 Chinese Bandits

They were born from LSU football coach Paul Dietzel's need to create three-platoon depth for the Tigers' 1958 national championship teams. Though they played both sides of the ball like the rest of the team did, their value was on defense. They were the Chinese Bandits, who time and again saved the Tigers from defeat during LSU's 11–0 national title quest.

When Dietzel had been defensive line coach at the University of Cincinnati in 1949, he wanted to give his defensive platoon a name. As a comic strip fan, Dietzel happened upon *Terry and the Pirates*, an action-adventure strip centered around a young American boy (Terry) who—along with his journalist friend— matched wits with an assortment of villains, including a group called the Chinese Bandits. Dietzel, wanting his defense to play fiercely, tagged it with the name the Chinese Bandits and told his players that the Chinese Bandits are "the meanest, most vicious people in the world."

It served a purpose in Cincinnati. But when Dietzel revived it at LSU, it worked better than he ever imagined. The Chinese Bandits' first tight situation was in Game 2 against Alabama in Mobile. Locked in a scoreless game, Alabama had first down at the LSU 3-yard line after a Tigers turnover. Dietzel thought the White Team, his first unit—with the 11 best players on the team—was tired. So he sent in the Bandits. "History records indicate after three downs that Alabama was still on the 3-yard line and on fourth down they were forced to kick a field goal for a 3–0 lead at the half," Dietzel recalled of the game LSU won 13–3. "That moment provided the cornerstone in the Bandits' stature."

It was in Game 5 against Kentucky in Tiger Stadium as LSU started a four-game home stand on consecutive Saturdays that the Chinese Bandits became "a thing" with the LSU fan base. "I had told our public address announcer to point out the Chinese Bandits' first entrance in the game," Dietzel said. "Midway through the first quarter, he proclaimed to 68,000 fans, 'Here come the Chinese Bandits!' when they entered the field to replace the White Team.

"On the very first play, a Kentucky fullback was met in midair, he fumbled, and a Bandit recovered it immediately. As the Bandits ran off the field to a deafening roar, the P.A. announcer said, 'And here come the Chinese Bandits right back.' From that moment on, the Chinese Bandits were electrified."

The Chinese Bandits consisted of juniors Mel Branch, Emile Fournet, John Langan, Tommy Lott, Duane Leopard, and Merle Schexnaildre as well as sophomores Andy Bourgeois, Gaynell Kinchen, Darryl Jenkins, Henry Lee Roberts, and Hart Bourque. They began coming to and from practice together. They ate meals together in Broussard Hall, the dorm housing LSU's athletes. Once when a Bandit guard was temporarily moved to the White Team to replace an injured player, Dietzel had to assure him he'd return to the Bandits as soon as possible. "I'm sure glad, Coach," he told Dietzel, "because I want to play with the Bandits."

While Dietzel and his staff wondered how the athletically limited Bandits kept getting the job done, they marveled at their toughness. "The fierce amount of pride they generated among themselves was almost unbelievable," Dietzel said. "Collectively, they were a ferocious bunch."

The Chinese Bandits saved their best performances for LSU's two biggest games of the season, a 14–0 win over No. 6 Ole Miss and a 7–0 Sugar Bowl victory over unranked Clemson. When Dietzel graded the Ole Miss game film, he saw what he described as "one of the greatest exhibitions of pure desire I have ever witnessed in football." So what did he see? "Time after time, all 11 Bandits would be in on the tackle," Dietzel said. "On the first six plays, we counted nine Bandits hitting ball carriers each play before he hit the ground. They didn't pile on; they just swarmed him and pyramided him."

Against Clemson, the Bandits allowed 2.87 yards per rushing attempt. They stopped Clemson's last-gasp drive for victory at the LSU 24. "God bless the Bandits; they never played more courageously than they did on that final drive," Dietzel said. "The Bandits came through in the clutch. Throughout the season, they were an inspired group of young men. They played like champions. Fans loved them for their hustle and utter abandon.

"Coaching the Chinese Bandits is one of the greatest thrills I've had in sports. I've never forgotten them."

44 Fourth Down and Florida

This one had it all: Three separate 10-point comebacks, all from LSU. A quarterback, Florida's Tim Tebow, jokingly gesturing to a rabid home student section. A whopping five fourth-down conversions, all of 'em from the Tigers and two of them for touchdowns. A midgame announcement over the stadium speakers that incited LSU's pair of second-half rallies and drew one of the biggest roars of the night. This was LSU 28, Florida 24, on October 6, 2007— one of the most exciting, top 10 duels in Tiger Stadium history. "It remains the single greatest football game I have ever seen in person," lifelong LSU fan Billy Gomila wrote for AndtheValleyShook.com, the *SB Nation* site covering the Tigers. "Nothing before it had ever featured the same sustained emotional roller coaster."

Running back Jacob Hester bulled his way to 106 yards, serving as a late-game bulldozer for his risk-taking head coach. LSU coach Les Miles attempted five fourth downs and his team converted them all, including the last two on the final, game-winning drive. Hester carried the ball on those two fourth-and-1 attempts—the first from LSU's own 49-yard line and the second from the Florida 7, well in range of a game-tying field goal attempt with about two minutes left. Hester fell so close to the first-down marker on both carries that officials needed measurements. He capped the drive by barreling into the end zone on a third-and-goal from the 2 with 1:09 left. "We pretty much knew it was going to be a chance to win the game," Hester said of those conversions afterward. "Coach Miles said, 'I believe in you. I don't want a tie. I want to go out and win this thing.' When your head coach has that kind of respect and trust in you, you want to prove something to him."

That last drive finished off a third 10-point comeback by Miles's squad. LSU trailed 10–0 and 17–7 in the second quarter and fell behind 24–14 in the third at the hands of the defending national champion Gators and their snazzy quarterback. Tim Tebow gouged the Tigers on the ground (67 yards and 1 touchdown) and through the air (158 yards and 2 touchdowns).

He had motivation. In the week leading up to the game, LSU students tracked down Tebow's cell number. They harassed him with phone calls and text messages. After completing the game's first touchdown, Tebow glared toward the student section pretending to make a phone call, his hand mimicking a phone placed up to his ear. "It was not planned at all," Tebow told *SB Nation* in an interview in 2017. "When I got to the end zone, and I looked up right in front of the student section and there were like 30,000 people giving me the bird. It was just instinct. Most of them had probably been calling me earlier that week, so it was just a little friendly reminder, saying hey."

LSU's motivation came from across the country. The Tigers entered the game against Florida No. 1 in the AP poll but No. 2 in the Coaches' poll behind undefeated Southern Cal. Midway through the third quarter, an announcement blared through the Tiger Stadium speakers that Stanford had upset USC 24–23. What transpired was something altogether wacky. Tiger Stadium roared to life. Chants of "L-S-U!" swept through the sold-out crowd, and CBS cameras caught LSU players celebrating wildly on the sideline.

Their coach glanced around stunned, his team trailing 17–14. "I can only tell you that was the dangdest thing I've even been a party to. I actually asked someone, 'Why are they celebrating? We haven't taken the lead yet,'" Miles told reporters at a news conference in 2015. "It made a difference. There was some juice, some energy in that stadium that these Tigers feed off of."

LSU scored two touchdowns on fourth-down plays and another after pulling off a fake field goal. Backup quarterback Ryan Perrilloux scored on a fourth-and-goal run from the 1 in the second quarter. Starter Matt Flynn executed a fake field goal to lead to a four-yard TD run in the third. Flynn tossed a four-yard scoring pass to Demetrius Byrd on fourth-and-goal with 10:15 remaining in the game. "I gamble more than you think," Miles said in the postgame news conference.

The win was significant. Miles eventually led the Tigers to the national championship later that season, despite having two losses. Florida was knocked out of title contention with a second straight loss in early October, dashing any hopes of a repeat.

45 Honey Badgers

During LSU's march to the 2011 National Championship Game, the Tigers picked up a critical victory in one of their toughest tests—a road game at No. 16 West Virginia. A sophomore named Tyrann Mathieu had a whale of a performance in the 47–21 win. He deflected and picked off a pass. He forced a fumble, tearing the ball away from a ball carrier, and he returned three punts, each for at least 10 yards. He had six tackles too, and he knocked away a Hail Mary pass.

This is where the Honey Badger was born. "I got on the bus after the game, and our defensive coordinator, John Chavis, was on the Internet. Coaches always tell you not to get on the Internet, but they read everything on the Internet," Mathieu said in a 2020 story published in the *Advocate*. "So anyway, he's going to blogs, all the gossip sites, and he says, 'Hey, man, this is your new nickname!'" At that point, Chavis showed Mathieu the viral video of a honey badger, a weasel-like mammal known as the world's most fearless animal.

"I'm like, 'What?'" Mathieu continued. "He showed me the video and goes, 'Trust me, go with it; you'll make a lot of money one day.'"

Mathieu became known as the Honey Badger because of his reckless, tenacious play on the field, mimicking that of the animal itself, a carnivorous species that has few natural predators because of its thick skin, strength, and ferocious defensive abilities. The real honey badger is courageous enough to attack animals twice its size or shove its nose in a hive of bees.

The football Honey Badger was known to rip away the football from running backs and receivers; return interceptions, punts, and fumbles for big chunks of yardage; and harass quarterbacks on timely blitzes. Mathieu's moxie resulted in so many electric plays that he was invited to New York City as a 2011 Heisman Trophy finalist.

Despite his success, Mathieu's career ended in a flameout. The Tigers lost 21–0 in the National Championship Game against Alabama to end the 2011 season, and then days before his much-ballyhooed junior season began, Mathieu was dismissed from the team for a rules violation that stemmed from failed drug tests.

Years later, Coach Les Miles called his decision to remove Mathieu from the team "one of the worst things [he's] ever done," saying he's "a Tyrann Mathieu fan." In the past, Mathieu has described his dismissal as a needed wake-up call, a point at which he told himself, "Something's got to change. I got to turn a corner."

He entered a rehabilitation program, and then the Cardinals picked him in the third round of the 2013 draft. The New Orleans native landed on the NFL All-Pro teams in 2013 and 2015, and he became the highest-paid safety in the league in 2016.

In only 26 games at LSU, Mathieu produced some of the best defensive statistics in program history, racking up 133 total tackles, 16 tackles for loss, and 4 interceptions. He also forced 11 fumbles, which ranked first in school history and seventh in NCAA history.

He scored four touchdowns for the Tigers, two on punt returns and two on fumble returns.

"I'm so grateful for the journey I've traveled, you know?" Mathieu said in 2020 in an NBC Sports story. "But I couldn't do it alone. So many great people really had my best interest, so I'm grateful for that."

46 Golden Girls

No halftime performance in Tiger Stadium would be complete without the Golden Girls performing on the field. The glitzy dance troupe has been a staple at LSU since 1959, when they were initially known as the LSU Ballet Corps. "The Golden Girls are one of the oldest traditions at LSU, because when you think LSU football, you think Golden Girls," Golden Girl alumna Andree Leddy said in a university feature on the dance line's 50th anniversary in 2009.

The group took on the Golden Girls moniker in 1965, and today they are officially part of the LSU band program, practicing alongside the Golden Band from Tigerland and joining the marching band at official events. Among their ranks are members who have gone on to become New Orleans Saintsations, Dallas Cowboys Cheerleaders, and even Radio City Rockettes.

The Golden Girls are most known for their sparkling leotards (often made by designers who also fashion attire for Mardi Gras royalty), starting with their original all-gold skirted version. After new takes on the attire that included gold and purple turns, the troupe returned to white leotards with golden fleur-de-lis accents in 2005. "When we have our reunions, the current Golden Girls wear the 1959 version," Golden Girl director Blair Buras Guillaume, who was captain of the 1982 line, told the *Advocate* in 2018.

47 If Tiger Stadium Could Talk

My name is Tiger Stadium, and I'll turn 96 years old in November 2020; at least that's what my construction certificate says. But I don't feel that old. It's my theory that I lose 10 years in age every time LSU wins a national football championship. So by my calculation I'm 56 years old, maybe even 50 if I give bonus years for perfect seasons such as 11–0 in 1958 and 15–0 just last year.

I've got to tell you that I've had a helluva lot of great times, but it's going to be hard to top 2019, when the Tigers averaged 47.6 points and scored 43 touchdowns in my seven home games. Heisman Trophy winning quarterback Joe Burrow, the Ohio State graduate transfer who was 13–1 in two seasons as a starter in my house, threw 22 touchdown passes. Then, before his last home game when LSU put 50 points on my scoreboard in a 43-point beatdown of mouthy Texas A&M, he ran onto the field for the pregame Senior Night wearing a jersey with his name spelled B-U-R-R-E-A-U-X. If he wasn't one of us before, then that clinched it. Done. He can come back and visit me any time and I'll give him a free running tab at my beer concessions.

Which was another thing memorable about the 2019 season. For the first time, the SEC allowed its schools to sell beer and wine throughout their stadiums, not just in select areas such as my premium suites and my beer garden that I opened in 2018. Naturally when I heard the news from the SEC, I said, "Hell yeah! Where do I sign up?" I'm proud to say we sold $2.259 million in net revenue in beer and wine sales (not counting the suites sales) in 2019. Hey, your throat would get dry too, cheering all those touchdowns thrown by Heisman Jeaux.

My capacity when I opened on November 25, 1924, just in time for the last game of the season—a 13–0 loss to Tulane—was 12,000. Now I'm at 102,321 seats as the sixth-largest on-campus stadium in college football. It seems like I've had more expansions, renovations, nips, and tucks than Dolly Parton. But like Ms. Dolly, you've got to always look good no matter your age and give the people what they want.

At last count, I've had seven expansions and four renovations. Some have been simply for aesthetics, such as adding my name in huge gold lights outside along my west facade. It looks great, but my first thought was, *Doesn't everybody know who I am by now?*

My strangest expansion came when I was just seven years old, in 1931. LSU athletic director T.P. "Skipper" Heard wanted to expand my capacity by 10,000 seats. So he persuaded LSU president James Smith to use $250,000 that had been earmarked to build new dorms to raise the stands on both the east and west sides, extend them into the end zone, and then build student dorm rooms inside me underneath the stands. Now, we're not talking five-star hotel accommodations. My rooms, which stopped being used as student housing in the late 1980s, were tiny, with no central air or heat and community bathrooms only. Any student who lived in one of my cracker boxes has worn it as a badge of honor forevermore. The football team even lived in my rooms in the fall of 1986, when the athletic dorm was being renovated. By the way, the Tigers won the SEC championship that season. Coincidence? I think not.

That same year I first had dorms was the first year I had lights, and Skipper Heard began scheduling night games because he wanted to avoid the Louisiana heat and humidity of day games. Since Tulane and Loyola also played day home games in New Orleans, Skipper wanted the night slot so more fans could see the

Tigers play. It was a strategic move that suddenly accelerated. By the mid-1950s, when Jim Corbett became athletic director, I had 67,720 seats and he was brilliant at marketing night football.

There was such a ticket demand for home games by the late 1950s that LSU Heisman Trophy–winning running back Billy Cannon was smart enough to cash in before the 1958 season when the Tigers won the national championship. Using almost his entire savings, he bought 200 tickets each for the Ole Miss and Tulane home games at $2.50 each in Section 32 in my north end. "The truth is," wrote the late Cannon in his 2015 autobiography, "I would have bought more tickets if I'd have had more money. I was that enthused about our team and prospects."

Billy was correct. So when the Tigers won their first six games to shoot to No. 1 in the nation, ticket demand was at an all-time high when No. 6 Ole Miss visited me, Billy, and the boys. The pregame atmosphere was electric. As Billy and teammate Johnny Robinson (a future Pro Football Hall of Famer) stood fielding punts, they exchanged chatter. "How are you feeling? Are you nervous?" Robinson asked Billy. "Nervous?" repeated Billy, who then pointed to Section 32. "I'm feeling great. My whole section sold out!"

No matter how many seats they've added to me with all the bells and whistles, I've retained a hint of originality. I remain one of three major college football venues—Florida State's Doak Campbell Stadium and Washington State's Martin Stadium are the others—who have the old school *H*-style uprights anchored by two goal posts rather than one.

The original *H*-style uprights, which have been on my field for decades, were temporarily removed in 1984 when some idiot decided I should get the more modern look. Someone took apart the north end zone crossbar and mounted it with the word WIN! on it above the Tigers' dressing room exit to the entrance chute at my north end zone. It's tradition that my Ti-gahs touch the bar as they run out onto the field before the game and halftime.

When LSU celebrated its 100th year of football, they reinstalled the *H*-style uprights on my field. Occasionally they get torn down in postgame celebrations, such as in 1997 when the Tigers scored their first-ever win over a No. 1 team, beating defending national champion Florida 28–21.

Late in that game, when it became apparent LSU would win, our concerned game operations manager, John Symank, entered athletic director Joe Dean's press box suite. "Mr. Dean, the students are going to tear the goal posts down," Symank said. "What do want me to do?"

Dean gave Symank an incredulous look and replied, "We're gonna beat the No. 1 team in the country. The students should tear the goal posts down. I *want* them to tear the damned things down."

The charged nighttime environment, such as during that win over the Gators, is why I'm annually named as college football's best home field advantage. The Tigers have done quite well by me. Entering the 2020 season, they've won 74.1 percent (431–151–18) of their home games, including 74.8 percent (339–108–13) at night. With a home record of 121–19 in the last 20 years, including five perfect seasons in my house, I'm definitely the place where—as former LSU coach Les Miles (who had a fondness for chewing my natural grass field) liked to say—"opponents' dreams come to die."

Through the decades, I've hosted visiting teams that included 8 Heisman Trophy winners, 6 national champions, 2 future Super Bowl MVPs, and 13 future No. 1 overall picks in the NFL Draft. Mix all that; the legendary LSU players through the years, such as Cannon, Burrow, Jerry Stovall, and Tommy Casanova; and the generations of fans, and you understand why Jim Corbett made me a priority and the focal point to build tradition. "The spirit of Tiger Stadium was already built in," he said before he died of a heart attack in January 1967. "LSU grew up with Baton Rouge and Baton Rouge with LSU, so there is a stronger personal identity with the players than is found in most places.

"Local following of home boys in places such as Lutcher, Reserve, Thibodaux, Gonzales, and so stimulates civic pride, and these small communities carry this enthusiasm with them to Baton Rouge on Saturday night.

"What we have is the Great Society of Equality at work. The doctor, the lawyer, the farmer, the plant worker, the society matron all band together in a single social strata. In Baton Rouge, [it is] the focal point of everything; the average fan doesn't seem to have a good week in his job if the Tigers lose." Corbett nailed it, and his words ring stronger today than ever before.

As for me, I'm just waiting for another season, eager to see new legends born and more memories created. And one more thing: my nickname—Death Valley—is the same as Clemson's stadium. Clemson had the nickname first; I can't deny that. But LSU hammered Clemson in January in the National Championship Game, so I get dibs on the nickname for the next season.

Come see me, people. I'm not hard to find.

48 Paul Mainieri

Somewhere in Paul Mainieri's home, likely within a dusty moving box, is a book on stocks he purchased in 1987. Decades ago, as a low-paid coach at a tiny college in South Florida, Mainieri wasn't just pondering a career change—he had promised his wife, Karen, he'd make one if he didn't land a bigger coaching gig in the next year. His backup plan was the stock market. He bought that book and never opened it. "I just stared at it every day," Mainieri said in a story published in 2016 in the *Advocate*. "I didn't really want to do it."

He didn't have to. In 1988 he landed the head job at Air Force, which turned into a gig coaching Notre Dame and then, starting in 2007, leading the LSU baseball team. At age 49 Mainieri began a revival of a program that had dipped in the post–Skip Bertman days, far removed from the dynasty of the 1990s.

By his second season, LSU returned to the College World Series, and the Tigers won it all the next year—a remarkable turnaround. The 2009 LSU baseball squad won 15 of its final 16 games and claimed both the SEC regular-season and tournament titles in one of the most impressive seasons in school history.

Under Mainieri, success extended for years, more than a decade of dominance that stretched into the 2010s. In his first 13 years, Mainieri's clubs missed the NCAA tournament just twice, including a rebuilding squad in Year 1. They won four SEC regular-season titles, claimed six SEC tournament championships, and took five trips to the College World Series.

Mainieri entered the 2020 season with 1,455 wins, the second-most among active coaches. He's won nearly 80 percent of games at Alex Box Stadium, and he has no plans to call it quits anytime soon. In fact, heading into his 10th season in 2016, he told the *Advocate* that he hoped to coach LSU for at least another eight years. Oddly enough, later that summer he signed a contract with the school extending his deal eight years, through the 2024 season. However, Mainieri doesn't plan to coach forever. "I think some coaches want to die on the field," he said in 2016. "I don't."

In that same interview, Mainieri—affable and talkative—expressed an interest in becoming a TV analyst once he retires, and he'd also like to cross off items on his bucket list. He wants to visit the Grand Canyon, begin playing golf regularly, and attend the Masters Tournament. He wants to road-trip to a Major League Baseball game with his sons and travel to watch the Kentucky Derby.

A father of four originally from Miami, Mainieri is the son of longtime Miami-area junior college baseball coach Demie Mainieri.

With Paul's induction in 2014, the pair became the first father-son combination in the American Baseball Coaches Association Hall of Fame. Each has claimed a national title on his respective level too. Demie passed away in 2019 at the age of 90.

Paul learned plenty about the game from his pop, and from an assortment of other big names in the baseball and football worlds. They include MLB big shots Jim Hendry and Tommy Lasorda, coaches such as UNO's Ron Maestri and football coaches such as Don Shula and Lou Holtz. He used to watch Holtz's practices while at Notre Dame and observed Shula's Dolphins while in Miami.

Bertman called Mainieri an organized workaholic, a man who spends more time in individual meetings with his players—getting to know them and their strengths and weaknesses, likes and dislikes—than any coach Bertman has ever seen. Mainieri "outmaneuvers" his fellow coaches on the field too, Bertman said.

Mainieri credits much of his success to his practice philosophy: pressure players as much as possible. If you pressure them in practice, they'll be prepared to face pressure during the game, he explained. "I don't expect them to be perfect," Mainieri said, "but I put the pressure on them to perform perfectly."

Like any baseball guy, Mainieri holds certain superstitions. For instance, before each game, he completes a lineup card with a brand-new purple Sharpie marker. Ahead of each Friday night home game, Mainieri and his wife eat lunch at the same restaurant—Roberto's, a riverfront restaurant in south Baton Rouge serving Louisiana cuisine.

A smiling Mainieri calls these things "traditions," not superstitions. "I tell people I'm not superstitious," he said, "but why take a chance?"

And as for that stock market book, it might never see the light of day again.

49 Women's Final Four Runs

For five years, from 2004 to 2008, LSU women's basketball teams were a perfect 20–0 in the first four rounds of the NCAA basketball tournament leading to the Final Four.

The Tigers, under coaches Pokey Chatman, Bob Starkey, and Van Chancellor, won 84 percent (152–28) of their games, including 87.1 percent (61–9) in the SEC while winning three league championships. Yet even with such stars as two-time Naismith College Player of the Year Seimone Augustus and future WNBA Player of the Year Sylvia Fowles, LSU never made it to the national title game.

They suffered five straight semifinal losses on women's college basketball's biggest stage. Here's how the heartache played out each season:

2004
West Region Champion: No. 4 seed LSU
Records: 27–8, 10–4 SEC
LSU's NCAA Tournament Run: defeated No. 13 seed Austin Peay 83–66, defeated No. 12 seed Maryland 76–61, defeated No. 1 seed Texas 71–55, defeated No. 4 seed Georgia 62–60, lost to No. 1 seed Tennessee 52–50

LSU head coach Sue Gunter missed the last half of the season due to illness, so acting head coach Pokey Chatman stepped in and led the Lady Tigers to the program's first trip to the NCAA Final Four just down to the road in New Orleans.

Fourth-seeded LSU won its first two regional games, then won the West Regional with wins over No. 1 seed Texas (71–55) in the Sweet 16 and over Georgia (62–60) in the regional finals after the

Tigers trailed the Bulldogs by seven points with six minutes left. Augustus scored a career-high 29 points in both games.

In a Final Four semifinal against Tennessee, Augustus was limited to 16 points. The Vols' Shyra Ely picked up a loose ball off a tipped pass from LSU's Temeka Johnson and passed to LaToya Davis for an uncontested game-winning layup with 1.2 seconds left for a 52–50 victory.

"It's probably going to be unfortunate that we're probably going to talk most about the last six seconds of this game, and in my opinion that's not where this game was lost," Chatman said. "Bottom line, [Tennessee had] 18 second-chance points. That's the ballgame."

Tennessee lost 60–51 to Connecticut in the National Championship Game.

2005

Chattanooga Region Champion: No. 1 seed LSU
Records: 33–3, 14–0 SEC
LSU's NCAA Tournament Run: defeated No. 16 seed Stetson 70–36, defeated No. 9 seed Arizona 76–43, defeated No. 13 seed Liberty 90–48, defeated No. 2 seed Duke 59–49, lost to No. 2 Baylor 68–57

Armed with NCAA National Player of the Year Seimone Augustus and National Point Guard of the Year Temeka Johnson, LSU entered the NCAA tournament with a 29–2 record after claiming the program's first Southeastern Conference regular-season title with a perfect 14–0 mark.

The Tigers won their first four NCAA tourney games by an average of 31.3 points. But in the national semifinals in Indianapolis against No. 2 Baylor in a battle of runs, the Bears battled back from an early 15-point deficit with a first-half-closing 19–2 burst for a 28–28 halftime tie.

In the second half, Baylor scored 9 of its last 10 points from the free-throw line in a 68–57 victory over LSU. Baylor then won its first-ever national championship by beating Michigan State 84–62.

2006

San Antonio Region Champion: No. 1 seed LSU

Records: 31–4, 13–1 SEC

LSU's NCAA Tournament Run: defeated No. 16 seed Florida Atlantic 72–48, defeated No. 9 seed Washington 72–49, defeated No. 4 seed DePaul 66–56, defeated No. 3 seed Stanford 62–59, lost to No. 1 seed Duke 64–45

After LSU senior Seimone Augustus scored 26 points and hit two free throws after drawing a charging foul to clinch the Tigers' 62–59 regional finals win over Stanford, top-seeded Duke put the defensive handcuffs on Augustus and teammates in the national semifinals in Boston.

The Blue Devils held LSU to 29 percent field-goal shooting, the lowest field-goal percentage in the then-25-year history of the Women's Final Four in an easy 64–45 victory.

LSU scored only 15 first-half points. Augustus was held scoreless in the first 22 minutes of play before finishing with 14 points on 6-of-18 shooting.

2007

Fresno Region Champion: No. 3 seed LSU

Records: 30–8, 10–4 SEC

LSU's NCAA Tournament Run: defeated No. 14 seed UNC Asheville 77–39, defeated No. 11 seed West Virginia 49–43, defeated No. 10 seed Florida State 55–43, defeated No. 1 seed UConn 73–50, lost to No. 4 seed Rutgers 59–35

It was a miracle LSU made it to its fourth Final Four after head coach Pokey Chatman resigned before the start of the NCAA tournament amid allegations of an inappropriate relationship with a former player that was alleged to have begun when Chatman was coaching the player.

Assistant coach Bob Starkey took over and the Tigers sprang the upset of the tourney when they hammered top-seeded UConn 73–50 in the Fresno Regional Final. LSU avenged a 72–71 regular-season loss in a big way, thanks to Sylvia Fowles's 23 points, 15 rebounds, and 6 blocked shots.

But the Tigers got shut down in the Final Four semifinals for the second straight year, this time a 59–35 loser to Rutgers. Rutgers hit 8 of 10 three-pointers in the first half to take an 18-point lead. LSU finished only 14-of-53 shooting (26.4 percent) and Fowles was held to only five points, the second-lowest scoring game in her 109-game career. "It was a very emotional [postgame] locker room," Starkey said. "Every kid was crying. We [had] lost three previous Final Fours and I'd never seen a tear in there. This team really cared about each other. I think they were not just crying for themselves but crying for each other."

Rutgers lost 59–46 to Tennessee in the National Championship Game.

2008

New Orleans Region Champion: No. 2 seed LSU
Records: 31–6, 14–0 SEC
LSU's NCAA Tournament Run: defeated No. 15 seed Jackson State 66–32, defeated No. 7 seed Marist 68–49, defeated No. 3 seed Oklahoma State 67–52, defeated No. 1 seed North Carolina 56–50, lost to No. 1 seed Tennessee 47–46

First-year LSU coach Van Chancellor stepped into a great situation, taking over a team with eight seniors, and got a season-ending break by playing and winning the first four games of the NCAA tournament in Baton Rouge and New Orleans, respectively.

The Tigers took out top-seeded North Carolina 56–50 with the New Orleans Region's Most Outstanding Player Sylvia Fowles scoring 21 points, grabbing 12 rebounds, and blocking 5 shots.

LSU advanced to the Final Four semifinals in St. Petersburg, Florida, to play Tennessee after the Tigers beat the Lady Vols at Knoxville in the regular season and Tennessee defeated LSU in the SEC tournament finals.

As in their 2004 Final Four semifinals two-point loss to Tennessee, the Tigers again lost in almost an identical heartbreaking fashion. After LSU's Erica White hit two free throws with seven seconds left for a one-point lead, Tennessee's Alexis Hornbuckle rebounded a missed shot and dropped in a layup with 0.7 seconds left to play for a 47–46 win. "I thought we had it won, up one point and they've got to go the full length of the court," Chancellor said. "And it's really a tough loss when I think about these kids and what all they have gone through for four years. I really feel for them."

Since that gut-wrenching loss, LSU has never advanced past the Sweet 16, the last time a 26-point regional semifinal loss to Louisville in 2014.

50 PMAC and Ag Center

It's hard to believe that as LSU opens its 2020–21 basketball season, the Pete Maravich Assembly Center will be a year shy of the 40th anniversary of its opening. Plans for building the Assembly Center, as it was originally known, were on then–LSU athletic director Jim Corbett's drawing board as early as 1965. But the project never gained traction to obtain funding because a mediocre

LSU basketball program never drew enough attendance to create a ticket demand.

That all changed when new Tigers head coach Press Maravich and his son Pete showed up on campus in 1966. For the next four seasons—one on the freshman team and three on the varsity—Pete Maravich became college basketball's all-time leading scorer while entertaining fans with Harlem Globetrotters–like passing and ball handling.

Suddenly, the John M. Parker Agricultural Center, site of LSU's home games, was packed to the rafters. There were plenty of enthralled fans but none more important than Louisiana governor John McKeithen, who persuaded the state legislature to make the funding and construction of LSU's proposed new arena a high priority.

In 1972—two seasons after Maravich finished his LSU career—the $11.5 million Assembly Center opened. It was nicknamed the House That Pete Built and Pete's Palace. It seemed light years ahead of the Ag Center in design and amenities, the Tigers' former hoops center appropriately nicknamed the Cow Palace because of the walking horse shows and rodeos that the building hosted.

The John M. Parker Agricultural Center—named for former Louisiana governor John M. Parker, who pushed for LSU's campus to be moved to its current location—was built for a cost of just more than $1.33 million as a Works Progress Administration project. Seating 12,000, it opened in 1937 and was the largest coliseum in the United States at that time. Through the 1940s, LSU still split playing home games between the on-campus Gym Armory and the Ag Center. By the 1950s the Ag Center became the sole home of LSU basketball and hosted the LSU boxing team's home fights.

The late Paul Dietzel, head football coach of LSU's first national championship team in 1958, in his autobiography recalled being introduced at an LSU boxing match in the Ag Center upon his hiring in 1955. "The place was absolutely packed, I was stunned," Dietzel recalled. "When I stepped into the ring, the crowd went ballistic for a good five minutes. I was shocked, but gratified, too."

LSU basketball didn't draw nearly as many fans as boxing. In fact, when NBC decided to televise LSU hosting powerhouse Kentucky in 1959, LSU authorities moved the fans' seating on the south side of the arena to the north side. That's because the two NBC cameras pointing at the north side would show more fans than empty seats.

The arena didn't have air-conditioning or heating until 1965. When there were heavy rains, the copper roof leaked, forcing LSU to move two home games to local high schools. The basketball court was laid over the dirt floor. Sometimes when there was a breeze from the lower open end of the arena leading to the livestock barn, the smell of horse and cow manure would waft over the court. There were also the occasional horseflies that made it from the barn to the court.

And because of an annual horse show in November and rodeo in February, the basketball team didn't get into the Ag Center for preseason practice until about a week before the first game and always ended the season with a string of road games. "We had to practice at University High School on campus with its short floor," Pete Maravich remembered. Maravich loved playing at the Ag Center, a place he described as having "the smell of livestock mingled with popcorn and cigarette smoke."

Former LSU basketball trainer Billy Simmons explained in the book *Maravich*, by Wayne Federman and Marshall Terrill, why Pistol Pete truly had a fondness for the Cow Palace. "He always commented that the floor was great for his legs," Simmons said, "because it was set on piers and beams rather than a concrete slab, making the floor soft." Shortly after Maravich's death in 1988, then–Louisiana governor Buddy Roemer signed an act to rename the Assembly Center in Maravich's honor.

In the heyday of former LSU coach Dale Brown's best teams in the late 1970s, 1980s and early 1990s, the PMAC earned the nickname Deaf Dome for its intimidating noise level. At one time, the building was a prime concert venue for the biggest names in the music industry. The Rolling Stones opened their 1975 U.S. *Made in the Shade* tour in the Assembly Center. "They were a very good audience," lead singer Mick Jagger said afterward. "We had never played here. They had never seen us before."

After flooding from Hurricane Katrina devastated New Orleans in August 2005, the PMAC served as the largest triage center and acute care field hospital ever created in U.S. history. The 800-bed facility under the direction of FEMA was staffed by volunteers (some displaced from New Orleans), including doctors.

Today, the PMAC is home to LSU men's and women's basketball teams, the women's gymnastics and volleyball teams, May and December commencement ceremonies, and special events such as the Tigers' 2019 football national championship celebration.

51 Bert Jones

In LSU's storied football history, the Tigers have had just two quarterbacks earn All-America honors. One is obvious: 2019 Heisman Trophy winner Joe Burrow. The other was Bert Jones, almost 50 years earlier.

Burrow played in an offense considered the greatest in SEC history with a 5,000-yard passer, a 1,000-yard rusher, and two 1,000-yard receivers. Jones—a Ruston, Louisiana, native nicknamed the Ruston Rifle—played in an offensive system tilted toward the run game and under a coach who used a two-quarterback system for most of Jones's college career, from 1970 to 1972. "The LSU coaching staff was old-school, with a system that adapted the players to the system," Jones said. "They were playing two quarterbacks all the time, primarily a run-option type. That wasn't conducive to my style. I only played half the time at LSU."

Despite that, Jones became the program's first consensus All-American quarterback in 1972 after throwing for a school-record 1,446 yards and 14 touchdowns. He was named the National Player of the Year in 1972 by the *Sporting News* and finished fourth in the Heisman Trophy balloting. He capped his LSU career as the school's then-all-time leader in passing yards (3,255), attempts (418), completions (220), and touchdowns (28).

As a youngster, it seemed obvious that football would emerge as Jones's favorite sport. His dad, Dub Jones, played running back at LSU and Tulane (stints split by military service) and then had a 10-year pro career as a running back, during which he was a key cog in three NFL championship teams with the Cleveland Browns.

But Dub never insisted Bert play football, though Bert served as a ballboy for the Browns when his father was an assistant coach from 1963 to 1968. "My father was the exact antithesis of what you would think a professional athlete would be, as it relates to his son," Jones said. "His theory was, 'If you haven't got anybody to throw to, I'll catch for you.' But never once can I ever recall him saying, 'Hey, you need to go throw the football so you can become a good thrower and be a player.'"

In junior high school Jones also played baseball and basketball and ran track. "I was a talented baseball pitcher," he said. "But for some distorted reason, I made the conscious decision that I did not want to choose between football and baseball. And so I stopped playing baseball when I was a sophomore in high school."

His excuse to quit was he needed to run track to get faster for football. He didn't become a starter until his junior year and wasn't considered a blue-chipper as a senior. "I wasn't that good a football player in high school, and I didn't have a whole lot of signs of interest from college recruiters," Jones said. "I also came out the same year that Joe Ferguson did. He was just 50 miles down the road [playing for Shreveport Woodlawn], was highly recruited, and [was] regarded as probably the best QB in the country.

"I went on just two recruiting trips, to Tulane and LSU. I only had a few schools that offered me a scholarship opportunity. I took the one that played the toughest football there was, and that was LSU."

Ferguson, who was being wooed to sign at LSU by Louisiana governor John McKeithen and former LSU QB and future Pro Football Hall of Famer Y.A. Tittle, signed with Arkansas. He played in a passing offense in which he threw for 4,431 yards and eventually had a 17-year NFL career.

Jones, who waited to sign at LSU after Ferguson chose Arkansas, didn't have Ferguson's good fortune of playing in a college offense conducive to his talents. Before his sophomore season began, Jones tore knee cartilage. He spent the year as a backup to senior starter Buddy Lee, then started the season opener in his junior year against Colorado. But when he threw three interceptions in the 31–21 loss, he lost his starting job to Paul Lyons, a converted cornerback who suited LSU head coach Charles McClendon's option offense. Jones often played in obvious passing situations. "I probably threw more third-down passes than any man in history but never a first-down pass," said Jones, who contemplated transferring but who eventually regained his starting spot later in the season in one of the most historic wins in Tigers history.

In No. 7–ranked Notre Dame's first-ever trip to Tiger Stadium, McClendon started the 6'3" Jones against the Fighting Irish's tall defensive line. He responded by completing 7 of 9 passes for 143 yards and 2 touchdowns of 36 and 32 yards to his cousin Andy Hamilton, and he ran for a 5-yard TD.

Jones completed 60 of 90 passes for 9 TDs and no interceptions in the last 6 games as a junior, then started every game as a senior in LSU's 9–2–1 1972 season. His signature performance was engineering a game-winning 80-yard TD drive in a 17–16 win over Ole Miss, throwing a scoring strike to running back Brad Davis as time expired.

Jones was the No. 2 overall pick by the then–Baltimore Colts in the 1973 draft. He threw for 18,190 yards and 124 TDs in his 10-year career, the first nine with the Colts. He was named the NFL's MVP in 1976. He retired due to a serious neck injury after spending the 1982 season with the Los Angeles Rams.

The shortness of his career prevented him from being elected to the Pro Football Hall of Fame, but coaches such as New England's Bill Belichick still hold him in high regard. "As a pure passer, I don't think I could put anybody ahead of Bert Jones," Belichick said. "I know he had a short career and the shoulder injury, but when I was there and he was just starting his career, the success that he had and his ability to throw the ball as a pure passer and as an athlete—it would be hard to put anybody ahead of Bert Jones at that point in time."

These days, Jones attends LSU home games as much as possible, arriving to Tiger Stadium in unique style. "I ride my bicycle to the game, slip in and slip out," Jones said. "It's the best way to go. We stay downtown most of the time, go straight down the levee and come straight in the door. Takes me 12 minutes from downtown Baton Rouge to Tiger Stadium."

Jones said he loved watching Burrow's Heisman season. "If I played in this offense, I would probably feel like Joe did," he said. "It doesn't get any better. I can't think of anything better than just sitting back there and playing sandlot football and watching everything develop in front of you and knowing where to go."

52 Mark Emmert

Never say never, but LSU may never again have a chancellor with the skill set of Mark Emmert. Because Emmert, now president of the NCAA, perfectly matched two characteristics required to succeed in the job and fuel growth in the university. The first was finding a way to get funding benefitting LSU from the Louisiana legislature. The second was realizing funding and contributions to universities fall like pennies from heaven when the football team succeeds mightily.

Emmert was 46 years old when LSU hired him in April 1999 from the University of Connecticut, where he served as chancellor for academic affairs. Since Emmert is a Washington native and graduated from the University of Washington, he had no clue about how state politics and LSU intertwine. He learned quickly. He became fast friends with Louisiana governor Mike Foster, who soon had so much trust in Emmert that he gave him any monies he wanted for LSU. If Emmert needed money appropriated from the legislature, Foster had his staff go behind the scenes to make it happen.

The money funded many new academic constructions and renovations, starting with buildings and renovations for marine biology and coastal studies, biology, music and dramatic arts, residence halls, and the student union. Fund-raising began obtaining alumni contributions for drastic improvements to the Roger Hadfield Ogden Honors College, the E.J. Ourso College of Business, and the College of Engineering.

But the part of LSU Emmert deemed most important was the football program, which he felt illuminated the entire university worldwide. "The critical role of our football program is clear,"

Emmert said in November 1999, when he fired head football coach Gerry DiNardo and hired Michigan State's Nick Saban as his replacement. "It is of vital importance to the entire LSU community: our students, our fans and alumni worldwide, and the state of Louisiana. Simply put, success in LSU football is essential for the success of Louisiana State University."

It may have been one of the first times ever a university chancellor or president anywhere in the United States spoke the truth that the rest of academia didn't want to hear: a national championship–caliber football program usually results in an increase in new students and donations from extremely happy alumni. It's why LSU couldn't screw up the pursuit and the contract negotiations of Saban, a Bill Belichick disciple who had a master plan to build a powerhouse if he had total cooperation from the administration.

Saban wanted a commitment from Emmert at their first meeting that LSU would build a football operations building and an academic center for athletes as well as provide better living quarters for the players. Emmert didn't flinch. He said yes to all of that and agreed to pay Saban $1.2 million annually as the first LSU football coach to clear the $1 million salary barrier.

Too much money? Not at that point. Emmert and the coaching search committee were convinced after their initial meeting with Saban at his agent's home in Memphis that he was the guy. They wanted someone who could not only lift LSU's program from being in the gutter for the majority of the 1990s—with 7 losing seasons in the previous 10 years—but who was a dynamic visionary with a sound plan to lift the Tigers to national status. "We liked his attitude toward the student-athlete and his analytical approach of how to build a program," Emmert said of Saban. "We all came away feeling this was somebody who could do what we wanted."

So Emmert made the hire that saved LSU's football program and pointed it in the direction of winning three national championships in the following 20 seasons. Saban stayed five seasons and won two SEC championships and the 2003 national title before leaving for the Miami Dolphins after the 2004 season.

Emmert left LSU before Saban, lasting five years before becoming president at his alma mater, Washington, in 2004. If Emmert had stayed at LSU, maybe Saban wouldn't have left. When the news that Emmert was leaving LSU broke, Saban described him as "the best boss."

"He's the most significant reason I was interested in the job," Saban said. "Never once has he disappointed me. He's a natural leader who's got great vision. I know he did a tremendous job in the academic areas in attracting quality people here. I can't tell you how different even the academic situation is around here. It has all been extremely positive.

"Leaders at any institution can create that atmosphere one way or the other with their attitude. Mark Emmert was good for athletics, but he was good for LSU in a lot of ways. We improved dramatically as an institution."

During Emmert's time at LSU, enrollment increased, especially from out-of-state students. New research initiatives improved the school's research profile. Besides Saban's wish list, there were other athletic facility–related improvements Emmert was responsible for, such as expanding Tiger Stadium and building a new state-of-the-art campus habitat for live school mascot Mike the Tiger.

Emmert didn't leave LSU unscathed. He was largely criticized for a token investigation he conducted into academic fraud allegations made against the football program in 2001–02. A university professor alleged players submitted plagiarized papers and that unenrolled students were attending class and taking notes for football players. Ultimately, the investigation uncovered only minor infractions. Emmert noted in his report, "despite isolated incidents, the allegations were largely unfounded."

The NCAA accepted LSU's finding and self-imposed minor penalties (loss of two football scholarships) and declined to put the school on probation. Subsequently two women sued the university for forcing them from their jobs as a result of whistleblowing about the academic fraud. The lawsuits were settled for $110,000 for each person. During the case, an employee of the academic counseling center confirmed the women's claims under oath, including changed grades for football players.

In an interview with *USA Today* in April 2013, Emmert said he "had no reason to believe it's a true allegation" when addressing the women's job termination accusations.

53 Joe Brady

Joe Brady wanted to be an NFL quarterback. Because of injuries, he couldn't even play the position in high school, let alone in the pros. Brady shifted his focus to receiver. But he was moved to running back as a freshman at Air Force. To make matters worse, he then broke his wrist. "Every little kid's dream was to play in the NFL," Brady said. "Freshman year of college, I knew that dream might not be a reality."

OK, so Brady's football-playing career didn't turn out so great, but his football-coaching career is another matter. Brady's ascent through the coaching ranks is historic in nature, one of the more meteoric rises the sport has ever seen. He rocketed up the tiers of the industry, moving from FCS assistant (William & Mary) to Power 5 graduate assistant (Penn State) to low-level NFL aide (Saints) before landing his big break as LSU's pass game coordinator at age 28.

He was responsible for overhauling an offense that eventually shattered passing records, produced Heisman Trophy–winning quarterback Joe Burrow, and helped the Tigers claim the 2019 national championship. Less than 24 hours after that title, Brady moved on to a multimillion-dollar-a-year gig as the offensive coordinator for the NFL's Carolina Panthers.

In less than a calendar year, this Florida native and William & Mary graduate went from making five figures to seven. He was a millionaire at 30. "If there's one thing I've never done, I've never thought about my age or talked about my age," Brady said in his introductory news conference with the Panthers. "You'll never hear me talk about my age. I don't believe that your age determines how good of a coach you are."

Brady forever left a mark in Baton Rouge. The wunderkind not only installed the spread scheme that vaulted LSU out of a decade of offensive slumber, but he also split play-calling duties with offensive coordinator Steve Ensminger, old enough to be Brady's father. The two worked in harmony in 2019. "Sometimes he'll just . . . it could be a third down, 'Hey, you got it on this one.' It could be a red-zone situation or a drive. It's all predicated off of how he's feeling and if he's in a groove," Brady said in an interview with *Sports Illustrated* during the season. "There's certain situations, and every great coordinator trusts certain coaches in certain situations. If there's a situation I [don't] feel strongly on or confident on throughout a week, he's going to have the final say and be able to call it, but if he trusts that I'm confident on a scheme, on a certain down and distance, he has no issues with saying 'You got it.'"

Brady related to LSU players because he's not so different from them, only seven to eight years older than some. He wears Air Jordans and a fancy gold chain. He's "cool," says one LSU assistant. More than anything, Brady installed an up-tempo spread offense to utilize Burrow and a talented group of weapons such as receiver Ja'Marr Chase, tight end Thaddeus Moss, and running back Clyde Edwards-Helaire. It resulted in a historic season for a program that had for years leaned on a slow, traditional offensive scheme.

LSU led the nation in total offense (568.4) and scoring offense (48.4). The Tigers became the first team in SEC history to have a 4,000-yard passer (Burrow), two 1,000-yard receivers (Chase and Justin Jefferson), and a 1,000-yard rusher (Clyde Edwards-Helaire) in the same season. They scored more points (725) than any other club in college football history, surpassing 2013 Florida State (723).

Brady oftentimes attributed the success to the players and coaches around him—namely quarterback Burrow, coordinator Ensminger, and head coach Ed Orgeron, the man whose bold decision got him to Baton Rouge. "It's hard to put in words," Brady said during an interview in December 2019. "It felt like everything happened so fast."

His scheme wasn't so different from the ones seen on Sundays in the NFL. During his two years in New Orleans, he adopted Saints coach Sean Payton's passing concepts that quarterback Drew Brees flourished with and brought them to Baton Rouge, where Burrow did the same. There were wrinkles of others things too, such as the run-pass option scheme he learned from Joe Moorhead, the former Penn State offensive coordinator and Mississippi State head coach.

Burrow had authoritative control over the offense, with freedoms that many college quarterbacks don't have. Ensminger and Brady trusted their quarterback with pre-snap play-calling decisions based on defensive formations. "If I see we have leverage to the boundary, I'll just give Ja'Marr a different route and we'll throw that," Burrow said in an October 2019 interview. "Or if we have a deep route called and they're playing off, I just check to a shorter route and complete the ball. Stuff like that."

In the end, the 2019 season might be remembered most for the Joes—Burrow and Brady, two guys benefiting from each other to lead the Tigers to the title.

54 The Down Years

LSU entered the 1989 football season poised to contend for a national championship. The Tigers were ranked No. 7 in the AP preseason poll, were fresh off a shared SEC title in 1988, and were returning with most of their key players: leading passer Tommy Hodson, leading receiver Tony Moss, and leading rusher Eddie Fuller. Head coach Mike Archer, meanwhile, had won more games in his first two seasons (18) than any LSU coach in the previous 50 years. Fan support was high. Expectations soared. A title was on many minds.

All of it came thundering down in a hurry. The Tigers won just one of their first seven games and ended the season at 4–7. The campaign was so disappointing that some in the LSU community describe it as the worst season in school history. The worst part? It was just the start. Things were about to get really ugly in Baton Rouge.

The 1989 campaign marked the first of six consecutive losing seasons, the longest stretch in LSU football history, a stunning skid that few saw coming. From 1957 to 1988, a 31-year stretch, the Tigers had four losing seasons. Before 1989 and 1990, they hadn't endured back-to-back losing years in more than three decades.

The six-year skid started in Archer's third season, forced him to resign after year four, and completely covered the forgettable four-year tenure of the next coach, Curley Hallman. During the slide, LSU never finished better than fourth in the new SEC West, amassed a 25–41 overall record and, at its lowest point, lost 13 of 15 SEC games, a stretch that spanned the 1991 to 1993 seasons, all under Hallman.

Decades later, Hallman's name in Baton Rouge still sends Tigers fans running in the opposite direction. In 2013 the sports fan site *SB Nation* published an opinion piece describing Hallman as "the worst thing to ever happen to LSU football."

Hallman, a former assistant at Alabama under Bear Bryant, is the only LSU coach in history to have coached at least 10 games and posted a losing record (he was 16–28). His four teams never produced an All-American, despite having offensive lineman Kevin Mawae, a future Pro Football Hall of Fame inductee. His 1994 team blew a 24–9 lead against Auburn after quarterback Jamie Howard inexplicably threw four interceptions in the fourth quarter, and he was responsible for the worst loss in LSU history—a 58–3 defeat at home against Florida in 1993.

Things under Hallman were such that the LSU football team one year got into a brawl with the LSU basketball team. Fans were so down on their football Tigers that players sometimes avoided wearing team apparel around campus, Todd Kinchen, an LSU receiver from 1988 to 1991, told Baton Rouge's WAFB in 2020. "We were one of the few classes to actually never go to a bowl game," Chad Loup, quarterback for LSU from 1990 to 1993, told the news channel. "If you think about it, that sounds wild now with LSU's success, but it was a great experience."

During the final season of his tenure in 1994, anger and frustration spilled into the coach's weekly radio show, where he at times became argumentative with callers. Hallman's situation at LSU went national. Vultures Circling Moribund LSU Program, read a headline in the *Chicago Tribune*.

At one point during his final days as coach, Hallman said of his future, "They'll have to carry me out of here before I resign." A few weeks later, athletic director Joe Dean offered Hallman the opportunity to resign. He refused and was fired. The final blow came in his last home game, a 20–18 loss to his former team, Southern Miss. Hallman landed the job at LSU for the most part because of his three-year run with the Golden Eagles, a stretch that included upsets of Alabama and Auburn. His quarterback for all of those years: Brett Favre.

55 Tommy Casanova

Tommy Casanova had the surname to match his good looks and the game to live up to both. It didn't take LSU coach Charles McClendon long to realize he wished he could clone Casanova, who played defensive back, running back, and punt returner. "He was one of the most gifted athletes I've ever had," McClendon said of the Crowley, Louisiana, native. "We needed him more on defense, but there's no doubt he could have been an All-America running back."

Instead, he was a three-year first-team All-American defensive back from 1969 to 1971. In his sophomore and junior seasons, Casanova had 72 rushing attempts for 302 yards and intercepted three passes each year. "I wanted to play both ways," Casanova once said. "Just about everybody who ever played football fancies themselves as a running back. But I knew if I had a pro career, it would be as a defensive back."

In his senior year, after appearing on the cover of the September 13, 1971, issue of *Sports Illustrated*—a college football preview issue—and being touted as the nation's best college player, Casanova pulled a hamstring muscle in Game 2 vs. Texas A&M. He missed the next five games.

Casanova's talent was obvious. A pro scout once said of him, "My wife could scout Tommy and put him down as a first-round draft choice." Had the NFL allowed early draft entries back in the early 1970s, Casanova would have been a first-round draft choice after his junior year in 1970. He capped that season with the greatest performance of his college career, scoring on punt returns of 61 and 73 yards and intercepting Ole Miss icon Archie Manning in a 61–17 blowout that sent LSU to the Orange Bowl. "There's no way we were that much better than Ole Miss," Casanova said. "It was just one of those games where things started rolling our way and never stopped."

The Cincinnati Bengals chose Casanova in the second round of the 1972 NFL Draft after his injury-riddled senior season. He played in the NFL as a safety, lasting six seasons with the Bengals as a three-time Pro Bowler who had 17 interceptions.

From the moment Casanova entered the NFL, he began preparing for life after football. As the son of an ophthalmologist, Casanova was a premed major at LSU. Starting in his second year in the NFL, he began attending medical school part-time at the University of Cincinnati. "That became really rough; I wouldn't want to do that again," Casanova said. "If I had to do it again, I'd choose one career or the other."

By the end of the 1977 season, Casanova's aching knees told him to retire, something he had no problem doing. "My last year, football wasn't fun," he said. "I was in pain virtually the whole season. I was concentrating more on limping than my assignments. If I'd played another year, it would've been strictly for the money. I told myself I wouldn't do that."

Paul Brown, Casanova's coach at Cincinnati, paid him the ultimate compliment. "We never had anyone else like him," Brown said of Casanova. "On defense, he played the ball like a center fielder. On punt returns, he was excellent. A very good football player and always a gentleman."

Upon retiring from football, Casanova had a residency in New Orleans and an oculoplastic surgery fellowship at the University of Utah before returning home to join his father's practice. Specializing in eye surgery and eyelid reconstruction, Casanova was named to the board of trustees for colleges and universities of Louisiana, worked with an environmental society, and worked on visual surgery for those with leprosy.

In 1995 Casanova entered the world of politics. He defeated an incumbent to win a four-year term in the Louisiana state senate. He would have won if he decided to run again in 1999, but he was dismayed by repeated struggles to pass legislation he deemed important. Still, he didn't regret his foray into politics. "Sometimes people tell me they won't run because they hate politics," Casanova said. "Heck, that's why you should do it. If you don't like what's going on, get in there and change it."

Casanova, who continues to run his ophthalmology practice in Crowley, was inducted into the College Football Hall of Fame in 1995. Then in 2000 he was named to the Walter Camp Football Foundation All-Century Team honoring the best college players of the 20th century. In 2009 LSU retired his No. 37 jersey.

But of all the honors Casanova received, the one that touched him the most was receiving more votes than any other LSU player in history when fans were asked to vote on a modern-day LSU all-century team. "That's crazy," Casanova said.

Not really.

56 DBU

On page 158 of LSU's 2018 media guide, you'll find at the bottom right corner three letters synonymous with the football program: *DBU*. Those in the LSU community take pride in a great many things: their food, their drink, their night kickoffs. But none of these topics triggers such passionate debate as those in purple and gold defending their self-proclaimed nickname: Defensive Back University.

From administrators to coaches to players to fans, LSU believes no other university in America produces such a number of top-flight safeties and cornerbacks quite like the Tigers. At least somewhat recently, they'd be right. From 2007 to 2018 LSU led the nation in number of defensive backs selected in the draft with 18. They've produced a defensive back selection in 11 of the last 13 drafts, and 6 of those 18 DBs have been picked in the first round. These are recognizable figures, many of them still playing in the NFL as recently as 2020: Patrick Peterson, Morris Claiborne, Eric Reid, Jamal Adams, LaRon Landry, and Tre'Davious White. Since 2010 the university has produced three winners of the Jim Thorpe Award, given to the nation's best DB: Peterson (2010), Claiborne (2011), and Grant Delpit (2019).

The debate over what college can claim DBU has been one of the hottest in football, with players from opposing teams sparring across social media over the mythical title. In 2019, ahead of LSU's game at Texas, UT players wore shirts during warm-ups that read, THERE'S ONLY ONE DBU: TEXAS LONGHORNS.

At least one player has narrowed the race down to two: Florida and LSU. "If you're a defensive back and want to be *a guy*, you go to one of those two schools," UF cornerback Vernon Hargreaves told reporters in October 2019. "That's just how it is."

In 2019 the debate even reached the stage of ESPN's popular Saturday show *College GameDay*, with all three analysts dubbing LSU as DBU over a group of teams that included Texas, Florida, and Ohio State. "LSU has always been first in my mind," longtime *GameDay* character and ex-coach Lee Corso told a national audience. "LSU, there's no question about it." Former quarterback Kirk Herbstreit chimed in, "I give LSU the advantage."

Through the years, various LSU defensive coordinators and secondary coaches have taken advantage of the talents on their roster. They've reaped the benefits, producing some of the nation's best secondary units. From 2003 to 2018, a span of 16 seasons, LSU ranked inside the top 30 in passing defense 13 times and in the top 15 eight times. Coordinators such as Will Muschamp, John Chavis, Bo Pelini, and Dave Aranda all captained elite defensive back units.

Many herald Corey Raymond as a key cog not only in coaching LSU DBs but in bringing them to Baton Rouge. Raymond entered his ninth season on staff in 2020. He is a Louisiana native and former LSU player who has lured some of the nation's best defensive backs to the school, many of them hailing from South Florida, a hotspot that the Tigers have mined over the years.

Meanwhile, all around them, the debate over DBU rages on. In 2014 ESPN.com published a series of stories, *Position U*, that used a points-based system to rank schools by position for years spanning 2000 to 2013. Ohio State ranked No. 1 in the DBU category with Oklahoma second and LSU third.

Consider the debate settled! Or not.

57 Tailgating the LSU Way

There is tailgating, and then there is tailgating in Louisiana. Often referred to as the kings of college football tailgating, LSU fans turn a four-hour home game on Saturdays into a weekend-long festival of food, drink, and fun. The school estimates that an LSU home game can bring 150,000 people to campus, one-third of whom couldn't fit into Tiger Stadium if they tried.

The food is cooked in exorbitant amounts, and the booze is poured heavy-handed. Cajun favorites—gumbo, jambalaya, and boiled seafood—are often cooked in giant pots over open flames, the chefs with paddles to stir and beers to sip. There are alligators sizzling on grills and whole hogs roasting over fires.

The drinks are plentiful. Pop-up bars can go through 40 or more liquor bottles during a tailgating Saturday, and hundreds of kegs are tapped dry by kickoff. Temporary dance floors are erected, and at least one longtime tailgating spot features a stripper pole. Ice luges are common around campus, making the delivery of liquor shots more entertaining.

In 2017 *Sports Illustrated* called LSU the "tailgating national champions," and two years later, ESPN analyst Kirk Herbstreit told a national audience the Tigers were tops in pregame partying. "I'm from the Big Ten, and I'll never forget when I started going with *GameDay* to the SEC," Herbstreit said. "You'd have campers coming into Baton Rouge on Thursday and little kids throwing Nerf footballs and the smokers going everywhere and the smell of bourbon in the air. This is very different. I think LSU takes it to a whole different level."

It's not always pretty. For years the reputation of LSU fans nationally had been that of aggression, hostility, and inebriation. In a 2018 interview, former athletic director Skip Bertman recalled fans setting fire to an Auburn van in 2001. It was normal for others to drop drinks onto people from "the third deck," Bertman says. During a thorough combing of Tiger Stadium after the 9/11 terrorist attacks, law enforcement found liquor bottles taped to the backs of dozens of seats—some of them empty from the previous game and others full for the next one.

But the behavior started to wane in the early 2000s, coinciding with two things: the Tigers winning and sweeping security enhancements that Bertman championed. "It goes back to when we thought we were losers," Bertman said in a story published by *Sports Illustrated* in 2018. "You don't have a lot of wins and don't feel good about your program so you do some bad things. Those things don't happen anymore."

Law enforcement began monitoring the student section with a 180-degree camera, they set up a police booth in the Tiger Stadium press box, and undercover officers began dressing in the opposing team's apparel. By 2003 the culture began to change, said Mike Barnett, a now-retired member of the local sheriff's department who headed Tiger Stadium security for years. In fact, before one game against Georgia in 2003, Barnett's undercover officers, all clad in Bulldogs red, returned to the precinct without issue—well, almost. "They came back fat and half drunk," he laughed. "LSU fans were feeding them and giving them drinks!"

LSU's tailgating stretches deep into the night, well past the end of regulation and sometimes into the wee hours of Sunday. In fact, tailgating doesn't stop for the games either. Ronald Lahasky, a longtime LSU tailgater, claims at least 30,000 fans remain at tailgate spots reveling as the Tigers play inside Tiger Stadium. "Twenty thousand of them don't know the game's going on," he told *SI*. "The other 10,000 know, and they're just watching the other 20,000."

Tailgating at LSU is the game outside of the game, and they're competitive about it too. "We don't fish. We don't hunt. We don't play golf," said Jaime San Andres, an LSU fan and tailgater. "We do a party, and we don't want nobody to outdo our party."

58 Earthquake Game

The black blotch on the seismograph is small, but its significance in LSU football lore is large. Tommy Hodson's 11-yard touchdown completion to running back Eddie Fuller—on fourth down, no less, with fewer than two minutes remaining—lifted LSU to an improbable 7–6 victory over No. 4 Auburn on October 8, 1988. The burst from the Tiger Stadium crowd that night was so tremendous that it registered on an on-campus seismograph.

Thus was born the Earthquake Game, with a game-winning touchdown that, so they say, shook the very surface of LSU's Baton Rouge campus. That seismograph printout for years hung in an on-campus building, framed and labeled with a descriptor pointing to that small black blotch—despite some detractors debunking the claims.

The earth-shaking play is still very much felt in south Louisiana, a piece of the purple-and-gold fabric that is LSU football, up there with Billy Cannon's Halloween Run and Marcus Randall's Bluegrass Miracle. Some might say it was more important than either of those. The victory spurred LSU to a Southeastern Conference championship, something it shared with Auburn that season. "I remember it like yesterday," tight end Willie Williams told Nola.com in a story published in 2013. "It would be hard to forget that one. I've never felt anything like that. The field was vibrating, the entire field. It's amazing that human beings can get that loud that the ground is moving."

His team down 6–0 and suffocated for much of the game by one of the nation's stiffest defenses, Hodson marched the Tigers down the field on a 75-yard, 15-play drive. He capped it with that pass to Fuller on fourth-and-10 at the Auburn 11-yard line.

Hodson, throwing sidearm to elude pressure from a would-be sacker, threaded his pass between AU defenders and found an open Fuller in the back of the end zone for the thunderous score. David Browndyke knocked in his all-important extra point with 1:41 left.

In a story published on LSUSports.net in 2008, Fuller said he first began to realize the magnitude of the Earthquake Game in the early 1990s. While on vacation, he visited Ripley's Believe It or Not Museum, which featured the play. "I was going through this Ripley's museum in Niagara Falls, and I looked up and there it was!" he said.

The play capped a miserable offensive outing for LSU in a game against a squad that would finish the year statistically as the nation's No. 1 defense, led by defensive tackle Tracy Rocker and linebacker Craig Ogletree. The hometown Tigers were outgained in yardage 316–213, and they mustered only two drives of longer than 11 yards before that final march. They limped into the game at 2–2 and unranked after losses to Ohio State (36–33) and Florida (19–6), on the brink of being removed completely from the SEC title hunt.

Two of the nation's stiffest defenses clashed on that cool night in Tiger Stadium. The quarterbacks combined to complete 46.5 percent of their passes, and the game's leading rusher didn't crack the 50-yard mark. Auburn managed only two field goals, and LSU's best drive before the game-winning march finished at the Auburn 40.

LSU started its final drive at its own 25 with 6:07 left. Hodson completed passes of 17 and 20 yards to receiver Tony Moss before a more significant play unfolded. On fourth-and-9 at the Auburn 20, Hodson found the 6'7" Williams open on a five-yard route in the flat. He tussled past defenders to gain the four extra yards needed for the first down. "There were four defenders in front of me. I dodged one and split the other one, but he grabbed my leg," Williams said. "I just stretched and got the first down. I remember the crowd going nuts. I was screaming and couldn't hear myself."

On the very next play, Hodson attempted a pass to Fuller that was similar to the one that would win LSU the game a few moments later. On first down, Fuller—corralling the pass in the back of the end zone—could not get his foot down in bounds. Three plays later, he got that foot down—both of them, in fact. "I was so happy Tommy had the confidence to come back to me," Fuller said. "It seemed like it took it forever for the ball to get to me. I caught the back of the ball; it slid through my hands. After that I don't remember anything. I threw the ball into the stands, and Coach [Mike] Archer wasn't very happy with me."

59 The North Gate and Tigerland

Tiger Stadium might be known for its festive atmosphere, but the real party unfolds down the street from LSU's colossal football venue. Tigerland, a complex of low-budget warehouse bars, is about 1.3 miles southwest of the stadium, and North Gate—a historic restaurant community—is about a mile to Tiger Stadium's north. These entertainment districts hug campus to provide thirst-quenching dives for students and out-of-towners alike, especially before and after games.

Tigerland is home to places such as Fred's, a 30-year-old bar known for its free-drinks nights and little-person wrestling competitions. There's also Reggie's and Mike's, and don't forget the House and JL's Place. These bars' clientele is almost exclusively students or those in their early to mid-twenties. If you're in your thirties here, you're old. On certain nights, you can buy a pitcher of beer for a penny, and on others, you can get a shot for 50 cents. You can always count on sticky floors, and as closing times arrives, their parking lots turn into booze-fueled after-parties, where sometimes anything goes—and we do mean *anything*. In fact, the crime rate around Tigerland bars has recently escalated.

North Gate, once known as Tiger Town, is a bit different. The occasional dive bar is woven among dozens of eateries along the famous Chimes Street, from the original Raising Cane's chicken tender restaurant to the Chimes, a Baton Rouge staple that opened in 1983 with delectable Cajun favorites such as seafood gumbo, shrimp po' boys, and blackened alligator. Highland Coffees is a favorite studying spot and brews a mean cup of joe, and Insomnia Cookies is there for your late-night sweet tooth cravings, just a stone's throw from the north gate of LSU's campus, hence the neighborhood's name.

Chain places are scattered about too, from Pita Pit to Buffalo Wild Wings to Chipotle to Jack in the Box. Don't forget about Louie's Café, a popular, classic 24-hour diner that opened in 1941, and the historic Varsity Theatre, host to musical acts and rented out for private soirees.

"Since the mid-1920s, North Gate has been the second-oldest continually operating commercial and residential neighborhood in Baton Rouge," Clarke Cadzow, owner of Highland Coffees, said in a story published in the *Advocate* in 2017. "The neighborhood has been the center of off-campus life for the LSU community since that time."

In a story published in 2007, one local told the LSU student newspaper, the *Daily Reveille*, that Tigerland had emerged as the new North Gate, at least for student nightlife. Both entertainment districts have experienced their share of adversity. The headline of a 2007 story in the *Daily Reveille* reads, Chimes Street Lost Luster with Time. Some long-standing neighborhood restaurants have shuttered, and many others are a revolving door of ownership. The community isn't far from a turbulent, poverty-stricken stretch of Baton Rouge dubbed the Bottoms.

Tigerland, meanwhile, has become increasingly dangerous as area residents have changed over time. Students have moved out of many of the neighborhood's apartment complexes and into newer, more upscale housing developments. In stories in both the *Advocate* and the *Daily Reveille*, residents speak of late-night gun violence and alcohol-related incidents. The reputation is bad enough that the owner of Fred's, Marc Fraioli, told the *Advocate* in a 2019 story, "When you hear 'Tigerland,' you get a negative connotation. There's been a lot of times where I've wanted to just be able to pick Fred's up and move it to a different location because of that."

In the same story, the newspaper reported on the increase in crime in the community. In the first 11 months of 2019, Tigerland saw a reported 163 assaults and batteries, 254 reported incidents of vehicle burglaries, and 463 instances of theft. LSU football players have found trouble there. One was involved in a stabbing in 2015, and another was accused of digging through an unconscious man's pockets and punching a woman in the parking lot.

A 2018 editorial in the *Daily Reveille* described Tigerland as "a cesspool for violence, crime, binge-drinking and other deplorable activities, making it a trashy and dangerous place for students and other visitors." In the piece, the newspaper also cited accusations of racism against some bars, from their dress code to the Confederate flag hanging on the wall. "Tigerland needs to be shut down for the safety and self-respect of students and residents in the area," the editorial read.

Despite it all, the parties go on—in and outside of Tiger Stadium.

60 LSU Saints

During Senior Bowl week ahead of the 2018 NFL Draft, in January 2018, the New Orleans Saints invited LSU defensive lineman Greg Gilmore to an interview. Gilmore sat down with Saints officials and, first off, asked them a question: "You going to draft LSU?"

The Saints, Louisiana's only professional franchise, located 80 miles from Tiger Stadium, went seven consecutive years without drafting an LSU player, something not lost on the Tigers fan base, including players such as Gilmore. He knew the history as he walked into that meeting in January 2018. Three months later, the Saints ended that streak, selecting offensive lineman Will Clapp in the seventh round. Clapp, at the time, was the 11th former LSU Tiger drafted by the Saints, and half of those are legendary figures you've probably heard of: Eric Martin, Dalton Hilliard, Hokie Gajan, and Devery Henderson.

In a way, the Saints and LSU hold a symbiotic relationship—they are by far the state's two largest athletic endeavors, coexisting an hour apart. Saturday nights in Tiger Stadium are lively, hostile, and full of an indescribable energy, the unique Louisiana culture pouring out into the usual murky night sky. Sunday afternoons in the Superdome are equally as intimidating for an opponent, the noise from beer guzzlers and Bloody Mary drinkers trapped inside an indoor facility at times seemingly ready to blow. Many fans double dip, watching their Saints from the Dome's cushioned-chairback seats 12 hours after rooting for their Tigers from the aluminum bleachers of Tiger Stadium.

"It's amazing how the success of both of those teams, LSU and the Saints, affects the psyche for everyone on Monday morning and how it sets the tone for the week as well," Saints quarterback Drew

Brees said in a story published on the *Athletic* in 2018. "You can feel it. It's a different vibe when we're coming off a big win or LSU is coming off a big win. Or the combination of the two. It's always a good feeling when everybody has an extra pep in their step."

Some of the greatest Saints wore the Purple and Gold. Martin, a receiver drafted in 1985, is second all-time in New Orleans history in receptions (532) and yards (7,854), and fourth in receiving touchdowns (48). Gajan spent his entire injury-shortened career with the Saints, running for more than 1,300 yards and scoring 11 touchdowns in a 45-game stretch that began in 1982 and ended in 1985. Later on, he became a Saints scout before moving into the booth as the team's radio color analyst, a role for which he was beloved. Gajan passed away in April 2016 after a bout with a rare form of cancer called liposarcoma. Henderson, a wideout the Saints selected in 2004, had his best season during the Saints' Super Bowl run in 2009, catching 51 passes for 804 yards. Hilliard, a running back picked in 1986, racked up more than 4,000 yards rushing and caught more than 240 passes in his career in New Orleans, even garnering a Pro Bowl invite in 1989.

The two programs have shared more than players recently. LSU head coach Ed Orgeron hired as an analyst former Saints special teams coordinator Greg McMahon in 2017, later promoting him to special teams coordinator. In 2019 Orgeron plucked away New Orleans offensive assistant Joe Brady to be his passing game coordinator.

They've even shared home turfs. The Tigers have played more than 20 games in the Superdome, as recently as a season-opening duel in 2017 against BYU. In 2005 the Saints played three designated home games in Tiger Stadium after Hurricane Katrina caused extensive damage to the Dome.

61

No. 1 Pick

Each spring, as the NFL Draft approaches, a cautionary tale is often shared in pro football circles. It's been more than a decade since the Oakland Raiders selected JaMarcus Russell out of LSU with the first pick in the 2007 NFL Draft, but Russell's short-lived, drama-filled pro career is a lesson for all NFL personnel.

Many consider the former LSU quarterback the biggest bust in NFL Draft history. NFL.com proclaimed such in a 2010 story, sermonizing that Russell had surpassed quarterback Ryan Leaf for the top spot on their all-time bust list. The Raiders paid Russell $39 million in guaranteed money. He started one season, was on their roster for only three years, and finished with a horrific stat line: 18 touchdowns to 23 interceptions, 52.1 percent completion rate, 7–19 starting record, and 15 lost fumbles. Russell began his third season in the league as the starter in 2009. By midseason he had dropped to third on the depth chart. His 2009 passer rating of 50 was the lowest rating by a starting quarterback in the NFL since 1998.

Few saw this coming. All Russell did in Baton Rouge was throw for more than 6,600 yards, complete 62 percent of his passes, toss 52 touchdowns to 21 interceptions, and finish 25–4 as a starter. Before that he was a three-sport star out of high school near Mobile, still holding Alabama's prep passing record. "I can't remember being in such awe of a quarterback in my decade of attending combines and pro days," ESPN's Todd McShay said in a piece in *Sports Illustrated*.

But during the pre-draft process, warning signs emerged. Matt Millen, then the president and CEO of the Detroit Lions, said in a radio interview in 2015 that he called Raiders owner Al Davis before the draft to encourage him not to select Russell because of Russell's peculiar visit to Detroit that spring. Millen claimed he threw Russell out of his office after the quarterback couldn't handle a simple question-and-answer segment. For the next three years, Russell's reputation only got worse in the league. As a rookie, he missed all of training camp and the first week of the season while holding out for more money. He often arrived to camp overweight, at times reaching close to the 300-pound mark, some 30 to 40 pounds heavier than during his playing days at LSU. His lack of work ethic spread across the league. The assault on his character was such that no team ever signed him after the Raiders released him in the spring of 2010, despite at least four tryouts. He later told *Sports Illustrated* in a 2011 story that a bout with sleep apnea was behind much of his troubles.

"Basically, Al Davis fell in love with [Russell], and if anyone had doubts, he didn't want to hear it," a former Raiders executive told *Sports Illustrated*. "You could justify JaMarcus, but it was based mostly on his arm strength. Great, but how many times a game does a guy throw 60 yards on the run?"

In 2016 he ramped up another comeback attempt, sending a letter to the 32 NFL teams pledging to play at least one year for free and begging for a tryout. According to *Sports Illustrated*, he wrote in the letter:

> As a former NFL player, I understand the daily grind that football operations can be. I am prepared to be physically examined and to have my football IQ evaluated. I would sincerely like an opportunity to come…meet with you and the coaching staff. I know that my name does not carry much weight in the NFL right now, but I am more than the image that others have bestowed on me. I've been labeled as a bust, I have been labeled as lazy, and I have been the target of many insults by the media. The blame for any negative press that I've received rests squarely on my shoulders.

No team responded to the letter. In 2010, just after the Raiders released him, he was arrested and charged with possession of codeine syrup without a prescription. A grand jury did not indict, but the incident further cast doubt on his search for employment.

And where is Russell now? As of 2020, he was a quarterbacks coach at his alma mater, Williamson High School, just outside Mobile. "I never thought I would want to do this, but it just came to my heart," Russell said in a 2018 interview with AL.com. "There comes a time in your life when you have done so many things, and you just want to give back. Right now, the best thing for me is to continue to help my community thrive in any way I can."

62 Down Goes No. 1

After a night game as LSU's head coach, Gerry DiNardo normally arrived home well after midnight to unwind and eventually drift to sleep. That did not happen in the wee hours of the morning of October 12, 1997.

He returned home to the Five Oaks neighborhood of Baton Rouge to an all-out party. "[My wife] Terri and I were right in the thick of it," DiNardo said in a 2017 interview with *Tiger Rag* magazine. "We were out partying in the streets in Five Oaks."

LSU's 28–21 win over top-ranked Florida in 1997 is one of the biggest upsets in Tigers football history, when the team beat a No. 1–ranked team for the first time in program history. DiNardo's neighborhood party was far from the only one in town that night. Part of the capacity crowd of more than 80,000 stormed the field immediately after the victory, toppling the goal posts and mingling among players in a wild scene. LSU quarterback Herb Tyler is still searching for his helmet from the win, he said in an interview with WAFB-TV in 2017. All-American guard Alan Faneca, as he did on the field, cleared a path through the fans afterward, guiding LSU players to the locker room.

Seconds after the win, a volley of student sent the archaic *H*-style goal posts collapsing onto the turf. "I could see over my shoulder that the thing was swaying and it was coming down," Herb Vincent, LSU's sports information director, said in the afore-mentioned article in *Tiger Rag*. "I remember our head of facilities went to [athletic director] Joe Dean and said, 'If we win this game, the students are going to take down those goal posts.' Joe Dean told him, 'Let them take them down!'"

The highlight of DiNardo's five-year tenure as LSU's head coach transpired that night, when his 14th-ranked Tigers shocked the college football world. LSU was a 17-point underdog and had lost to Florida nine consecutive times, dating back to 1987—a stretch in which the Tigers were outscored 297–94.

Florida and coach Steve Spurrier entered the game having won 25 consecutive Southeastern Conference games, four straight SEC titles, and the 1996 national championship. Spurrier held a 10–0 record against LSU, as a player and a coach, and he had built a powerhouse in Gainesville, Florida, that had won its previous 25 SEC games by an average of 28.6 points. "Who's going to slow down this juggernaut?" broadcaster Ron Franklin asked just before kickoff on the ESPN telecast. "Can it be the LSU Tigers?" Surely not, many thought. "We were sick and tired of hearing that we had no chance to win this game," LSU running back Kevin Faulk said.

DiNardo's team had barely beaten Vanderbilt 7–6 the week before, a lowly performance that caught their coach's ire. DiNardo spent much of that week chastising his team and praising the Gators, at one point referring to the Tigers as an "also-ran."

While he publicly berated his team, DiNardo and his staff privately made changes. They implemented a new offensive and defensive package that week in practice—a significant key to the program's first win over a No. 1–ranked team. The coaches installed a new option play with dual-threat QB Herb Tyler, and on defense they installed a substitution or platoon-style scheme similar to the one the program used in the 1950s and 1960s.

Tyler ran for touchdowns of 40 and 11 yards—both on option plays—and LSU's defense sacked UF quarterback Doug Jones five times and intercepted four of his passes. Florida failed to complete a touchdown pass, snapping its NCAA-record streak of 62 straight regular-season games with at least one score through the air.

Defensive back Cedric Donaldson picked off two passes for a combined 99 yards in returns. His first set up LSU for an early 14–0 lead, and he returned his second for a 31-yard touchdown to break a tied game in the fourth quarter. Fellow DB Raion Hill intercepted Jones with three minutes left to secure the victory. "The week before the game, I invited all the DBs to my house after practice," Donaldson said. "We had pizza, we had some beers, and we would watch film. All the things they tried to do, we had it all down."

In order to keep his defense fresh against pass-heavy Florida, defensive coordinator Carl Reese, on each third-and-long, substituted six players at linebacker and in the secondary—a group of younger, fresh guys who coaches referred to as the Chinese Bandits. The nickname had previously been used for the No. 1 defensive unit on LSU's 1958 national championship team, among others, during those glory years of Tigers football.

"Gerry DiNardo had told me before the game that we were going to do something different with our defense, but he said not to tell anybody until the game start[ed]," Vincent said. "He said to wait until we got into the game to tell anybody and see if it works. LSU was getting to the Florida quarterback a lot, so I started going through the press box telling people about the Bandits defense. It was evident when that group came in. It was the star of the game."

Florida did not help itself. Along with the four interceptions, the Gators lost a fumble on a critical kickoff return in the fourth quarter. The Tigers capitalized with a touchdown for a 28–14 lead. LSU blocked a Florida field goal attempt too, just before halftime.

The game's outcome resulted in LSU running back Kevin Faulk landing on the cover of *Sports Illustrated*, paired with the headline See You Later, Gators. But it did not, however, send the Tigers soaring. They lost 36–21 at home the very next week to an unranked Ole Miss team.

63 Glenn Dorsey

For a year of his life, Glenn Dorsey's legs were locked in metal braces so intrusive that some family members avoided carrying the young child for fear of scratching themselves. "I don't really know the scientific medical term, but I was bowlegged," Dorsey said in an ESPN interview that aired in 2007. "My toes pointed at each other."

That boy eventually grew out of braces to become the most decorated football player in LSU's history. As a senior, the defensive tackle from Baton Rouge won four national awards and was considered the top player at his position in college football.

Beside Dorsey's name in LSU's media guide are pictures of four trophies—all of Dorsey's hardware from that remarkable 2007 season: Bronko Nagurski Trophy (most outstanding defender), Lombardi Award (best lineman), Outland Trophy (best interior lineman), and Lott Trophy (most impactful defensive player). At that time, no LSU player had won even a single one of those trophies. Dorsey won all four.

He was such a dominating force that many coaches in 2007 admitted to scheming around him. "He's the most explosive big man we've had in the league in a very long time," one SEC coach told ESPN. "If you don't account for him on every play, you're crazy. He'll ruin your day, and you'll never get plays off."

The scheming didn't always help. Despite playing a position that normally doesn't lend itself to a lot of tackles, Dorsey finished with 69 in 2007, including a whopping 43 unassisted, along with 7 sacks to help LSU win the national championship. Offenses attempted anything and everything to slow him. They used two and sometimes three offensive players against him on a given play. "I make a move on a guard, and the center's ear-holing me," Dorsey explained in 2007. "I get past him, and the fullback cuts me."

Some teams went beyond that. Dorsey was involved in what many around LSU still believe is one of the dirtiest plays in recent Tigers history. In a home game against Auburn in 2007, Dorsey went down with a knee injury that lingered for the rest of the season. Auburn tackle Lee Ziemba blocked high as AU guard Chaz Ramsey bashed into Dorsey's right knee. When asked about it later, coach Les Miles suggested foul play. "I thought stuff like that went out in the '70s," he said.

Many believe Dorsey should have won the 2007 Heisman Trophy, or at least advanced to New York as a finalist. He finished ninth in the voting that produced Heisman winner Tim Tebow.

His defensive coordinator at LSU, Bo Pelini, called the 6'2", 305-pound Dorsey the "total package"—he had the athleticism of a 275-pounder and the power of a 320-pounder. Dorsey attributes his success to his inner motor. "Sometimes I'll be surprised at myself," he said in 2007. "Most of that just comes from doing whatever it takes to get to the ball. Sometimes I go back and watch film and say, 'I didn't know I did that to him!'"

Dorsey was ranked as the No. 5 defensive tackle in the nation in 2004 coming out of East Ascension High School in Gonzales, just south of Baton Rouge. He went from a reserve to a rotating player to a full-time starter as a junior. He decided to return for his senior season despite being a first-round projection for the 2007 NFL Draft. A year later, that hardware in tow, Dorsey was selected as the fifth pick overall in the NFL Draft by Kansas City.

Dorsey's transformation from a leg-braces-wearing kid to a sack-craving lineman still baffles his mother, Sandra. "To look at him now," she said in 2007, "you'd be surprised to know he wore braces as a kid."

64 Ice Bowl

On the LSU sideline, crates of hay and barrels of hot coals served as warming devices. In the stands, fans reportedly created fires. Snow encircled the field, and icicles hung from the hat of Arkansas coach Jim Barnhill. LSU quarterback Y.A. Tittle claimed it to be the coldest game in which he ever played, and at least one Arkansas defender played while wearing carpenter gloves.

The 1947 Cotton Bowl pitted the Razorbacks and the Tigers in a game in which temperatures hung in the 20s. A stiff wind, freezing rain, and sleet made it feel colder, the aftermath of a wintry storm that dumped two inches of snow on Dallas. The final score spoke of the icy temperatures: LSU 0, Arkansas 0.

According to a 247Sports.com piece published in 2016, an Associated Press story in the *Arkansas Gazette* summed up the game with its headline In Which a Good Time Wasn't Had by Anybody. "Flurries of sleet and rain the temperature of a Kentucky colonel's mint julep fell alternately," the story in the *Gazette* read.

Despite the tie, the game is one of the more memorable in LSU football history. The Tigers finished that season 9–1–1, their best mark in 10 years and just one misstep—a homecoming loss to Georgia Tech—from claiming the Southeastern Conference championship.

Led by future Hall of Famer Tittle and longtime coach Bernie Moore, the Tigers entered the game against Arkansas as a 12-point favorite and, for the most part, played like it. They dominated in yards (271–54) and first downs (15–1) but failed to score in four trips inside the 10-yard line, two of those in the final six minutes of the game. Their last chance came in the final seconds of the game, but holder Ray Coates fumbled a slick and icy football during a 15-yard field-goal attempt.

Earlier in the game, the Tigers got as close as they would to scoring. Tittle flipped a pass to receiver Jeff Adams at the 1-yard line on a fourth-and-goal from the 6. Clyde Scott, from his defensive position, collided with Adams in one of the biggest hits of the day, knocking him out of bounds. Officials marked him short of the goal line.

The Hogs' offense was helpless on this day. Each of their four passes fell incomplete, and they never reached LSU's red zone. Arkansas fumbled five times, two more than LSU, as the teams jostled in terrible conditions.

According to the story from 247Sports.com, after the game, Moore argued that LSU deserved to take home the trophy because the Tigers finished with more first downs. Barnhill countered that his squad had more tackles. A coin toss awarded Arkansas with the trophy. Weeks later, a replica was sent to Baton Rouge.

65 Odell Beckham Jr.

Odell Beckham Jr. had no choice but to be great. His father, Odell Sr., was a starting LSU running back. His mother, Heather Van Norman, was a six-time NCAA track All-American at LSU. "[Odell Jr.] hit the genetic jackpot," Heather said.

"Odell Jr. always jokes about, 'I'm gonna make sure I find a track girl so I can make one like me,'" Odell Sr. said. "I'm like, 'Boy, it's *not* that easy. It just so happened you got blessed.'" Indeed, he did.

He also got lucky in 2013, in his junior (and final college) season, when Cam Cameron became LSU's offensive coordinator. Realizing he had future NFL Draft choices sprinkled throughout his lineup, with receivers such as Odell Jr. and Jarvis Landry, quarterback Zach Mettenberger, and running back Jeremy Hill, Cameron turned his horses loose. He opened up the offense, threw the ball downfield at the drop of a hat, and masterminded an attack that featured two 1,000-yard receivers, a 3,000-yard passer, and a 1,000-yard rusher.

Odell Jr., who had 84 catches for 1,188 yards and four touchdowns in his first two LSU seasons combined, jumped to 59 receptions for 1,152 yards and eight TDs in his final season with the Tigers. "The offense we had before didn't allow the receivers to produce the way we were capable of producing," said Odell Jr., who starred in high school for Isidore Newman School in New Orleans, which is also the alma mater of Super Bowl champion quarterbacks Peyton and Eli Manning. "It was great to get in a scheme like that where you were getting touches. It wasn't just about putting up numbers but also being able to show what I'm capable of doing," he continued.

NFL Draft expert Chris Landry agreed with Odell Jr. about Cameron's impact. "Odell had always been a really good route runner with good hands," Landry said. "But with Cam Cameron coming in, the change of the offensive system, the development of Mettenberger, and the fact he played with another good receiver [Jarvis Landry] to prevent coverage to rolling to one side, what you saw with Odell was a perfect example of the production starting to match his potential.

"Without the new offense, he still would have had some production. But with the receiving depth in this [2014] draft, he would have been a first-round talent who would have probably been picked in the second round."

The fact that Odell Jr. was the 12th overall pick in the 2014 NFL Draft by the New York Giants wasn't a surprise, not to the general public who saw him win the 2013 Paul Hornung Award as college football's most versatile player. Of his 15 TDs in his three-year LSU career, 12 came on plays of 25 yards or more and 7 of them were 50 yards or better.

Odell Jr. certainly had a flair for the dramatic, a knack for making game-breaking plays. There was his game-tying 89-yard TD punt return that rallied LSU from a 35–28 deficit with 11 minutes left to help the Tigers beat Ole Miss 41–35 in 2012. And his 100-yard TD return of a missed UAB field goal in 2013 that he actually caught just under the crossbar.

Despite becoming one of the world's most recognizable athletes during his current, ongoing NFL career, Odell Jr. has never forgotten where he came from and how he was raised. Odell Sr. and Heather Van Norman didn't marry, yet they met the challenge of raising their son while both were college athletes at LSU. "My mother was pregnant with me, training for track, and had a 4.0 grade point average," Odell Jr. said. "I don't know how she and my dad did it."

Well, it took a village. "I'd take [Odell Jr.] to class, Heather would take him to class," Odell Sr. recalled. "He'd run around Broussard Hall [then the athletic dorm], he'd run around the track field, we'd play basketball in the dungeon [the windowless old practice court] in the Pete Maravich Assembly Center. Shaq [former LSU and NBA star Shaquille O'Neal] would lift him up and dunk. Shaq was like his uncle, and still is."

At LSU Odell Jr. was noted for his tireless work ethic, which he has carried over to the pros. But as his mother knows, he has been that way since he could run and throw a football to himself. When he was almost five years old, she watched him throw a football to himself repeatedly one chilly day. She noted her son's intensity, his look of total concentration. Her curiosity got the best of her, so she finally stepped outside. "Hey, son," she said. "What are you doing exactly?"

"I'm training for Sunday," replied Odell Jr., his NFL career path already mapped.

66 A Tour of LSU's Campus

The LSU campus is filled with timeless, iconic landmarks that have spanned generations. These are the most notable.

The Memorial Clock Tower

The Memorial Tower, also known as the Campanile, is a 175-foot clock tower in the middle of the LSU campus. It was erected in 1923; builders took the cornerstone, located in front of the tower, from the early LSU campus in Pineville. The stone describes the history of the campus and lists the names of the first Board of Supervisors and faculty.

The tower was officially dedicated in 1926, paid for by the American Legion of Louisiana and given to the university as a memorial to the 1,447 Louisianans who gave their lives during World War I. On the rotunda walls are bronze plaques bearing the names of those to whom Memorial Tower is dedicated. Each quarter hour, everyone on campus can hear the sound of chimes coming from the bells of the clock tower.

The Westminster Chimes are used each day until 10:00 PM. Valentine's Day is the only day the chimes ring at midnight, because there's a superstition-turned-tradition that says to become an official LSU student, one must be kissed under the Memorial Tower when the chimes ring at midnight.

The plaza area in front of the Memorial Tower is a place of celebration and ceremony, such as the university's annual Christmas tree lighting ceremony. Also, the student government holds the annual formal induction ceremonies for its new president and vice president there each spring. In 2003 the LSU Corps of Cadets placed a time capsule on the plaza honoring all former, present, and future cadets.

The building is currently undergoing a facelift funded by private donations and state funds. The tower will eventually serve as a military museum honoring all LSU students who have served our country.

LSU War Memorial

The LSU War Memorial, which sits in front of the Memorial Tower, was dedicated on October 8, 1998, in a ceremony that featured former president George H.W. Bush. It was built in memory of those who gave their lives in military conflict from World War II through the present and beyond into the future. The LSU Alumni

Association raised the money necessary to construct the memorial and then donated it to the university.

The Parade Ground

It's the large grassy gathering area along Highland Road bound by Dalrymple Drive and Veterans Drive that sits in front of the Memorial Tower and borders the LSU Student Union.

Former LSU chancellor Bud Davis eloquently described the Parade Ground:

> There are ghosts on the LSU Parade Ground. You have only to close your eyes, and visions of massed troops in World War II uniforms pass in review—and behind them, bringing up the rear, are long lines of soldiers in LSU gray. These images stretch back over a hundred years, back to a distant past. This broad, level field in front of Memorial Tower in the heart of the campus, indeed, is hallowed ground—a memorial to the veterans of this nation's armed forces—a place of tribute to absent comrades. It is a place where the past, the present, and the future come together in overlapping generations and overlapping memories.
>
> It is a special place—this Parade Ground with the American flag snapping and popping in the breeze, the well-trampled field surrounded by sentinels of live oaks. From the very beginnings of the new campus established on this site in 1926, it has been a landmark and focal point for LSU. It is a sacred place, a place of dreams of things that were and dreams of things that might be, a place where generations of students in times of peace prepared for war and in times of war went forth to lead in every branch of this nation's armed forces. It will ever be a reminder that students and members of this University community have led and served in every war, from the outbreak of the Civil War in 1861 to the present.

From the distant past, from the founding of that primitive seminary that blossomed into a prestigious state university, the military presence has been intertwined with LSU's great history. That presence also has impacted and helped shape the lives of generations of students representing this revered institution.

LSU Student Union

It took 25 years from the germination of the idea of a student union being constructed until the time it actually happened. The idea was first broached as early as 1939, but it didn't receive widespread support until 1955, then the school's Board of Supervisors authorized the construction in 1958.

Designed by Baton Rouge architect John Desmond, well-known union consultant Porter Butts, and the first director of the union, Carl Maddox, the building was funded by a $1.7 million allocation from the Board of Supervisors and a $10-per-student fee. Construction began in 1962 and the Union was opened officially in January 1964.

The LSU Union was conceived as a place where students could spend their leisure time in a variety of pursuits. The building originally featured a cafeteria and snack bar, a barbershop, a bowling alley, study rooms, separate men's and women's quiet rest areas, a browsing library, a music listening room, and a bookstore.

The Union has been renovated three times. The first was in 1987 to give the bookstore a second floor, the second was in the 1990s to convert the cafeteria and snack bar into a food court, and the third was in 2011 renovating the theater and adding a four-story addition on the southeast side of the building.

Memorial Oak Grove

The 30 magnificent live oak trees in Memorial Oak Grove, located just south of the LSU Union, were dedicated in 1926 to a fallen soldier who had given his life in service to the United States of America. One tree is dedicated to "the Unknown," representing those missing in action but remembered for their valor.

The Campus Mounds

The Campus Mounds are the oldest monuments on campus, estimated to have been built during the Archaic period about 6,100 years ago. They are two hills located in the northwest portion of campus near Graham Hall and the Huey P. Long Field House. The mounds are part of a cluster of Archaic Native American mounds found throughout the state because of the state's abundance of resources available to migrating and hunting American Indians. The mounds are believed not to be burial sites but to house mounds or temple mounds. The LSU Campus Mounds are listed in the National Register of Historic Places.

Greek Theatre

Opened in 1925, the 3,500-seat natural amphitheater was built into a hill. It was originally used for commencement exercises, rallies, pageants, and convocations. During Louisiana governor Huey P. Long's term in office, he used the Greek Theatre when he had announcements for the entire student body. A large gong sounded on campus to summon students to hear Long. In the 1930s gardens were installed behind the amphitheater. It was called the Sunken Garden, landscaped with shrubs and existing trees for cover. A 150-foot-long, 30-foot-high reflecting pool that was two feet deep was also installed. An eight-foot statue of Spanish explorer Hernando de Soto was located at the far end of the pool. ROTC cadets threw officers into the reflecting pools after the final parade of each year.

The reflecting pool was filled in 1960, and the area was replaced with a formal garden. Then, in the late 1990s and early 2000s, the Sunken Garden was used to form an open, tree-shaded area. The Greek Theatre is still used today for outdoor concerts, performances, religious ceremonies, and as a place for students to congregate.

The LSU Lakes

Four donors gave LSU a tupelo cypress swamp next to the campus in 1933. The donors' stipulation was that LSU was to turn the swamps into lakes and parks for public use forever.

University Lake was dug from that swamp by hundreds of men employed by the Works Progress Administration. The work of those 900 men removed the threat of malaria-bearing mosquitoes and created forever-cherished public space. They also built a sewer system that let LSU claim land for Sorority Row and formed land for roads that surround the lakes.

Expansion of residential development and the LSU campus resulted in the subdivision of the original University Lake into the current Lake District System, which includes six urban lakes ranging from 3 to 196 acres, with a cumulative area of approximately 275 acres. University Lake is the largest lake of the system at approximately 196 acres in size. There's also City Park Lake (58 acres), Crest Lake (9 acres), Campus Lake (7 acres), College Lake (5 acres), and Erie Lake (3 acres).

TAF

Have you noticed the 8,000-seat addition to Tiger Stadium's south end zone? Or the giant videoboard hanging from the ceiling of LSU's basketball arena? Have you sat in the seats at Tiger Park, eaten a hot dog from Alex Box Stadium, or watched LSU's live Bengal tiger crawl across the ground of his $3.7 million habitat?

None of these niceties are possible without donations made by LSU fans through the school's fund-raising arm, the Tiger Athletic Foundation (TAF), a private, nonprofit corporation. TAF has been raising money for LSU athletics since 1987, providing the necessary dough for facilities construction and improvements as well as scholarship endowments. Their membership has tripled since 1990 to about 9,400 donors giving an average annually of about $45 million, says Rick Perry, the president of TAF.

It wasn't always such a lucrative endeavor. In fact, as recently as the early 2000s, LSU's athletic fund-raising lagged behind many other universities, specifically those in its own conference, the SEC. "We were way behind," said Herb Vincent, then an LSU administrator who left the school in 2013 to take a job with the SEC.

At the turn of the millennium, two events changed LSU's athletic donor situation: 1) on-field success from the Nick Saban–coached football Tigers and 2) a controversial off-the-field fund-raising initiative by a group of LSU administrators.

Football experienced its most success in decades. Saban won two SEC titles and the 2003 national championship, transforming a middling program into a perennial juggernaut. Meanwhile, then–athletic director Skip Bertman and his lieutenants privately operated from behind the scenes, spearheading a movement to connect seating priority in Tiger Stadium to financial donations to TAF. Administrators toured the state to convince LSU's fan base that the plan would benefit the university in the long run. Seat prices for many longtime season ticket holders jumped significantly. Emotions were high. Tempers flared. In the end, it was all worth it.

Years later, LSU is one of the nation's richest athletic departments, and those administrators are among college football giants. Mark Emmert, then the LSU chancellor, became president of the NCAA, and Scott Woodward—a former political lobbyist in Louisiana who then served Emmert in a liaison role—was named LSU's athletic director in 2019. Verge Ausberry, the ranking No. 2 in LSU athletics; Chris Howard, overseeing football for the NCAA; and Vincent, the right-hand man to SEC commissioner Greg Sankey, were all administrators then. So were Eddie Nuñez, who became New Mexico's athletic director, and Dan Radakovich, who moved on to lead departments as AD at Georgia Tech and Clemson.

Decades earlier, Paul Dietzel—LSU's former football coach and then athletic director—formed the first fund-raising group to help LSU athletics. The Varsity Club began in 1978, a time of financial distress for a department that now brings in more than $150 million in revenue each year. Back then, LSU was "in the red," James H. Wharton, the university's chancellor from 1981 to 1988, told the *Daily Reveille* for a story in 2004.

To dig out of the hole, LSU discontinued dispensing free tickets to legislators and raised student ticket prices. The Varsity Club turned into Tigers Unlimited, and it was granted 501(c)(3) status from the IRS in 1984. Three years later, Baton Rouge businessman Richard Lipsey took over as president and changed the name to the Tiger Athletic Foundation. Why? Lipsey, a member of Ducks Unlimited, did not like the commonality in the names, Wharton said.

More than 30 years later, TAF lives on, supporting LSU athletics with its vast array of boosters—Lipsey included.

68 Doc Fenton

LSU's football program was 15 years old when it had its first legitimate star. George Ellwood Fenton, better known as Doc because his father was a singer who traveled with American Indian medicine shows, led the Tigers to a 23–5 record from 1907 to 1909 as a running, passing, and kicking whiz. Included was a perfect 10–0 season in 1908 when LSU won the SIAA championship. It was the Tigers' first 10-win season in program history, and they didn't experience another until LSU won its first national championship in 1958 with an 11–0 record.

Fenton was actually the source of a recruiting battle when he starred in high school for Mansfield Normal in his home state of Pennsylvania. He already had an offer to Mississippi State. But that was before LSU coach Edgar Wingard managed to get his foot in the door. Fenton's parents were impressed by the well-spoken Wingard and his wife.

Fenton was happy to discover Baton Rouge's cheap beers and liberal drinking laws, so he signed with LSU. "Baton Rouge was a nice little town, but I have to be honest and say the thing that really sold me was the nickel beers," Fenton said in Peter Finney's 1968 book *The Fighting Tigers*.

He started at end in his first LSU season in 1907 when the Tigers traveled to Cuba for a 56–0 Christmas Day win in Havana. His performance as an elusive runner not only earned him a Cuban nickname of El Rubio Vaselino (which translates to the Vaselined Redhead), but it convinced Wingard to move him to quarterback in 1908. Fenton didn't like the idea, but Wingard bribed him by buying him clothes from a downtown Baton Rouge store. "For a

$70 haberdasher's bill, I was quarterback for the rest of my career," Fenton admitted.

Fenton's move to quarterback in Wingard's version of a T-formation offense fit Fenton to...well, to a T. In the Tigers' unbeaten 1908 season, in which they scored 442 points (508 points in today's scoring system) in 450 minutes of play, they allowed only 11 points and recorded seven shutouts. Many years later, in awarding retroactive national titles to colleges, the 1908 Tigers were named co-national champions with Penn by the National Championship Foundation. Fenton set four school records that year, including scoring 125 points (132 by today's rules) and kicking six field goals—including a 45-yarder—and 36 extra points.

LSU's most challenging game of the year was a 10–2 win at Auburn, played on a field surrounded by fans standing behind ropes. It was a memorable day for Fenton for two reasons. The first is his 35-yard touchdown pass and the other came when he had a punt blocked in LSU's end zone. "The ball was bouncing around so I picked it up and was getting ready to run it out of the end zone when a fan reached over the rope and cracked me over the head with a cane," Fenton said. "It knocked me cold."

Auburn coach Mike Donahue, who later became LSU's coach for five seasons from 1923 to 1927, called Fenton "the consummate football player, born to run, who lived and loved the attacking side of football."

Just before the start of Fenton's senior season in 1909, Wingard resigned as LSU's coach after battling charges the previous year he had recruited professionals. Vanderbilt coach Joe Pritchard quickly filled Wingard's vacancy, and the Tigers won their first three games of the season by a combined 95–0. The victories stretched LSU's winning streak to 15 dating back to the last two games of the 1907 season.

There was no 16th straight win. With President William Howard Taft in attendance, Sewanee edged LSU 15–6 before

6,000 fans in New Orleans's Heinemann Park. Four games later, Fenton ended his marvelous three-year college career with 36 touchdowns, 298 points, and a legion of admirers.

"Doc could do more with a football than a monkey can with a coconut," said Cap Gandy, Fenton's teammate. "He was the greatest field general who ever donned a uniform, a fellow who could punt on the run and catch the football one-handed. Doc was the hub of our team and we were the spokes."

After he graduated from LSU, Fenton coached at high schools in Baton Rouge for a couple seasons before entering the oil business. He was also a star semipro baseball player. Three years after he died in 1968 at the age of 80, Fenton was elected to the College Football Hall of Fame as a member of the class of 1971.

69 LSU and SEC Championships

Imagine the football champion of the SEC opening the season with a home loss to Rice. Well, that really happened in 1935. Three years after the founding of the SEC as a conference, the LSU Tigers, led by coach Bernie Moore, opened the season with a 10–7 loss to Rice in Tiger Stadium. LSU wouldn't lose another regular-season game that year, winning nine straight to claim the program's first-ever SEC football title.

LSU would go on to win 11 more SEC championships on the gridiron, including the very next year in 1936. After a 22-year gap, Paul Dietzel captained the Tigers to a third SEC title in 1958, along with the national championship. Twelve years later, in 1970, coach Charles McClendon's ninth season as coach resulted in his only league title in 18 years at the helm of the program.

In 1986 freshman sensation Tommy Hodson passed the Tigers to the SEC championship under coach Bill Arnsparger, and he did it again two years later under coach Mike Archer.

The Nick Saban–coached 2001 SEC championship team began what many believe to be the golden years of LSU football, a nearly 20-year run that would include five SEC titles (2001, 2003, 2007, 2011, 2019), three national championships (2003, 2007, 2019), and a whopping 11 10-win seasons (2001, 2003, 2005–07, 2010–13, 2018, 2019).

The 2001 team rallied to produce one of the most remarkable championship seasons in school history, roaring back from a 4–3 start to win its final six games, including a rescheduled quasi–SEC West title game against Auburn, an upset in the league championship game over Tennessee, and a whipping of Illinois in the Sugar Bowl. Big underdogs against the then–No. 2 Volunteers in the Georgia Dome, LSU lost its starting running back (LaBrandon Toefield) and quarterback (Rohan Davey) but survived with steady backup QB Matt Mauck and a defense that recovered two fumbles and allowed only 50 yards rushing.

In 2003 freshman running back Justin Vincent piled up an SEC Championship Game–record 201 yards rushing, and the Tigers rolled over Georgia to advance to the national title bout against Oklahoma, a game they won 21–14.

In coach Les Miles's third season, the 2007 championship season was beset with the bizarre. The Tigers' only losses that year came in triple overtime, at Kentucky and against Arkansas. They beat Florida by converting all five fourth-down attempts, many of them during a game-securing drive on the legs of running back Jacob Hester. They beat Auburn on a last-second touchdown pass from quarterback Matt Flynn to receiver Demetrius Byrd, and they won the SEC title game over Tennessee despite missing Flynn. Backup quarterback Ryan Perrilloux garnered the game's MVP honors before Flynn returned to lead the Tigers to a 38–24 win over Ohio State for the BCS championship.

Before 2019 arrived, the 2011 Tigers were thought by many to be the school's most dominant team. The Miles-coached club spent 11 consecutive weeks at No. 1 and won 12 of its 13 games by double digits. Led by Heisman Trophy finalist and Chuck Bednarik Award winner Tyrann Mathieu, LSU held opponents without a touchdown in 44 quarters, and the Tigers set an NCAA record with eight victories over top 25 teams.

LSU walloped Georgia—one of the greatest teams in college football history—42–10 in the SEC Championship Game before ending the season with a dud: a 21–0 loss to Alabama in the BCS championship in New Orleans.

The 2019 Tigers finished the job, led by Heisman winner Joe Burrow and Biletnikoff Award winner Ja'Marr Chase. LSU capped a magical season with three postseason wins by a combined 79 points: a 37–10 thumping of Georgia in the SEC title game, a 63–28 victory over Oklahoma in the CFP semifinal, and a 42–25 crushing of Clemson in the title bout. In one of the most dominant seasons in college football and SEC history, LSU won seven games against teams ranked in the top 10—the most ever—and became the first team to beat preseason AP Poll's top four teams (Alabama, Clemson, Georgia, and Oklahoma).

70 Rival-Less

The argument at LSU is ages old, and everyone believes they've got the right answer: Who is the Tigers' biggest rival? A large group would say Ole Miss. Another might claim Alabama. A third group likely contends it's Auburn, and the old-timers may harken to the now-defunct clash with little Louisiana brother Tulane. Younger LSU fans might tell you it's the new SEC foe from the neighboring state, Texas A&M, and others may point to the bordering neighbor to the north, Arkansas.

No one can really make up their minds and settle on the team to put in their purple-and-gold crosshairs. It's a long-standing argument, partly created because of Louisiana's absence of a second major conference football program. LSU stands alone as the only Power 5 football team inside the borders of the Bayou State.

Other surrounding states possess deep-seated in-state feuds. Mississippi's got Ole Miss vs. Mississippi State in the Egg Bowl. Alabama has Auburn vs. Bama in the Iron Bowl. Texas and Florida have a great many in-state rivalries, starting with a trio in each state: Texas, Texas A&M, and Texas Tech and Florida, Florida State, and Miami. In Oklahoma there's Oklahoma State vs. OU. In Georgia you've got the yearly season-ending match between the UGA and Georgia Tech. There's Kentucky and Louisville, South Carolina and Clemson, and even Tennessee and Vanderbilt, no matter how lopsided those series are.

LSU's predicament is such that the Southeastern Conference, hoping to find a year-ending rivalry clash for the Tigers, situated Arkansas as the regular-season finale in what they hoped would become a heated series. It never really developed. Once Texas A&M and Missouri joined the conference in 2012, the league switched up the schedule in a geographically engineered decision to, again, ignite border rivalry series. LSU and A&M meet to end the season while Arkansas and Missouri do the same.

The Tigers are involved in a couple of series that include trophies. There's the Battle for the Boot with Arkansas and the Magnolia Bowl with Ole Miss, but neither side has truly embraced these unusual, clunky monstrosities. The Golden Boot, for instance, weighs nearly 200 pounds and stands 4 feet tall. You need two or three hulking defensive linemen to lift it into the air. The Magnolia Bowl trophy is so fragile that, during a celebration after a 2013 victory over the Tigers, Rebels players broke the thing. The new trophy is a depiction of a Magnolia flower—flowers in football?—resting on a wooden base.

In reality, LSU's rival has changed through the decades. Before Tulane left the SEC in 1966, the Green Wave and the Tigers were embroiled in a sometimes-intense battle. Ole Miss and LSU football experienced their peaks during similar stretches. Starting in 1958, the Rebels and Tigers met five times in a five-year stretch while both ranked inside the top six. They accounted for five SEC championships in an eight-year span beginning in 1954. By the mid-1970s, most LSU fans had turned their attention to coach Bear Bryant and Alabama, a program that, at one point, held an 11-game winning streak over the Tigers. Florida became LSU's permanent cross-divisional opponent in football in 1991, and that rivalry was brewing more than ever by 2018. LSU and Auburn have been involved in some of college football's most incredible games (I mean, an actual barn burned down next to Jordan-Hare Stadium during one game). One of the two, LSU or Auburn, represented the SEC West in the league championship game five times in a six-year span ending in 2005. After that, it was back to Alabama. The Tide and Tigers tangled in some of college football's most elite affairs from 2008 through 2013. They were both ranked in five meetings over that stretch, clashing as No. 1 vs. No. 2 twice in 2011.

As of 2020, a new rivalry is budding. Texas A&M and LSU, now season-ending opponents, are on a sizzling path. The Aggies snapped a six-game losing streak to the Tigers in 2018 by winning a seven-overtime affair that clocked as the longest game in college football history and included a host of late-game officiating calls that irked LSU fans. At various points in history, LSU notoriously attempted to hire Aggies coach Jimbo Fisher while he led Florida State; the two programs fight for the same talent, their recruiting territories overlapping near the Texas-Louisiana border.

So who is LSU's rival? Depends on who you ask and when you ask them.

71 Sing All of LSU's Fight Songs

LSU has football fight song depth. The Tigers go four deep with fight songs and somehow mix and match all flawlessly, especially on game day.

The first composed was "Touchdown for LSU," a 1935 collaboration between Louisiana governor Huey Long and Castro Carazo. It began in 1934 when Long visited the Blue Room in New Orleans's Roosevelt Hotel, where Carazo was leading the hotel's jazz band orchestra. Long sent a bodyguard to bring Carazo to his table. When Carazo met Long, the governor reportedly told him, "You are now the bandleader at LSU. Come with me; we're returning to LSU."

Once in Baton Rouge, Carazo and Long wrote "Touchdown for LSU," which remains part of every Tiger Band pregame show.

The Lyrics:

Tigers! Tigers! They've come to town,
They fight! They fight! Call a first down,
Just look them over, and how they can go,
Smashing the line with runs and passes
high and low.
Touchdown! Touchdown! It's Tigers' score.
Give them hell and a little bit more.
Come on you Tigers, Fight them, you Tigers,
Touchdown for LSU.
Rah! U. Rah!

Two years later, in 1937, Castro and W.G. Higginbotham wrote the music and lyrics for "Fight for LSU."

The Lyrics:

Like Knights of old, Let's fight to hold
The glory of the Purple Gold.
Let's carry through, Let's die or do
To win the game for dear old LSU.
Keep trying for that high score;
Come on and fight,
We want some more, some more.
Come on you Tigers, Fight! Fight! Fight!
for dear old L-S-U.
RAH!

"Hey Fighting Tigers" is a 1962 adaptation of the song "Hey, Look Me Over!" written by Cy Coleman for the Broadway musical *Wildcat*. According to former LSU sports information director Bud Johnson, the idea came from Tigers athletic director Jim Corbett while attending a business meeting in New York City. "Jim was on the NCAA television committee, so he goes to New York on

TV business," Johnson said. "He saw Lucille Ball in the musical *Wildcat*, which had a very lively tune called 'Hey, Look Me Over!'

"That song sounded like a college fight song to Jim. He turned 'Hey, Look Me Over!' into 'Hey Fighting Tigers' for Charles McClendon's first game as LSU's coach in 1962 in Tiger Stadium.

"Jim got somebody on campus [director of social recreation Gene Quaw] to write the words and got permission from the people to use it.

"Tom Tyra, LSU's band director, initially wasn't sold on the song. I was in this staff meeting when Tom Tyra said, 'It'll always be known as 'Hey, Look Me Over!'

"Now, you find me somebody in Tiger Stadium today that knows 'Hey Fighting Tigers' was 'Hey, Look Me Over!'"

The Lyrics:
Hey, Fightin' Tigers, Fight all the way
Play, Fightin' Tigers, win the game today.
You've got the know how,
you're doing fine,
Hang on to the ball as you hit the wall
And smash right through the line
You've got to go for a touchdown
Run up the score.
Make Mike the Tiger stand right up and roar.
ROAR!
Give it all of your might as you fight tonight
and keep the goal in view.
Victory for L-S-U!

And of course, there's the song "Tiger Rag," written in 1917 by New Orleans trumpeter and bandleader Nick LaRocca. His Original Dixieland Jass Band made the first recording of the song on August 17, 1917, in New York. "Tiger Rag" is regarded as one of the most important and influential jazz standards of the 20th century. There were 136 cover versions of LaRocca's copyrighted composition "Tiger Rag" by 1942 alone. Among the artists who have recorded "Tiger Rag" are Louis Armstrong, Charlie Parker, Benny Goodman, Frank Sinatra, Duke Ellington, and Les Paul.

The Lyrics:
Long ago, way down in the jungle
Someone got an inspiration for a tune,
And that jingle brought from the jungle
Became famous mighty soon.
Thrills and chills it sends thru you!
Hot! so hot, it burns you too!
Tho' it's just the growl of the tiger
It was written in a syncopated way,
More and more they howl for the 'Tiger'
Ev'ry where you go today
They're shoutin'
Where's that Tiger! Where's that Tiger!
Where's that Tiger! Where's that Tiger!
Hold that Tiger! Hold that Tiger!
Hold that Tiger!

Current LSU football coach Ed Orgeron uses the "Hold that Tiger!" refrain in a unique way. Because NCAA rules don't permit schools to publicly announce names of athletes when they commit to sign a scholarship, Orgeron has found a way to skirt the rules using social media. Every time a prospect commits to LSU, Orgeron tweets "Hold that Tiger!"

72 Gator Hate

Martez Ivey grew up in Apopka, Florida. It's a 40,000-person town just north of Orlando and about 110 miles south of Gainesville. Apopka is Gators country. You'll find Florida flags waving outside of homes and Gators license plates along the roads. Ivey, in 2017 a junior offensive lineman at UF, learned quickly to hate Florida State, the Gators' longtime rival. "Ever since I've been a Florida fan, it's about FSU," Ivey said in a story that ran in the *Advocate* in 2017. "Lately, it's been all LSU."

The Florida-LSU series—one played every year since 1971—has developed into one of the Tigers' more spicy matchups. Hate for the Gators oozes from the pores of Baton Rouge as steadfastly these days as it does for Ole Miss.

Their most recent drama was a public and sometimes nasty back-and-forth between the two programs surrounding the postponement and eventual relocation of a 2016 game because of Hurricane Matthew. LSU officials, upset over the postponement, refused to travel to Gainesville later that year, forcing Florida to give up its home game with the Tigers and travel to Baton Rouge. Florida won that game 16–10 to claim the SEC Eastern Division championship, stuffing LSU running back Derrius Guice on a fourth-and-goal from the 1-yard line and then madly celebrating on LSU's home turf.

At least one Florida player planted a giant school flag in LSU's south end zone, and Florida coach James McElwain seared LSU in postgame remarks. "The way I look at it, they got what they deserved," he said. "And it should have been worse."

This rivalry began to brew years ago. During a search to replace coach Bill Arnsparger in 1986, LSU officials interviewed a young hotshot former Florida quarterback named Steve Spurrier. They passed him over for the job, making the in-house hire of Mike Archer instead. Funnily enough, Arnsparger, as Florida's athletic director, hired Spurrier to coach the Gators three years later. He led them to a national title and six SEC crowns, and beat LSU in his first seven games against the Tigers.

He's still twisting the knife into LSU's collective fan base. At a function in Shreveport in 2017, Spurrier took a jab at the Tigers. "You can have a bunch of good ballplayers and not win, also," he said, according to KSLA-TV in north Louisiana. "All you LSU fans know about that, I'm sure."

Since Spurrier's dominance over LSU (he was 10–1), the Tigers have made this a tight battle. In fact, they've won 10 of 16 games starting in 2004, and four consecutive games (2014 to 2017) were decided by a combined 17 points. The overall series is tight too. In 66 games played, Florida is up 33–30–3.

The height of the rivalry came in the 2000s. The programs met when both ranked in the top 10 in 2006, 2007, 2009, and 2015. Those seasons included slobber-knocker wins that resulted, at times, in national championships. No. 5 Florida beat ninth-ranked LSU 23–10 in 2006 on the way to the championship. Top-ranked LSU, in one of the school's greatest games, converted five fourth downs and beat the No. 9 Gators 28–24 en route to the 2007 title.

Florida's 19–7 upset win over No. 6 LSU in Baton Rouge served as the Tigers' only loss during their 2003 national championship season under Nick Saban. LSU upset the top-ranked Gators in 1997, ending their 25-game SEC winning streak.

73 David Toms

David Toms, the most successful golfer ever to play for LSU, started his 32nd year as a pro in 2020. The résumé of 53-year-old Toms speaks volumes: 13 PGA tour victories, including the 2001 PGA Championship; a win at the 2018 U.S. Senior Open; and lifetime earnings of $41,901,709, which ranks 17th all-time.

But the best part about Toms is he has never forgotten his roots. In 2003 he created the David Toms Foundation in Shreveport. It has raised and donated more than $3.7 million to local organizations, specifically those with programs to help underprivileged, abused, and abandoned children.

Then in 2013, the foundation created the David Toms 265 Academy, where underprivileged and at-risk youth learn important life lessons through the sport of golf. "I know I'm blessed to have the talent to play this game and be in the right place at the right time on more than one occasion," Toms said. "You're always tested in life. But I really believe the Good Lord does that for a reason. It makes you appreciate the good times even more."

It's true that golf is a sport anyone can play. But it's not a sport everyone can play exceptionally. Toms, who was raised in both south Louisiana (Denham Springs) and north Louisiana (Shreveport–Bossier City) because of his parents' divorce just before he became a teenager, had an edge because he had some athletic genes. His father, Buster, was an All-State player in baseball and basketball, and went on to then–Northeast Louisiana University, where he played baseball. Later in college, he quickly became a scratch golfer.

Toms inherited his father's athletic versatility. He was an unruffled point guard in basketball and one of the best pitcher-shortstops in his Little League age group, sans the day he gave up a homer to a strapping Shreveport youngster named Albert Belle, who later played for LSU and then had a 12-year major league career as a five-time All-Star. "I threw a fastball to him as hard as I could, he hit it to dead center, and I still think the ball is goin' today," Toms said.

When Toms got to high school, baseball and basketball got shelved. He wasn't even six feet tall and didn't have a growth spurt in him. But that little sucker could sure take a golf ball for a ride. "David looked at his size and abilities and decided if he was going to make a living in sports, that it was going to be golf," Buster said. "He was so good as a junior golfer that he would have to play really bad to lose a tournament. He'd get that far ahead of the field."

Yet it was only when Toms moved in with his grandparents that he realized golf was his thing. He fit right in with his late grandfather Tom, who had a regularly scheduled Saturday round of golf with his old cronies at Palmetto Country Club in Bossier City. "We had a bunch of old men in our group, and old men usually don't like anybody playing with them," Tom Toms said before his death in 2010 at age 88. "But because he could keep up with us and was so well-behaved, the group accepted him. They were all crazy about David."

It was Tom, a former military man, who showed his grandson that when he needed to master a certain shot, there were no short-cuts. "Like when he thought I needed to work on hitting a 60-yard sand wedge, he'd take me out to a field at Barksdale Air Force Base, drop a shag bag 60 yards away, and have me hit balls at [it]," Toms said. "If my shots got within a close enough distance to the bag, then he picked them up. But I had to pick up the ones that weren't anywhere close."

The time Toms spent with his grandfather amounted to his golf lessons. He had a natural swing that belied his age, turning heads when he shot a 67 in a local charity tournament staged by

Hal Sutton, Shreveport's first hot touring pro. Also playing in the charity round that day were Ben Crenshaw and Lee Trevino.

So in an event that had three PGA veterans with an eventual combined 62 tour victories, including 9 majors, the little ol' high schooler blitzed 'em in front of about 4,000 people. "It was one of those days that made me think that I might be good enough to be a pro golfer one day," Toms said.

Well, if he didn't know it, his friends and competitors did, such as Rob Akins, another local prep golfer from Captain Shreve High School. "There were 8 to 10 kids who had the potential to play professionally, but David just stood out," said Akins, who eventually became his swing coach. "A lot of us always said, 'If David doesn't make it, none of us will.'"

Toms won the Junior Worlds at age 17 and was a Southeastern Conference individual medalist as a sophomore, which came as no surprise to his college coach. "David had one of the most natural swings of any golfer I've ever coached," said Buddy Alexander, who coached Toms at LSU.

Even as Toms's career blossomed, he and his family never moved from Shreveport. "The fact David chose to live in Shreveport, and not Arizona or Florida or Texas like a lot of pro golfers, says a lot about him," said Adam Young, executive director of Toms's foundation. "He can be himself here."

When Hurricane Katrina destroyed the Mississippi Gulf Coast and flooded New Orleans and surrounding parishes in late August 2005, it drove many evacuees north and west to such locales as Houston, Memphis, Dallas, and Shreveport. A day after Katrina hit, Toms walked through the LSU-Shreveport gymnasium, which had been turned into a shelter, and handed out 500 $100 Walmart gift cards to grateful evacuees. He also got one of his corporate sponsors, Tommy Hilfiger, to outfit the entire St. Bernard Parish Sheriff's Department with new pullover windbreakers.

Aided by a $500,000 donation from Bighorn Golf Club, Toms's foundation raised $1.5 million in Katrina relief. In his first visit back to New Orleans following Katrina for the Zurich Classic, the annual PGA tour stop, his foundation gave $100,000 each to four New Orleans charities.

74 When Time Stood Still

In the week of practice leading up to LSU's game against Ole Miss in 1972, Charles McClendon and his coaching staff installed a new wrinkle to their team's arsenal: a flare route to the pylon of the end zone. It was implemented for use on a two-point conversion, if the sixth-ranked and undefeated Tigers needed such against the unranked 4–3 Rebels.

That two-point play turned into one of the more incredible touchdowns in LSU football history, as quarterback Bert Jones hit running back Brad Davis for a game-tying 10-yard scoring completion as time expired. Rusty Jackson made the game-winning extra point with no time left on the clock, and LSU beat Ole Miss 17–16 in epic fashion.

The circumstances made the result so improbable. For one, LSU ran two plays in the final four seconds of the game, a controversial issue that still lingers with some Ole Miss faithful. Many in the stadium, including LSU's own quarterback, assumed the clock had expired after an incomplete pass to Jimmy LeDoux in the end zone on first down. "I really thought that there was pass interference against Jimmy LeDoux in the end zone," Jones said in a 2012 story published on LSUSports.net. "I did not realize there was a second left until I looked at the clock after arguing with the referee for a pass interference call."

During a timeout before the final snap, McClendon selected the play he'd installed earlier that week for a two-point conversion. Davis lined up as the inside receiver in a three-receiver set to the left, a choreographed mismatch with an Ole Miss linebacker. The mismatch never really transpired. Gerald Keigley, the middle receiver of the three, chipped the linebacker who was on man coverage against Davis while running his route. The subtle nudge knocked the defender off the route in what was possibly a designed pick play, an illegal but widely used strategy even in today's football games.

Davis made a mad dash toward the left goal-line pylon, but there was a problem as he turned back toward Jones for the ball. Stadium lights temporarily blinded him, and he lost the pass. Davis tipped the ball to himself, caught it, and lunged inside the pylon, barely squeaking in. "It was an elated feeling," Jones said. "It was my dream of hitting a home run in the World Series, or better yet, an LSU victory over Ole Miss in Tiger Stadium."

Hysteria descended on what was a then-record 70,502 fans packed into the venue. Some fans raced onto the field even before the game-winning extra point, and LSU players scattered about in a massive celebration in the south end zone. "In all my years in the game, I don't believe I've ever seen a game won after time expired," McClendon is quoted as saying afterward about a game known around Baton Rouge as When Time Stood Still.

According to one LSU expert in attendance, the stadium shook on the final completion. "Tiger Stadium exploded, not in a wall of noise but in a surreal surround-sound of massive vibration that permeated everything and was, for a moment, frightening," longtime LSU beat reporter Jim Kleinpeter wrote in a first-person account of the game published at Nola.com. "I felt like I might be lifted in the air. I could feel the stadium shaking for the only time in my life, but I couldn't hear myself screaming. I know I was."

The Rebels' loss that night in Tiger Stadium further dented the brief stay for Ole Miss coach Billy Kinard, working in the shadow of his predecessor, Johnny Vaught. That 1972 Ole Miss team finished 5–5 a year after producing 10 wins in Kinard's first season. Kinard coached Ole Miss for five more games after the loss to LSU. Vaught returned as head coach and athletic director, replacing Kinard after the third game of his third season, in 1973.

Oh, how close he came to toppling the Tigers on that November 4 night. The Rebels were positioned to win. Kicker Steve Lavinghouse, who had made three field goals already, missed a 27-yard chip shot late in the game. The Tigers took over at their 20-yard line with 3:02 remaining and down 16–10. "Bert was very cool and was smiling the whole time," Davis said of that touchdown march. "He knew we would score. He made us very confident."

Jones led the Tigers 80 yards on 13 plays. He opened the drive with a 23-yard completion under duress and then completed a 10-yard pass to convert a fourth-and-2. LSU needed a fourth-and-1 conversion and then got a pass-interference penalty on Ole Miss. The flag set up LSU with a first down from the Rebels' 10 with four ticks left. Turns out, the Tigers got two downs.

"The Jones-to-Davis game will never go down as one of the biggest LSU victories in Tiger Stadium history, but it was the most dramatic, the most sudden, and if you're an Ole Miss fan, perhaps the most controversial," Kleinpeter wrote in his 2012 first-person piece. "For years afterward, travelers on a highway leaving Mississippi and entering Louisiana were greeted by a billboard that read, Entering Louisiana. Set your watch back four seconds."

75 Coach Nader

Gerry DiNardo had no real plans to retain many people on LSU's former football staff when he took over as head coach in 1995. Curley Hallman had won 15 games in four years and been fired days earlier. Why in the heck would he keep any assistants at all? "When I got there," DiNardo said, "the AD, Joe Dean, said, 'We've got a guy, Sam Nader, been here a long time. If you don't like him, you'll be the first person I've met who doesn't.' It was Joe's way of saying, 'You're keeping Sam.'"

You might not know much about Sam Nader, but for more than four decades, Nader has labored in the darkness at LSU, silently and diligently, unassuming and inconspicuous. He is the man behind this football program, a living connection to the past, a confidant for thousands of players and a consigliere to dozens of coaches. He is the grandfather of this place, having completed his 45th consecutive regular season as a member of the LSU staff in 2019. He's a survivor in a cutthroat industry, outlasting nine head coaches and six athletic directors, nine times retained through coaching transitions.

Since arriving at the school as a graduate assistant in 1975, Nader has been on the sideline for 512 games; 16 division, conference, and national championships; and two perfect regular seasons (2011 and 2019). He's seen Tiger Stadium expand four different times, and he's worked out of four different office buildings. "I don't know that there's many more like Sam," Les Miles, coach at LSU from 2005 to 2016, said in a 2019 story published in *Sports Illustrated*. "He's an original. He's one of a kind. He's a serving man. He has no peer. He's special."

Though it's difficult to prove, Sam—who turned 74 in 2019—may be the longest-serving football staff member in the country. He's certain to be one of the longest, his tenure spanning eight U.S. presidents. While all around him this place has changed, Nader has remained mostly the same, right down to his spectacles and balding head.

Nader grew up in Louisiana along the Texas border in both Lake Charles and then later Shreveport, a son to a traveling Methodist minister. In 1975 the Naders moved to Baton Rouge from Columbus, Georgia, where Sam coached prep football after a stint as a backup quarterback at Auburn. He first appeared in the LSU media guide in 1979 as the "junior varsity coach," the first of many titles he's held through the years: recruiting coordinator, administrative assistant, director of football operations, and assistant athletic director for football operations.

While the titles have changed, Sam's role has virtually remained the same: he oversees everything that is not conducted on the field. In other words, "He knows where all the bodies are buried," said former LSU defensive lineman Booger McFarland.

Through the years, as football budgets and staffs have expanded, Sam has delegated duties. He's done a little bit of everything, from making bed checks to coordinating recruiting trips to organizing the walk-on program to arranging players' summer jobs.

He even delivers impassioned motivational speeches to the team, such as the one before a win at Alabama in 2019, a key victory in the Tigers' national championship run. "It was legendary," said Tommy Moffitt, the Tigers' longtime strength coach. "He sounded like Steve Sabol up there from NFL Films."

He has other ways of motivating the troops too. In 2014, in an effort to inspire the team during a 30-degree outdoor practice, Sam showed up shirtless with a purple *T* painted across his 69-year-old chest, a photo of which went viral in the LSU community.

Through the years, Nader's most important job might be his role to the head coaches. DiNardo became the fifth different LSU head coach to retain Nader, and he realized days later in 1994 why Dean recommended it: Nader was good. Sam has been an advisor and organizer for the 10 head coaches under whom he's worked, some of his most important work coming as a recruiter during transitional periods from one coach to the next.

Sam helped secure a 1984 signing class that eventually delivered an SEC championship; had a significant influence on the Tigers landing prized running back Kevin Faulk; and guided Miles, in his first month on the job, through the winding Louisiana roads during recruiting trips, Nader on the other end of the phone giving directions.

Similar to many LSU head coaches, Miles confided in Nader. After a speech to the team, he sometimes privately sought Nader's approval, asking things such as, "How did I do? Is that what they needed?" Mike Archer, coach from 1987 to 1990, bounced ideas off Nader and used him to understand the nuances of coaching at a politically charged place such as LSU. "It's like no other place. It's unique," said Archer, now a coach in the upstart XFL. "He could tell you, 'This is the guy you've got to go to talk to.'"

Sam's relationship with Nick Saban—who coached LSU for five seasons, from 2000 to 2004—ran deep, said former LSU assistant Will Muschamp. "Nick trusted him more than anybody, and that's hard, especially if you've been with the former staff," Muschamp said in the aforementioned *Sports Illustrated* story. "Nick loved Nader. If we talked about anything in the state, he'd get the OK from Sam."

In 1998, when DiNardo's fourth team began declining in performance, the coach asked Sam for his thoughts. What he got was a 10-page-long handwritten letter that DiNardo still keeps to this day—a relic from a bygone era, the cherished work of an unsung legend.

LSU coach Ed Orgeron privately meets with Nader to discuss the makeup of the team and personnel. As he's done for decades, Nader sits in on every staff meeting, and he even sometimes watches film with coaches, silently seated in the back. "Sam is part of the fabric," said longtime athletic trainer Jack Marucci. "He's the hidden gem here."

One of Nader's most noteworthy accomplishments came in 1980, when he helped hold together LSU's football program after newly hired coach Bo Rein tragically perished in a plane crash. Darrell Moody, an assistant then at LSU, recalled Sam's leadership during that turbulent time in Baton Rouge. He manned the ship and kept it from sinking. "He may be as organized as any person I've been around," said Moody. "He told us all where to go and what we needed to do. I'm not sure that Sam hasn't meant more to that school than 90 percent of the coaches there." Moody paused and added, "They put statues up down there, right? They need to put up one of Sam Nader."

76 The History of LSU's Creation and Growth

The year 1860 wasn't an ideal time to start a college. Especially when the superintendent of the school resigned a year later to become a Union Army general in the Civil War, fighting against many of his faculty members and students who joined the Confederate Army. But that's how LSU—Louisiana State University—began under another name in a small central Louisiana town 100 miles northwest of its well-known home in Baton Rouge.

William Tecumseh Sherman was the first superintendent of what began as the Louisiana State Seminary of Learning and

Military Academy near Pineville, Louisiana. He and five faculty members taught the first students in one building, the seminary, where classes were offered in liberal arts and engineering along with rigid military discipline. The next year, when Louisiana joined other Southern states in seceding from the Union to start the Civil War in April 1861, the school closed, and stayed closed for the better part of the next four years. Sherman left to help lead the Union forces, and most of the students and faculty members left to fight for the Confederacy.

In September 1865 the school reopened with original faculty member David F. Boyd as superintendent. The seminary building had made it through the war, but most of the books and equipment were destroyed or missing. It seemed the school was getting firm footing in June 1869 when it held a commencement ceremony for its first graduating class, but a fire four months later destroyed the seminary building.

On November 1, 1869, the cadets moved the school to the State Institution for the Deaf, Dumb, and Blind in Baton Rouge. The following year, in 1870, the seminary was renamed Louisiana State University.

For most of the 1870s, LSU struggled financially and had to compete for almost nonexistent state funding against the Louisiana Agricultural and Mechanical College (1874–77) and the University of Louisiana (Tulane University after 1884), both based in New Orleans. Finally in 1877, LSU and the Agricultural and Mechanical College merged to form Baton Rouge–based Louisiana State University and Agricultural and Mechanical College.

In 1886 LSU—steadily increasing the number of agriculture classes offered and needing more space for its experimental farm—moved to the 200-acre former military post in north Baton Rouge where the State Capitol Building is situated today.

Four years later, the campus started a major 15-year building project and LSU began an athletic program with teams in football, baseball, tennis, and track and field. In 1906 women were admitted as students on a regular basis, and the law school was established.

By 1918 there was no more room for campus expansion. Then–LSU president Thomas Boyd began scouting for a large piece of land to build a larger campus. Boyd decided on the Gartness Plantation. Owed by C.P. Williams of Mississippi, it was located south of Baton Rouge along the Mississippi River. His selling price was $82,000.

Thomas Atkinson (dean of the College of Engineering), William Dodson (dean of the College of Agriculture), O.B. Steele (owner of Windrush Plantation), and other prominent Baton Rouge citizens paid Williams $500 on May 23, 1918, for an option to buy the property until the state legislature could pass a bill to allocate the $82,000 asking price. Just a few weeks later, on June 4, the legislature passed Act 6, which provided the funding to purchase Gartness. This property, along with portions of Arlington and Nestledown Plantations, comprise LSU's present campus in Baton Rouge.

With the land obtained, LSU utilized severance tax revenues with the support of Governor John M. Parker as construction began on March 29, 1922, with the groundbreaking for the dairy barn. Barns and other buildings associated with farming were constructed first, keeping with LSU's mission as an agricultural university.

The Olmsted Brothers landscape architecture firm, which had already designed campuses such as Stanford University and the University of Chicago—as well as Audubon Park in New Orleans— was hired to create the overall plan for the new campus. For LSU the Olmsted brothers visualized a northern Italian Renaissance architectural style of pantile roofs, archways, and stucco walls along with arches and towers.

Architect Theodore Link, hired in 1922 to design the campus buildings, modified the Olmstead Brothers plan. Link died in 1923 and his son C.Y. Link took over briefly before the New Orleans architectural firm of Wogan and Bernard finished overseeing the construction using Theodore Link's designs.

Although there were a few classes on the new campus in the fall of 1925, the official three-day formal dedication ceremony began on April 30, 1926, and featured speeches by Parker and U.S. senator Edward J. Gay. The ceremony also had performances by the LSU Cadet Band and the Stanocola Refinery Band (the latter named after the predecessor to Exxon). It ended with a track meet between LSU and Tulane and a barbecue on the Campus Mounds.

There was no landscape plan for the new campus. Four years after it was dedicated, Steele Burden was hired in 1930 as a campus landscape architect. He didn't have a plan either. If he spied a place he thought needed a tree or garden, he simply planted it. He is responsible for the many magnificent oak trees and blooming magnolias that have shaded the campus through the decades.

LSU's greatest growth started when Huey Long was elected Louisiana's governor in 1928. He wanted LSU to be the best university in the nation, so funding the school became a priority. Despite the Great Depression that stretched from 1929 to 1939, Long somehow found the money to build more campus classrooms and dorms and offer more courses to increase enrollment.

During World War II, LSU became a major center for the Army Specialized Training Program. By 1947 GIs, many married with families, returned from the war and increased LSU's student population to just more than 10,000. Another major building program took place to house and provide classrooms for the new students and their families.

Throughout the 1950s, 1960s, and 1970s, LSU grew and evolved from a teaching university with a mainly agricultural research component to an institution where teaching and research went hand in hand. The school was fueled by tax revenue from the oil and petrochemical industry. As a result, research in medicine, engineering, computers, nuclear science, and fisheries prospered, in addition to agriculture. Branch campuses opened in New Orleans, Alexandria, Eunice, and Shreveport.

LSU suffered during the 1980s and into the mid-1990s because of declining revenue from the oil and gas industries. Also the school and other Louisiana colleges and universities were the targets of an expensive federal lawsuit alleging that the state operated a dual system of higher education in violation of the Civil Rights Act. The lawsuit questioned every program offered by all universities and required court approval for any new funding or academic programs.

By the late 1990s, LSU recovered from those roadblocks. Despite shrinking funding from the legislature and rising enrollment costs, LSU's enrollment in the fall of 2019 was 31,761.

77 Bo Rein

No coach wants to be the coach who follows a legend. Usually it's better to be the coach who follows the coach who follows the legend. Bo Rein was hired to replace Charles McClendon, the winningest football coach in LSU history. At age 34, having been a head coach for only four seasons at North Carolina State, he charged into the Tigers job in late November 1979 with unabashed enthusiasm and confidence. "It's an honor to be here and be the head coach at LSU," Rein said at his introductory press conference. "The program athletically is so rich in tradition, not so much in wins and losses, but in its heroes and the character of its heroes."

Then–LSU athletic director Paul Dietzel chose Ohio State grad Rein, who was a running back under Woody Hayes from 1964 to 1966 and an outfielder on the Buckeyes' 1966 College World Series championship team. Rein had worked under Hayes,

Lou Holtz, and Frank Broyles, three of the best coaches in college history—all of whom recommended him. "Bo is probably the best young coach in the country," Hayes said at the time.

Rein was 27–18–1 in his four years at North Carolina State, winning two bowl games and the 1979 Atlantic Coast Conference championship. He also was ready for bigger challenges. In the first week of October 1979, he wrote a note to Dietzel on hotel stationery. It read, "Dear Paul, I would be very interested in talking to you at some future date concerning the head coaching position at LSU. I would appreciate a response in the near future. Sincerely, Bo Rein."

Just less than two months later, Rein had the job, put together a staff, and hit the recruiting trail hard. Greg Williams, Rein's defensive coordinator, recruited north Louisiana. There was an overwhelming reception from high schools ecstatic to see an LSU coach recruiting in person rather than by phone. "At Woodlawn in Shreveport, the principal was so happy to see us that he called an assembly to introduce LSU's new head coach to the entire school," Williams said.

Williams planned a recruiting trip to Shreveport for himself and Rein on January 10, 1980. Rein and Williams drove to Shreveport together. But since he had to visit a prospect in Mississippi the next day, the plan was for Rein to fly home at the end of the recruiting day in Shreveport. Williams would continue to recruit his assigned area before driving back to Baton Rouge.

Rein and Williams had a 15-hour day. Then Williams drove Rein to the Shreveport airport to await a private plane coming from Houston flown by an experienced pilot named Lewis Benscotter. Williams shook Rein's hand, put him on the plane, checked into a Shreveport airport hotel, and immediately fell asleep.

Meanwhile, the Cessna Conquest 441 carrying Rein and Benscotter wandered off course as a line of storms appeared between Shreveport and Baton Rouge. The plane turned east and was eventually tracked out over the Atlantic Ocean by Captain Daniel Zoerb, a U.S. Air Force fighter pilot who could only see the red glow of the Cessna's cockpit but nothing else.

Zoerb made three passes at the plane about 500 feet away, giving all the standard intercept signals to get the plane to turn back. There was no response. Finally, about 100 miles east of Cape Charles, Virginia, at 1:34 AM ET, Zoerb watched one of the plane's engines quit. The plane rotated and went into a 5,000-foot-per-minute nosedive before it crashed into the Atlantic. "That was the first time I ever escorted a plane to a crash," said Zoerb, who made one pass over the crash site and saw nothing but an oil slick.

The FAA's Office of Accident Investigation speculated that something happened to the cabin's pressurization system, causing Benscotter and Rein to pass out and die from lack of oxygen. Their bodies were never found.

The LSU family was stunned, but not as much as Williams and the other N.C. State assistants who had made the move with Rein to LSU. "It was something you can't believe," Williams recalled. "He just disappeared. It was crazy. For about the next year, it was like I still didn't believe it happened."

Hayes gave the eulogy at Rein's funeral in Niles, Ohio. Bo Rein's widow, Suzanne, reached an out-of-court settlement for an undisclosed amount after filing a $10 million damages suit against a number of defendants linked to the plane. LSU paid for Rein's children's college educations at the universities of their choice.

At the 2014 Ole Miss at LSU game, Suzanne and Bo Rein's daughter, Linea Rein, were introduced to Tiger Stadium during a first-half break. The crowd roared long and loud.

Williams, who coached in 5 different capacities at 10 schools before retiring, has always believed LSU's program would have skyrocketed if Rein hadn't gotten on that plane. "With the players that were already there and the players we were recruiting, there's no doubt at all we would have won and won big," Williams said. "No doubt about that at all."

78 Trip to Cuba

At the end of the 1907 season, LSU and Tulane could not agree on a set of rules to play each other. LSU president Thomas Boyd turned down Tulane's final proposal, saying that the rules Tulane wanted were not those of the Southern Intercollegiate Athletic Association, of which LSU and Tulane were members.

Boyd played hardball because he had a scheduling curveball thrown at him that he couldn't resist. The city of Havana wanted to schedule an American football team to play the University of Havana on Christmas Day as the climax to Cuba's annual National Sports Festival. LSU was invited to play in the game, nicknamed the Bacardi Bowl. The Havana committee promised to pay LSU's travel expenses, which it finally did a week before the game, after the Tigers threatened to cancel the trip.

The University of Havana's team supposedly had many former American college men who played football, including former LSU player René Messa. But after scheduling the game, University of Havana officials began searching the island for the biggest and meanest players to be found. It was in violation of the contract that LSU signed stipulating Havana couldn't use American players not already on their team or players of African descent.

After LSU beat Baylor 48–0 on November 30, it took time off before practicing through December 20 in Baton Rouge. Then, the next day in New Orleans its 13-man team, one coach, and two student assistants boarded the Southern Pacific steamer *Chalmette* for Havana. The team was scheduled to stay through January 1.

LSU's appearance in Havana came only nine years after the Spanish-American War. President Theodore Roosevelt sent U.S. military forces to Cuba in September 1906. He wanted to end the country's civil war, protect U.S. economic interests there, and ensure free elections to establish a new government. Thus, U.S. soldiers from Camp Columbia and sailors from two U.S. Navy gunboats in Havana provided LSU's team with a built-in fan base. Also, nonmilitary Americans in Cuba feted the Tigers after they arrived, often buying them daiquiris and dinner in local restaurants.

Since no LSU fans made the trip, they raised $2,000 for LSU coach Edgar Wingard to place a bet on the game.

The University of Havana thought the game was going to be a financial bust and backed out of promoting it. A group of enterprising spectators jumped in and sold sideline tickets to Havana aristocrats for $10.

A crowd of 4,200 showed up for the game at Almendares Park, which didn't turn out to be much of a game after LSU made a key pregame discovery. When the Tigers took the field for warm-ups, they spied large glass demijohns filled with wine on the Havana sideline. Every so often, a Cuban player such as 300-pounder A.C. Infante-Garcia, who was recruited to handle LSU's 200-pound guard W.M. Lyles, would run to the sideline for a swig of wine. LSU star quarterback Doc Fenton told Lyles, "Hit that guy in the stomach with your head, and he's done for." On the first play from scrimmage, Lyles hammered his shoulder into Garcia's stomach.

"The big guy spouted wine like an artesian well," Fenton said. "We nearly had to swim to get out of there."

Lyle exclaimed, "Well, I'll be damned. Let's go to work."

LSU scored 10 TDs in a 56–0 win highlighted by Fenton's trademark broken-field running. He earned the nickname El Rubio Vaselino (the Vaselined Redhead) from the Cuban fans.

Every time LSU scored, sailors from the *Paducah* and the *Dubuque* would toss their blue hats in the air. "You would have thought there was a flock of blackbirds flying across the field," LSU end Pat Ryan said.

LSU's victory was celebrated heartily. Wingard lifted curfew. The Tigers players were welcomed in clubs and in private homes and never spent a dime, as Americans in Havana bought them anything they wanted. Even the LSU players' gray skullcaps with the *L* on the front were sold for $10 each as souvenirs.

Before the team returned to Baton Rouge, they arranged a second game in Havana to make money. "We found we could make $25 apiece," recalled LSU tackle Cap Gandy, later known as Doc when he became a veterinarian in Baton Rouge. "So we made up two teams from the two squads and played again. We only had 13, so we loaned Havana a couple of men. We still won it, something like 20–0."

Accepting payment, by college rules, should have made the LSU players professionals who were no longer eligible to play in college. But no one in Baton Rouge ever found out, and they all returned for the Tigers' 10–0 season in 1908.

79 Y.A. Tittle

One of the first and greatest recruiting steals in LSU football also happens be the first and only Tigers quarterback elected to the Pro Football Hall of Fame. Yelberton Abraham Tittle, best known as Y.A., was a Marshall, Texas, native who was swiped by LSU from the University of Texas campus. He was a committed recruit working a summer job but not officially signed to a scholarship and enrolled.

Tittle was originally an LSU commitment who was pressured by his Texas townfolk to play for the in-state Longhorns. But after three weeks in Austin, he'd had enough. He wasn't happy that he and fellow Texas recruit Bobby Layne both had summer jobs but Layne was being paid despite not showing up for work.

When LSU assistant coach Red Swanson visited Tittle and asked him if he wanted to change his mind and sign with LSU, Tittle said yes. Swanson didn't want to appear he was stealing a player, so he told Tittle to call Texas coach Dana Bible and tell him of his decision to leave. Tittle went to a phone and faked a call during which he pretended to be talking to Bible. Tittle hung up and told Swanson, "Everything seems to be OK." It was more than OK.

When LSU coach Bernie Moore switched from a single-wing to a T-formation offense in 1945, he made Tittle his quarterback. By the time Tittle's college career ended, he had thrown for 2,525 yards and 23 touchdowns, startling numbers in an era when coaches weren't yet enamored with the forward pass.

It seemed odd back then that LSU was able to land such an out-of-state gem as Tittle, who explained he was attracted to LSU because his older brother Jack was an All-SEC performer at Tulane. Jack Tittle recalled the hard work his younger brother put in to become a great passer. "I remember going out to the backyard and hanging up an old tire as a target," Jack said of Y.A. "He'd throw at it by the hour. And he didn't take the easy way out. He'd get that tire swinging and still hit it on the button."

Y.A. detailed his initial exposure to LSU in author Marty Mule's book *Game of My Life LSU Tigers: Memorable Stories of Tigers Football*. "Every year, we'd go see Jack play against LSU, and I was impressed even as a young kid with the enthusiasm, the tiger in the cage, the campus, just the whole LSU atmosphere," Tittle said.

Once enrolled at LSU, Tittle filled out a questionnaire for then–LSU sports information director Jim Corbett. Corbett noticed that Tittle wrote Y.A. as his first name. When Corbett told Tittle initials weren't enough and he needed to fill out his first name, Tittle confirmed that was his first name. A curious Corbett finally called the courthouse in Marshall, Texas, to request information on a Y.A. Tittle. There was no Y.A. Tittle, but there was a Yelberton Abraham Tittle, so Corbett went back to Tittle with the new information. "I'd appreciate it if you lay off using my name," Tittle told Corbett, who kept his promise as the Tigers went 21–6–2 with Tittle as a three-year starting quarterback and defensive back.

One of Tittle's unforgettable LSU moments came in his senior season against Ole Miss when he intercepted a fourth-quarter pass from Charlie Conerly at the Rebels' 15. As Tittle pulled away from the receiver, who was grabbing the top of Tittle's pants from the rear, the receiver yanked Tittle's belt so hard that the belt buckle broke. Tittle had a clear 70-yard path to the goal line. But trying to hold the football in one hand and hold up his pants with his other hand was too much. He was tackled at the LSU 38-yard line and Ole Miss ended up winning 20–18.

In 17 pro seasons, mostly with the San Francisco 49ers and the New York Giants, Tittle completed 2,427 of 4,395 passes for 33,070 yards and 242 touchdowns with 248 interceptions. He also ran for 39 TDs and remains tied for most TD passes thrown in an NFL game with seven vs. the Washington Redskins in 1962. He won three of his four NFL Most Valuable Player awards at age 35 and older.

He retired after the 1964 season at age 39, saying rookie quarterback Gary Wood not only "took my job away, but started to ask permission to date my daughter." Tittle was elected to the Pro Football Hall of Fame in 1971. His final Tiger Stadium appearance came in September 2014 when he was introduced to a roaring crowd before the LSU–Mississippi State game.

Tittle passed away in October 2017 at the age of 90.

80 Visit the Andonie Museum

There's a simple reason why the museum on the LSU campus that houses artifacts of the Tigers' storied athletic history bears the names of a Metairie, Louisiana, obstetrician-gynecologist and his wife. It's mostly his stuff in there, making her very happy it's no longer in their house.

The Jack & Priscilla Andonie Museum includes more than 13,000 pieces from Andonie's personal LSU memorabilia collection gathered over three decades. Also included is the former school's athletic Hall of Fame, previously in the school's athletic administration building. The museum, located at the Lod Cook Alumni Center on West Lakeshore Drive near Sorority Row, cost $348,000 to construct and opened to the public in late 2003.

Andonie offered his entire collection, worth more than $1 million, when he discovered LSU was the only school in the SEC not to have an athletic museum. "I miss it, but I know it's going to a lot better place than just having it in someone's home," longtime former LSU Board of Supervisors member Andonie said when he made his donation.

His fascination with everything LSU began in 1974 when he met and befriended former Tigers football coach Charlie McClendon. As Andonie's love of LSU grew, so did his quest to find collectable items he displayed in his house in a special area he called the Purple and Gold Room. When the Andonies moved to a larger house, a bigger room was designed to hold the ever-expanding collection. "LSU games and all the memorabilia became a hobby that I could share with my three kids," Andonie said. "My wife raised them. I was working all the time. But we bonded over the Tigers."

Andonie was dogged in his pursuit of memorabilia. He purchased a basketball autographed by LSU legend "Pistol Pete" Maravich that Maravich used to set an NCAA record. Andonie also donated a fake Ole Miss jersey with the words Go to Hell Ole Miss imprinted on it. McClendon wore the jersey around campus the entire week before the LSU–Ole Miss game to get everybody pumped.

Andonie also gave his collection of autographed pictures of LSU All-American athletes from every sport, such as Naismith Memorial Basketball Hall of Famers Maravich, Bob Pettit, and Shaquille O'Neal; 1959 Heisman Trophy winner Billy Cannon; 1962 Heisman runner-up Jerry Stovall; and 1989 Golden Spikes Award winner pitcher Ben McDonald. He gathered that collection by finding pictures of each athlete, and then writing or calling them to request their autograph on the pictures.

The museum has 54 separate displays with at least one area in the room for each of LSU's sports. Each of LSU's athletic programs is featured in its own area with a large photo gallery spanning the history of the sport.

There are also two dozen large wall-mounted TV sets throughout airing footage of past and present LSU events and a history of the formation of the museum. Large banners hang around the museum for each of LSU's national championships. There are also displays featuring LSU's retired jerseys, the "early years" of LSU athletics, the Tiger Band and Golden Girls, cheerleaders, and Mike the Tiger.

Fans entering the museum are greeted by a photo opportunity in front of a larger-than-life picture of the Tigers celebrating a national championship. Kids and adults can put on various past and present LSU football helmets for photos as well as don the head of a Mike the Tiger mascot costume.

The Andonie Museum is a private, nonprofit facility. Admission fees help support the daily operation of the museum.

81 Jerry Stovall

Jerry Stovall has had a few notable disappointments in his life. There's no doubt he should have won the 1962 Heisman Trophy as an LSU senior. All he did for the No. 6–ranked 9–1–1 Tigers that season was lead them in rushing, receiving, scoring, punting, and kickoff returns, and he was tied for first in interceptions and was second in punt returns. For all of that, he finished second in Heisman voting to Terry Baker, an Oregon State quarterback, who led the nation in total offense with 2,276 yards (the second-most ever at the time). Baker got 172 first-place votes and 707 points to Stovall's 112 first-place votes and 618 points in the closest Heisman balloting ever to that point.

Twenty-three years later, Stovall was fired by the school he deeply loved. It came after he was thrust into the role as LSU's head coach as the emergency hire to replace Bo Rein, who died in a plane crash. A lesser man never would have forgotten being dumped by his alma mater. But Stovall, because of his strong Christian faith, couldn't stay away. He could not hate his school. He could not forget the people who became his friends for life at LSU—the coaches, the teammates, and even the trainers.

The only thing Stovall has felt about LSU all these years is gratitude. As an All-State back at West Monroe (Louisiana), he was the last player signed in the Tigers' 52-man 1959 recruiting class back in the day when there wasn't an NCAA-established 25-man scholarship limit per year. "I was the runt of the litter," Stovall said.

Stovall's recruitment process was simple. Four colleges contacted him: Louisiana Tech, Tulane, Northeast Louisiana, and LSU. Probably the only reason LSU finally offered to Stovall was because of the persistence and persuasion of Red Swanson, a former LSU player and coach who was a member of LSU's Board of Supervisors when Stovall was in high school. Swanson had seen Stovall play as a ninth-grade baseball player, believed in him, followed his high school football career, and drove him to Baton Rouge for five LSU home games during the Tigers' 1958 national championship season. "Coach Swanson is the gentleman I hold directly responsible for me getting a scholarship to LSU," Stovall said. "I think the last time he drove me down there, he told Coach [Paul] Dietzel, 'Look, I'm going to leave him on the steps. I'm not going to take him back. If you don't want him, send him home on a bus.'"

There were times in his freshman season when Stovall thought about returning home to West Monroe and never coming back to LSU. Those thoughts ended for good one day when he phoned his father, a no-nonsense, pound-the-pavement salesman whose day always started before sunrise and ended after sunset. "When I got to LSU, everybody was bigger and faster than me," Stovall said. "Bo Campbell was the state of Louisiana high school track champion in the quarter mile. White Graves, another back, was the state of Mississippi high school quarter mile champ. Stovall's school never even had a high school track. So I'm thinking my chances of ever playing for LSU don't look real good. I call my daddy and say, 'I may have made a mistake coming here. Everybody is really good.'

"He says, 'And so? You're there to do what?' I said, 'I'm here to get an education and play ball.' He said, 'Has anything changed since you got there?' I said, 'No, sir.' He said, 'Good, then don't call me anymore.' My daddy had a great way of dismissing me."

Stovall gradually proved himself, becoming the best all-around player in LSU history.

He was taken No. 2 overall in the first round of the 1963 NFL Draft by the St. Louis Cardinals, where he became a hard-hitting strong safety who earned All-Pro honors once (1966) and was named to the Pro Bowl three times (1966, 1967, and 1969).

He played 97 games in nine seasons, finishing with 18 career interceptions.

In the spring of 2010, Stovall got a call from then–LSU athletic director Joe Alleva, who told him he had been selected to the National Football Foundation College Football Hall of Fame. "Joe told me and I got real quiet," Stovall said. "I asked him to repeat it, and I said, 'It sounded just as good the second time as it did the first time.'"

Several months later, in December 2010, he was inducted with the rest of the class at the foundation's annual banquet in New York City at the Waldorf Astoria. They handed him a small box that contained his Hall of Fame ring. "I don't think I've ever cried in front of that many people in my life," he said. "I was thinking about coaches and players and teachers who meant so much in my life, like Dan McClure, my high school coach. It made me sit down and think, *How in the world did his happen?*

"I always felt God has a plan for everybody in life. Can you imagine skinny Jerry Stovall from West Monroe, Louisiana, coming to LSU on a football scholarship? And then to be surrounded by the greatest personalities in all of athletics like Paul Dietzel, Charlie McClendon, [assistant coach] George Terry, [trainers] Doc Broussard, and Herman Lang?

"When I sit back and think about the guidance they gave the skinny kid, I say, 'Thank you, Lord' for all those people making me better."

82 1933 National Championship Men's Track Team

As of January 2020, with LSU's victory over Clemson in the College Football Playoff finals, the Tigers have won 48 national team championships—more than any original SEC member—as recognized by the NCAA.

And back in 1933, seven months after the SEC was officially established on December 8 and 9, 1932, in Knoxville, Tennessee, LSU's men's track team was the first SEC squad in any sport ever to win an NCAA championship. On June 17, 1933, in Chicago's historic Soldier Field, the Tigers finished with 58 points, only four ahead of runner-up Southern Cal.

Those points were scored by just five athletes: future major leaguer Buddy Blair, eventual Olympic gold medalist Glenn "Slats" Hardin, unexpected NFL Pro Bowler Jack "Baby Jack" Torrance, LSU's future SEC championship winning head track coach Al Moreau, and Matt Gordy, a guy whose career athletic highlight began and ended with the pole-vault of his life that clinched the national championship. Their coach was Bernie Moore, who came to LSU as an assistant football coach in 1928. He took over as head track coach in 1930, also became head football coach in 1935, and eventually became SEC commissioner in 1948.

Moore, an assistant coach, a trainer, 10 athletes, plus luggage and equipment drove two cars 950 miles to Chicago after winning the first-ever SEC championship. Vaulting poles and javelins were tied to the cars and rattled incessantly during the four-day trip on mostly gravel roads. Moore's big black Plymouth had a huge Bengal tiger painted on its tire cover.

Immediately upon arriving in Chicago, Moore ran a red light. "Right there on Michigan Avenue, a cop stopped us," Moreau once told writer Ruth Laney. "Coach told him, 'Hell, we're country boys. We don't know about red lights.' The cop studied that tiger on the tire cover and said, 'I can see that.' But we were in town for the meet, so he let us go without a ticket."

Southern Cal was the favorite to win the national title. They were a squad with 14 or 15 athletes that included two Olympic gold medalists. They made the trip to Chicago in a private railway car (with a porter) attached to a Southern Pacific train. Moore's pre-meet assessment of his team's chances was, "We'll be lucky to place as high as fifth." But he may have underestimated his team's toughness.

He had athletes who lived and trained in physically and mentally taxing situations. There were no track scholarships. The athletes had to play football to earn their keep along with working odd jobs around campus that paid 25 cents an hour, such as delivering laundry, milking cows for the agriculture department, sweeping classrooms, and pruning azaleas. They lived rent-free, sharing tiny windowless rooms above the school's gym armory. Their track shoes had metal in their soles. With no laundry facilities, uniforms frequently went unwashed. They trained on a rough cinder track in the football stadium. Landing pits were sawdust piles. In retrospect, Southern Cal didn't have a chance against the Tigers' fearsome fivesome.

Here's how LSU won the title with the number of points scored by each athlete:

Blair (4): One of the greatest all-around athletes in the history of LSU athletics—he was a three-time letterman in track, basketball, and baseball from 1933 to 1935—Blair accomplished a fourth-place finish in the javelin with a throw of 195'6". He later played one season of Major League Baseball with the Philadelphia Athletics in 1942, hitting .279 in 137 games as the team's regular third baseman.

Hardin (20): The only non-Louisianan of the group, the Greenwood, Mississippi, native scored wins one hour apart, first in the 440-yard run—setting an NCAA record of 47.1 seconds—and then running a world-record 22.9 seconds in the 220-yard low hurdles. He went on to win a gold medal in the 400 hurdles in the 1936 Olympics.

Torrance (16): A 6'5", 265-pound three-time All-SEC honoree as an offensive lineman, he won the shot put with a world-record heave of 52'10" and then added a third-place finish in the discus with a throw of 147'10". Seven years later, Torrance was named an NFL Pro Bowl choice playing in his penultimate season with the Chicago Bears.

Moreau (9): He scored nine points in the meet with a narrow second-place finish in the high hurdles and a sixth-place effort in the 220-yard low hurdles. In the high hurdles, he and Stanford's Gus Meier were clocked with a world-record time of 14.2 seconds.

Gordy (9): The fate of LSU's national championship hopes came down to Gordy, the 5'11", 129-pound Abbeville, Louisiana, native who had taught himself to vault with a pole hacked from a stand of bamboo. His career best was 13'4", which came after he chopped his pole down from 16 feet to 12.5 feet, an idea he copied from Yale's pole-vaulters. "It produced better form, was much easier to handle coming down the runway, [and] provided perfect pull under the chest and better balance in the air," he said.

Moore only added Gordy to the traveling squad for the NCAA meet when he cleared 13'6" several times (several times coming close to 14 feet) in practice by twisting his body into a handstand at the top of the arc as he released his pole to curl around the bar. As it played out, Gordy cleared 13'6" in Chicago and found himself in a duel with world record holder Bill Graber of Southern Cal. Graber topped out at just over 13'11".

Gordy had one last vault attempt at that height. He knew what was at stake. If he cleared the bar, he would tie Graber for first, and they both would earn nine points, but LSU would win the national championship. If he missed, Graber would win the vault and LSU and Southern Cal would be tied for the title.

Just before midnight, with most of the 7,000 fans still in the Soldier Field stands and a slight breeze coming off Lake Michigan, Gordy stood on the runway about to make his final vault when he saw Moore at the top of the stadium. "Coach Moore [was] pacing up and down like an expectant father," Gordy said in a 1971 story in the *New Orleans Times-Picayune*. "I laughed and I guess that really relaxed me."

Gordy cleared the crossbar, which only wobbled slightly when he hit it with his thumb. His teammates mobbed him, and Gordy said that Moore somehow had raced down from the stadium and "was grabbing my hand before I picked myself out of the pit." When the celebration finally ended, Gordy discovered a souvenir hunter had swiped his pole.

Gordy didn't pursue an athletic career after college but eventually became vice president of Houston-based Pan-American Oil.

In 1967 when Moore passed away, Gordy flew to Baton Rouge in his private plane to pick up his four teammates from the 1933 title team. Together they flew to Moore's hometown of Winchester, Tennessee, to serve as pallbearers for the coach they had loved for a lifetime.

83 Alvin Roy

As years have passed since LSU's football team won its first national championship in 1958, the legends from that magical season have never faded. There's eventual Heisman Trophy winner Billy Cannon, Hollywood-handsome coach Paul Dietzel, and the Chinese Bandits, one of Dietzel's specialized groups in his three-platoon style.

But as much as anybody, the Tigers owed their national championship to Baton Rouge native Alvin Roy, who returned in 1948 from serving in the army to open Louisiana's first health and strength studio not more than a few miles from the LSU campus. When Roy was stationed in Europe in 1946 as a staff athletic officer, he served as trainer for the American weightlifting team under Bob Hoffman at the world championships in Paris. Roy learned that lifting weights made athletes faster and more flexible, as well as stronger.

It took Roy several years to spread his gospel, trying to get local schools interested in a lifting program. He started by training LSU and future NFL guard Piggy Barnes, who lied to his LSU coaches so he could go off campus to lift. Then he trained a Baton Rouge High School running back named Jimmy Taylor.

When Istrouma High School suffered an embarrassing loss to BRHS in 1954, Istrouma coach "Little Fuzzy" Brown and school principal "Big Fuzzy" Brown finally agreed to accept overtures from Roy, an Istrouma graduate, to train the team.

Roy chose a basic training program used by competitive lifters—one of power cleans, bench presses, rowing motions, dead lifts, dumbbell presses, and squats with low repetitions and lots of sets. The first person on the Istrouma campus Roy had to convince was a multisport phenom named Billy Cannon. "At first Billy said, 'I don't know if I want to do this,'" Astrid Clements, Roy's elder daughter, once recalled. "He said, 'You know, I hold a state record in the sprints, and what happens if I get all bulked up and I get slower?' And Daddy knew in the end, if [Cannon] ended up being slower when he did his sprints, that basically his concepts would not be accepted."

But Cannon got bigger and faster and became a believer after he and 20 other Istrouma players began training with Roy in May 1955. "He brought us along at our own pace and he kept telling us that all this was going to do was make us stronger than the guy we'd be facing across the line next fall," the late Cannon said.

Roy's program worked. Istrouma won the 1955 state championship and scored a state record 432 points, including 229 points by Cannon, who averaged 10 yards per carry. "We not only killed everybody we played, but we had fewer injuries than we'd ever had since I came to the school in 1935," Little Fuzzy Brown said. "Al made believers out of me and Big Fuzzy, and we not only kept the program for the football players, we added programs for our other sports and for all our junior high athletes."

Because it worked for Taylor—who went on to play at LSU under Dietzel—and for the athletes at Istrouma, Dietzel was sold that Roy could help the Tigers, who didn't have a strength program. "Back when I was in school, we always laughed whenever we saw anyone with muscles because we'd been taught that big muscles made you slow," the late Dietzel said. "What Jimmy and Billy were doing and what they were doing over at Istrouma was absolutely opposed to everything I'd always believed. All I can say is that after seeing what Taylor and Cannon could do and after listening to Al, I was sold."

Roy brought weights to LSU and started a weight room where he trained the team three days per week in the spring. He remained steadfast in his philosophy. "Every year in some country in the world a group of men gather for combat," Roy once wrote. "They meet to determine the strongest men in the world at the World Weightlifting Championships.

"I point this out for the simple reason that until football coaches from both high schools and universities in America start thinking along the line that these strength coaches do and until the football coaches start training their football players like these weightlifters are trained, they will always be following a second-best program.

"These weightlifters are the strongest men in the world. It is our belief that you must train your football players the same way."

When LSU won the 1958 national title and then Cannon captured the 1959 Heisman, Roy gained more believers.

In 1963 the San Diego Chargers won the AFL championship after Roy became their full-time strength coach, the first in pro football history. He also worked for Kansas City, Dallas, New Orleans, and Oakland.

At the time of his death in 1979, Roy had 38 fitness franchises, called Roy Studios. He continues to be honored by the LSU football program, which annually gives its Alvin Roy Fourth Quarter Award to the player who had the best off-season. Also, the National Strength and Conditioning Association annually gives the Alvin Roy Award for Career Achievement.

84 Battle for the Boot

The trophy weighs nearly 200 pounds, stands 4 feet tall, is molded from 24-karat gold, and is in the shape of a boot. The Golden Boot trophy is one of the most peculiar in all of sports—and it is the heaviest, according to LSU. The victor of the annual LSU-Arkansas clash takes this prize home with them. "It kind of looks like a bad neck chain from the '80s," former Arkansas coach Bret Bielema said about the trophy in an SBNation.com story published in 2017. "It's a little gaudy. It's a little big. But it's gold-plated."

The Battle for the Boot began in 1996, but the series between these two border rivals started well before that. They met for the first time in 1901, played an annual game in Shreveport for nearly a quarter of a century (1913 to 1936), took a 30-year hiatus in regular-season meetings, and resumed their annual series when the Hogs joined the Southeastern Conference in 1992.

The rivalry, somewhat one-sided (LSU leads 41–22–2), picked up some spice over the last two decades. They've split two games with the SEC West title on the line (2002 and 2011), and they've been embroiled in some wild come-from-behind duels.

In 2002, with an SEC Championship Game berth at stake, Arkansas rallied from a 17–7 deficit early in the fourth quarter and, even more stunning, a 20–14 deficit with 40 seconds left. Taking over at his own 19, quarterback Matt Jones completed passes of 50 and 31 yards—the latter a touchdown strike with nine seconds left. The extra point served as the game winner and sent Arkansas and coach Houston Nutt to the SEC Championship Game.

In 2013 backup quarterback Anthony Jennings drove the Tigers 99 yards in 1:15, capped by a 49-yard touchdown completion to receiver Travin Dural in the final two minutes to win 31–27 over the 3–8 Hogs.

The two programs met ranked No. 1 and No. 3 in 2011, a 41–17 trouncing by top-ranked LSU that sent them to the SEC Championship Game. It was the highest-ranked matchup in Tiger Stadium since LSU hosted Ole Miss on Halloween night in 1959.

Since the Hogs joined the conference, they've won only 10 of 26 matchups with the Tigers. For years the series has been viewed as one taken more seriously by the Arkansas side, sort of a duel pitting little brother against big brother. That was never more evident than during a controversial schedule shift in 2014. LSU administrators lobbied for the SEC to replace Arkansas with Texas A&M as the Tigers' season-ending opponent. The league granted the request starting in 2014, ending 22 consecutive seasons of LSU and Arkansas meeting to end their regular seasons.

It was a sign, some might say, of LSU's attitude toward the series with the Razorbacks. "They were trying to take away the importance of it," former Arkansas tight end Jeremy Sprinkle said in a 2016 story in the *Advocate*. "It's still a rivalry game for us."

There was a time, though, when the Hogs stopped the series. LSU and Arkansas played in the Red River State Fair Classic 23 times in a 24-year span starting in 1913. Arkansas school officials ended the meetings after LSU won seven straight from 1930 to 1936.

The squads played in two Cotton Bowls: 1947 and 1966. The former is one of the most legendary college football games of all time. Dubbed the Ice Bowl, it saw the two teams tangled in Dallas on a field surrounded by snow and under sleeting skies. It was so cold that LSU players kept warm on the sidelines by gathering around a barrel full of hot coals. The game ended in a scoreless tie.

85 D-D Breaux

The longest-tenured coach in any sport in SEC history started her 44th season in January 2020. Yes, LSU gymnastics coach D-D Breaux was still in pursuit of her first national championship.

At the start of the 2020 schedule, Breaux's Tigers had placed among the nation's top 10 teams 30 times, finishing a program-best second in 2016, 2017, and 2019; third in 2014; fourth in 1988 and 2018; fifth in 2008 and 2013; and sixth on four other occasions.

A national title for Breaux has been the only missing element of a brilliant career. But anyone who knows Breaux—a Donaldsonville, Louisiana, native still spunky and fiery at age 67—understands she beams about the young women she has produced as model citizens through the decades and is fiercely proud she built a national powerhouse against all odds.

For most of her four decades after being hired as the Tigers' coach when she was an LSU graduate student, the former Southeastern Louisiana gymnast who had her college career cut short by a knee injury has had no other choice but to lead the victory parade by herself. That meant literally and figuratively—hiring the marching band, finding someone to fund it, and then devising and executing strategies to attract people to come watch it.

For many years, actual in-the-gym, face-to-face coaching was the last thing on Breaux's daily agenda. She was too busy raising money and finding sponsors to keep the program afloat. She was constantly promoting, because she got little or no help from the first four athletic directors she has served under. "For a long time," Breaux said, "I'd hear from my athletic directors, 'D-D, you are such a squeaky wheel. Just go do your job. Be happy that you got 2,000 people in the stands.' I'd reply, 'But there are 11,000 empty seats.' So I pushed. And I keep pushing and pushing and pushing."

In the beginning, winning the national championship wasn't Breaux's annual goal but rather doing what it took to make her program viable to financially survive year to year. "We were fighting, scratching and scraping, and worrying about the quality of our events," Breaux said. "We wondered if people [who went to a meet] would come back."

Breaux has watched a cavalcade of coaches filter through the other LSU major sports during her tenure—10 in football, five in men's basketball, four in baseball, and six in women's basketball. "It was survival of the fittest; I've never doubted my survivability," said Breaux, who has had to adjust to a parade of seven athletic directors.

AD No. 1 was former LSU football assistant Carl Maddox. He hired Breaux in 1978 when the school decided to start competing in women's gymnastics. He gave her a piece of advice that has served her well ever since. "Carl Maddox said to me, 'You're not going to get plan A and I'm going to tell you no, so you better come in here with a plan B, you better have something else to settle for,'" Breaux recalled. "That mind-set has paid dividends for me throughout the years. I'm totally not afraid to ask for something, because there's a 100 percent chance I won't get anything if I don't ask. I'm not afraid to make mistakes or get people mad."

AD No. 2 was Paul Dietzel, former football coach of the Tigers' 1958 national championship team. He wasn't enthused about women's athletics, to the point Breaux believed her program was on the chopping block. "One day he called me and asked that I come to his office," Breaux said. "I didn't go across the street to see him. I knew what he was going to do, and I just didn't want to deal with it."

AD No. 3 was Bob Brodhead, who had been chief financial officer of the Miami Dolphins. Shortly after LSU hired Sue Gunter as women's basketball coach in 1983, Breaux discovered her key suddenly didn't fit in her office door. "Bob Brodhead hired her and gave her my office," Breaux said. "They put my stuff in boxes in little cubicles underneath the PMAC. It was not a great day."

AD No. 4 was Joe Dean, a former All-SEC LSU basketball player and vice president of international promotion for Converse Rubber Company. He was most concerned about getting athletic department finances in the black. One of his moves was to eliminate Breaux's assistants, advising her to use graduate students instead. "It's no coincidence that I had some of my worst seasons when that happened," said Breaux, who has had only a handful of subpar years.

AD No. 5 was former LSU baseball coach Skip Bertman, who retired from the field after winning five national championships. He became athletic director at the start of his last season, in 2001. When Bertman took over LSU baseball in 1984, it wasn't long before he found a kindred spirit in Breaux. Like her, he had to scratch and claw to build a program with almost no help—financially or emotionally—from the athletic department and university administration. "Skip saw my hard work, my dedication, and my passion," Breaux said. "He was such a mentor and loyal friend when he was baseball coach that after I'd get turned down by our athletic director for something I needed for our program, I'd go to Skip. He'd pay for it out of his foundation. It was that kind of relationship.

"When he became athletic director, he was all about the marketing, promoting, putting out the energy to do what it takes to put people in the stands."

Bertman said he admired Breaux's tenacity in refusing to stop fighting for the elements she needed for her program to survive and thrive. "You talk about her fight and the things she's been through," Bertman said. "Every time they'd beat her down, she just turned around and came back for more.

"How many schools can say we draw the most fans for football, then unbelievably the next-most fans for baseball, and even more unbelievably the third-next-most fans in gymnastics? D-D is the greatest."

AD No. 6, Joe Alleva, finally greenlit the construction of a 38,656-square-foot practice facility that opened in February 2016. "Joe Alleva heard me and began to listen," said Breaux, now serving under AD No. 7 Scott Woodward. "The willingness for Tiger Athletic Foundation to fold our facility into the bond they were doing for the expansion of Tiger Stadium was the perfect storm."

After the personal and senseless hell Breaux has walked through battling her own athletic administration on simple things ("I was like a squirrel foraging for nuts," she said), such as having promotional billboards just like the football, men's basketball, and baseball teams, her program deserved a state-of-the-art abode. Her teams practiced for years in the Carl Maddox Field House. She and her team had to constantly reassemble their equipment, which had been broken down and stored to accommodate other LSU athletic teams needing workout space.

Occasionally Breaux will give her squad a glimpse of the often-difficult journey her program endured. "She told us one time she and her team handed out free tickets just to get people to come to a meet," said Ashleigh Gnat, one of the most decorated gymnasts in LSU history, who competed from 2014 to 2017. "It's a true story of growth and perseverance. It was an honor to be coached by somebody who has gone through so much."

All of which has made her success sweeter and keeps her more determined than ever. "It's been about an evolution of everybody getting on board," Breaux said. "You must be passionate in what you're doing. Then you need a village, a group of people who care as passionately as you do. You can share the responsibilities, with everybody doing what it takes to make things work.

"Having a consistent message is critically important. I don't think my message has changed. Now, I've just got some really good listeners."

86 Fournette Runs Wild

"It shouldn't be too difficult." That's how Auburn defensive back Rudy Ford described stopping LSU running back Leonard Fournette. The comment came in the days leading up to the meeting between the two teams on September 19, 2015.

Fournette, in the midst of his record-setting sophomore season, heard those words, used them as motivation, and ran slap over the

Auburn Tigers in a coming-out-party type of performance. He ran for a career-high 228 yards on 19 carries and had a pair of jaw-dropping, tackle-breaking, Heisman Trophy–worthy touchdown jaunts to lead LSU to a 45–21 victory.

"He knew what was said," coach Les Miles said after the game. During practice that week, Fournette said he told his offensive line, "They don't come into our house and talk crazy."

He ran crazy—completely wild, in fact, in one of the greatest rushing performances in LSU history. On the national stage during a CBS televised broadcast, the country learned more about the power, speed, and strength of the 230-pound sophomore from New Orleans.

Fournette signed with LSU in 2014 as the nation's No. 1 high school prospect. Recruiting analysts pronounced him as one of the most talented players ever to emerge from prep football. He followed a ho-hum freshman season with a sensational one as a sophomore.

All of it started with this game. Fournette scored on touchdowns of 1, 29, and 40 yards, and he sat for much of the second half, doing all of his damage in 40 minutes of a 60-minute game. He raced for 71 yards on the game's first play. He hit the 100-yard mark midway through the second quarter and broke the 200-yard barrier with his second scoring dash early in the third.

At the time, it was the seventh-most rushing yards in a game in LSU history, and it included a duo of runs that showed off his versatile potential: strength, speed, and elusiveness. His 29-yard TD in the third quarter included a nasty juke move against the first defender diving at his feet. His second move came against defensive back Tray Matthews. Matthews attempted to leap onto Fournette's back and head, but the running back tossed him off and kept trucking. "I can't explain that one," Fournette said afterward. "It was a reaction, man. Just kept my feet pumping. Tried to get into the end zone."

The third defender was Carlton Davis. Fournette easily moved out of his arm tackle and marched into the end zone. "He did some things today," Miles said. "He took one of their tacklers and threw him into another tackler."

His second run was a 40-yard scoring jaunt. Fournette used his speed to race by three defenders. At the 15-yard line, he lowered his right shoulder and bashed into AU defensive back Blake Countess. Countess was on his back moments later as Fournette stepped over the 5'10", 185-pounder. "Like I said I have a team full of savages words are just words . . . #DontplaywithUs," Fournette tweeted after the game.

His performance against Auburn was the first of three straight 200-yard rushing outings and the second in a line of seven consecutive games with 100 yards or more. He bolted up Heisman Trophy projections, the odds-on favorite in late September before a 31-yard outing against Alabama sent his stock tumbling.

Still, when folks point to a breakout game for one of LSU's most heralded running backs, they'll point to Auburn 2015. With about five minutes left in that game, during a TV timeout, Fournette walked onto the field—the only player on the playing surface. A one-third-filled Tiger Stadium roared as Fournette raised both hands like a gladiator strutting in front of his audience.

"I didn't do nothing," Fournette said afterward. "Big shouts out to the O-line."

87 Eat Near Tiger Stadium

Baton Rouge has a plethora of homegrown restaurants, some of which have expanded around the nation, while others have remained uniquely original. Here are six favorite eating places of LSU and visiting football fans that are located within about two miles of Tiger Stadium:

Walk-On's Bistreaux & Bar: Walk-On's founders Brandon Landry and Jack Warner are former LSU basketball walk-ons who visited restaurants and sports bars across the country during Tigers road trips. They soon believed Baton Rouge needed a great sports bar of its own. They sketched their first floorplan on the back of a napkin while the team flew home from a road game at the University of Tennessee. Despite having no restaurant experience, they opened their first Walk-On's on September 9, 2003, in the shadow of LSU's Tiger Stadium. In 2012 ESPN named Walk-On's the No. 1 sports bar in America. Three years later, New Orleans Saints QB Drew Brees became an investor (he is now a co-owner and partner in the business). There are now 18 Walk-On's in Louisiana and several locations in other states, and even more are planned in an expansion.

The original Walk-On's is located at 3838 Burbank, a quarter mile from Tiger Stadium. Hours: Sunday–Thursday 11:00 AM–11:00 PM, Friday–Saturday 11:00 AM–12:00 AM. Phone Number: 225-757-8010.

Mike Anderson's: Once upon a time in the late 1960s, Mike Anderson was an All-American linebacker for LSU. He opened Mike Anderson's College Town Seafood & Oyster Bar in November 1975 on Highland Road near LSU, offering four different po' boys and oysters on the half shell. When it outgrew its space, it moved to its current location on West Lee Drive and changed its name to Mike Anderson's Seafood Restaurant and Oyster Bar. The location has changed but Anderson's goal of "making sure customers get their money's worth by going home full and with leftovers" hasn't.

Mike Anderson's is located at 1031 West Lee Drive, 2.1 miles from Tiger Stadium. Hours: Monday–Thursday 11:00 AM–2:00 PM and 5:00 PM–9:00 PM, Friday–Saturday 11:00 AM–10:00 PM, and Sunday 11:00 AM–9:00 PM. Phone Number: 225-766-7823.

The Chimes: There are several locations, but the original Chimes that opened in 1983 is steps away from LSU's north gates. It was built in a building that had always been a pharmacy, Sitman's Drugs during the 1940s and Maxwell's Rexall Drugs (complete with a soda fountain dishing burgers and malts) in the 1950s. The Chimes has diverse food with a Cajun flair (try the Abita root beer pork chops) and is regarded as one of the most popular Baton Rouge eateries. In 2019 it opened a rooftop beer garden overlooking Highland Road. The Chimes has a huge beer selection with usually 75 or so beers on tap, most of which you've never heard of but can't wait to try.

The original Chimes is located at 3357 Highland Road, about a mile from Tiger Stadium. Hours: Monday–Saturday 11:00 AM–2:00 AM, Sunday 10:30 AM–12:00 AM. Phone Number: 225-383-1754.

The Pastime Restaurant: Tucked in a small brick building inconspicuously located under the newer of the two Mississippi River bridges, the Pastime is definitely old-school. The building was a grocery store in the 1920s until then-owner Joe Alesce transformed it into Pastime Lounge, a popular dance hall with air-conditioning. In the 1960s Bobby Wesley and J.L. Mallet bought the lounge and introduced snacks such as pizza and sandwiches. Wesley's son, Randy, runs the business today, and it is filled with LSU football pictures from the 1960s and '70s. You order at the counter, use any name you want, and they'll summon you on the house intercom system. It's the only historical landmark restaurant in Baton Rouge.

The Pastime Restaurant is located at 252 South Blvd., at the corner of Nicholson Drive, two miles from Tiger Stadium. Hours: Monday–Thursday and Saturday 10:00 AM–10:00 PM, Friday 10:00 AM–11:00 PM. Phone Number: 225-343-5490.

Louie's Café: A 24-hour diner on Lake Street, it originally opened on Chimes Street in 1941, moved to State Street in 1986, and then moved to Lake Street in 2014. It's the oldest continuously operating restaurant in Baton Rouge. Founder and owner Louie Sisk ran the restaurant until his death in 1977. His wife, Nana, took over the business for a few years but sold the café to its current owner, Jimmy Wetherford. Wetherford attended LSU and bought the restaurant with two friends when he was 22 years old. Cook Marcus "Frenchie" Cox dispenses legendary basic fare and advice on a daily basis. The hash browns are a must—diced potatoes seasoned and cooked with Tony Chachere's Creole Seasoning, browned with sautéed onions and covered with melted cheese.

Louie's is located 3322 Lake St. on the north edge of the LSU campus, about a mile from Tiger Stadium. Hours: 24 hours a day. Phone Number: 225-346-8221.

Raising Cane's: What started as a low grade from a college professor who told Todd Graves a chicken finger restaurant would never work is now a business that started near the LSU campus in 1996 and made an estimated $1.5 billion in 2019. Graves raised money to build his first restaurant by working 90-hour weeks as a boilermaker in a refinery and then 20-hour days as a commercial salmon fisherman in Alaska. He named his business after his first yellow lab, whose name was Raisin' Cane. As of April 2020 there are 474 domestic Raising Cane's locations in 28 states, and Graves's concept was ranked the fastest-growing restaurant chain in America a couple years ago. The chicken fingers are second to none.

The original Cane's is located at 3313 Highland Road, about a mile from Tiger Stadium. Hours: Monday–Wednesday and Sunday 10:00 AM–2:00 AM, Thursday–Saturday 10:00 AM–3:30 AM. Phone Number: 225-387-3533.

88 Alex Bregman

It's a good thing LSU coach Paul Mainieri had someone hit Alex Bregman a few ground balls a few days after he arrived in Baton Rouge as a freshman. Otherwise the baseball world might have been denied one of its current hottest major league stars. All Bregman did in his first three full seasons with the Houston Astros through 2019 as their starting third baseman is win a World Series ring while contributing a game-winning walk-off hit, win All-Star Game MVP honors, win the American League Silver Slugger Award for a third baseman, play in two All-Star Games and two World Series, and finish second and fifth in American League MVP voting.

Not bad for a guy who walked through the doors of Alex Box Stadium in the fall of 2012 as a highly regarded high school catcher who battled injuries most of his senior season. Mainieri, knowing he needed a shortstop to replace four-year starter Austin Nola, who had been selected in the fifth round of the MLB draft, told Bregman to field ground balls whenever he could in the summer before he enrolled at LSU. "He was catching for his summer league team," Mainieri said. "I told him to do whatever his summer coach told him, but every chance he got to try to take ground balls."

That first day on the field at LSU when Mainieri watched Bregman flawlessly gobble up grounder after grounder, he knew he had a diamond that didn't need much polish. "It took me about five minutes to realize he had all the attributes you need to be an excellent infielder," Mainieri said of arguably one of the best players in LSU baseball history.

From 2013 to 2015, when LSU went to the College World Series twice, Bregman started in all 196 games of his Tigers' career. He batted .337 (265 for 786) with 56 doubles, 10 triples, 21 homers, 148 RBIs, 153 runs, and 66 stolen bases. He committed only 9 errors in 359 chances. He was a first-team All-American in 2013 and 2015 and also won 2013 National Freshman of the Year and the 2013 Brooks Wallace Award as the nation's best shortstop.

What separated him from the rest of the pack was his insatiable competitive drive. "I came to college to put on the purple and gold, win a championship, and bring that ring back to Baton Rouge," Bregman said in his college playing days. "That's why I do what I do. To be the best, you have to win."

It didn't matter the opponent—a powerhouse fellow SEC foe or a midweek game against an in-state Louisiana school—Bregman showed up ready to win. Like when he was determined to play in a midweek contest just days after his beloved grandfather died. Bregman had eight RBIs including a grand slam and a three-run homer.

He was often driven by his rare failures, such as when he was a freshman and he booted an eighth-inning ground ball in the 2013 College World Series that allowed UCLA to win and start LSU toward a stunning two-game elimination. Bregman cut out a picture of that play from the Baton Rouge newspaper and hung it in his locker.

In the winter before the 2014 season, while ice storms blanketed Baton Rouge, he found ways to get to the stadium to get in his frozen hacks against a pitching machine. The only day he missed was when he had a staph infection and his doctor ordered him not to hit. "People look at him and see someone who's self-made through hard work and dedication," Mainieri said. "I haven't had too many like him in my coaching career who are that dedicated."

In fact, Mainieri said he couldn't stop talking about Bregman in the summer of 2018 when Mainieri coached Team USA through a 15-game schedule. "I talked to the players about Alex's dedication, his commitment, his obsession with the game," Mainieri said.

He continued, "I remember one time I was coming home with my wife, Karen, from downtown Baton Rouge after giving a speech. It was 10:00 at night, we were driving past the [Alex Box] stadium and the lights of the stadium are on.

"Karen says, 'Why are the lights of the stadium on?' I said, 'Bregman's probably out there taking ground balls.'

"The next day at practice, I asked Alex, 'What were you doing about 10:00 last night?' He said, 'I convinced one of the student managers to come over and turn on the lights and hit me ground balls. Is that OK?'

"Alex never wants to quit improving in anything he does. One time right after he delivered the keynote speech at our season-opening banquet, he sat next to me and asked me to critique his talk."

Mainieri said Bregman's love affair with baseball shines through in the way he interacts with his teammates, whether he's on a hot streak or whether he's struggling. "Remember his sophomore year when he had a 4-for-51 slump after being a Freshman All-American and helping us to the College World Series?" Mainieri asked. "You wouldn't have known he was 4-for-51 or 50-for-51 because he acted the same way. He sprinted on and off the field every inning, he believed every one of his at-bats was going to be the one that would turn it around, he played his best defense ever, and he'd stand at the top of the rail in the dugout rooting on his teammates. He got as much joy out of his teammates' success as if it was his own success. Because of that, you knew he'd come out of the slump, and he did."

Mainieri said Bregman acclimated quickly to new situations because of his mix of humility and quiet confidence. "Don't confuse his humbleness with a lack of self-confidence and arrogance in his own belief of his abilities," Mainieri said. "He wants to be the guy at the plate with the game on the line. His whole career has been one for the record books."

Bregman had the complete respect from Mainieri and his assistants, from his teammates, and from opposing players and coaches even when the Tigers fell short twice in their College World Series trips to Omaha. The 57–11 Tigers were eliminated in two games in 2013 when Bregman went 0-for-8. When he returned as a junior in 2015, 54–12 LSU lasted three games with Bregman going 7-for-13 with several acrobatic fielding gems.

"It's an honor to be on the same field with that team and that program, especially Alex Bregman," TCU coach Jim Schlossnagle said after his Frogs eliminated LSU with an 8–4 win. "I had a chance to coach him for a summer [with Team USA], and in 25 years of college coaching, there's very few players that you sit in the other dugout and just truly enjoy watching them compete. And so I'll always consider that an honor."

Mainieri said there's one thing about Bregman that will never change. "Because of his unflappable self-confidence, Alex is fearless on the baseball field," Mainieri said. "He is not afraid of game-winning situations in the biggest moments. He embraces them. Only special players think that way."

89 Catholics vs. Catholics

The predominant rooting interest of south Louisiana is wrapped in purple and gold these days, but that wasn't always the case. Just ask the head football coach of LSU. "In everybody's house in south Louisiana, Notre Dame games would replay every Sunday morning," said Ed Orgeron, a native Louisianan who became LSU's coach in 2016. "Notre Dame games were shown in every household in Louisiana."

The connection between the Tigers and the Irish, decades old, is rooted in the world's largest Christian religion: Catholicism. More than 1.3 million Catholics reside in Louisiana, according to the Association of Religion Data Archives, far exceeding most Southern states. The Cajun and French Creole settlers of the state brought the same beliefs to Louisiana as did those who founded Notre Dame, the Congregation of Holy Cross, a Catholic group of missionary priests and brothers.

During Orgeron's childhood growing up on the bayous of south Louisiana, the Tigers were an inconsistent program, struggling to beat SEC powers Alabama and Tennessee, while Notre Dame had reached championship caliber under coaches Ara Parseghian, Dan Devine, and Lou Holtz. Inside Louisiana homes, you'd find plenty of gold—some paired with purple and some paired with navy blue.

LSU and Notre Dame have met in the regular season eight times, holding games in 1970, 1971, 1981, 1984, 1985, 1986, 1997, and 1998. They've been paired together in four bowl games. Heck, in 1997 they played twice in a matter of about six weeks. They split those games, with LSU losing in the regular season and then beating the Irish in the Independence Bowl. Then there was the Sugar Bowl following the 2006 season—a 41–14 LSU drubbing over the Charlie Weis–coached Irish in New Orleans. That matchup featured two first-round NFL Draft picks in LSU's JaMarcus Russell and Notre Dame's Brady Quinn.

Notre Dame leads the all-time series 7–5. The LSU–Notre Dame series started back in 1970 when the Irish squeaked out a 3–0 win over the Tigers. That Notre Dame win prompted a *Chicago Tribune* writer to pen, "If Notre Dame is number one, LSU has got to be one-A," according to LSU's media guide.

One of Notre Dame's biggest wins in the series came off the field the year before. In 1969 Irish school officials lifted a self-imposed bowl ban to steal LSU's spot in the Cotton Bowl against top-ranked Texas. The one-loss Tigers, so dejected, turned down offers from the Sun and Bluebonnet Bowls. What might have been Charles McClendon's best team in 18 years at LSU stayed home for the holidays. "Before the season everyone was saying LSU wasn't going anywhere this year," one LSU coach told Peter Finney for his book *The Fighting Tigers II*. "They didn't mean it that way, but that's the way it turned out."

The Sugar Bowl that year had the option of taking one of three SEC teams to meet Arkansas: 8–2 Auburn, 7–2 Ole Miss, or 9–1 LSU. The bowl committee chose quarterback Archie Manning's Rebels. They beat the Hogs 27–22. "Some members of the Sugar Bowl committee were irked that LSU did not show interest in New Orleans until Notre Dame shut the door in Dallas," Finney wrote in his book. No McClendon team in Baton Rouge ever finished with a better record.

90 Charles Alexander

Charles Alexander has never been afraid to take that extra step. Not during his four years at LSU from 1975 to 1978, when he became the first running back in SEC history to rush for more than 4,000 yards and score 40 touchdowns in a career. Not when he retired after seven seasons with the Cincinnati Bengals, including one Super Bowl appearance. And not when he created a Cajun seasoning company called C'mon Man.

Well, there was one time when none of Alexander's steps came easy: September 13, 1975, the day he began an All-American career with the LSU football team. On that particular afternoon, however, the freshman from Galveston, Texas, wasn't exactly everybody's All-American when he squared off against the Nebraska defense. "I'll never forget that game," said a modest Alexander, who still chuckles about his debut. "It was sort of like, 'Welcome to college football.' I can remember my stats like it was yesterday."

Alexander, a strapping 6'1", 226-pound tailback with sprinter's speed, was tossed around Nebraska's Memorial Stadium turf like a rag doll. He finished the game with eight carries for minus-2 yards and enough bruises to last the season. "I don't think I made it back to the line of scrimmage all day," Alexander said of the game, which LSU lost 10–7.

But that certainly wasn't typical of Alexander's stellar career at LSU and later with the Bengals. He usually dished out more punishment than he took, running away from huge defensive linemen and linebackers and simply overpowering defensive backs who tried to bring him down. He finished his college career with 4,035 rushing yards, a school record at the time. He then gained 2,645 yards in the NFL.

Even today, Alexander admitted he would never have believed he would play in the NFL after his rugged college debut. He said he set his sights on three simple goals when he left Ball High School as an unheralded and unproven recruit. "I wanted to earn a degree, have some fun playing football at LSU, and go home to coach high school football," he said. Alexander accomplished the first two but came up way short on the final one. Instead of becoming a coach, Alexander was a 1979 first-round draft choice of the Bengals (he was the 12th player selected) and was a starter for most of his career.

That wasn't too bad for an athlete who didn't gain 1,000 yards in his entire prep career and who was sought by only a handful of colleges. "I really didn't get an opportunity to show my ability," Alexander said. "I had three different coaches in high school, and I was a blocking back."

But there was at least one college recruiter, LSU running backs coach Jerry Stovall, who saw Alexander's raw talent. Stovall had been tipped off about Alexander by a track coach who had gone to Galveston to recruit Ball track star Greg Edmonds. Until then, a couple Southwest Conference schools were the only ones mildly interested in Alexander, who was a junior at the time. Several months later, when recruits could sign two letters of intent before signing the binding national letter, Alexander went with LSU and the University of Houston.

When national signing day rolled around, Alexander had to choose between venerable UH coach Bill Yeoman and Stovall. "Coach Yeoman was in his car and Coach Stovall was sitting there waiting in his car," Alexander recalled. "It amazed me that Jerry was so persistent because I had told him no at least a dozen times. But thank goodness [Stovall] was out there that particular day because I might have made the wrong decision and gone to Houston."

Alexander still doesn't know why he picked LSU, except maybe that Stovall offered him trust and a genuine chance to be a big-time running back. It didn't take very long to realize he made the right choice. "As soon as I got to LSU, I knew it was the place for me," Alexander said. "I liked the atmosphere of the stadium and all the tradition. It was a great place to play football and get an education."

Alexander played his first two years behind Terry Robiskie but still piled up 1,177 rushing yards, including 876 yards and 7 TDs as a sophomore. He made four All-America teams in 1977 and five in 1978 when he rushed for 1,686 yards and 1,172 yards, respectively. Alexander averaged 4.7 yards per carry during his college career and scored 42 TDs. He also set nine Southeastern Conference records and 27 school marks, including most rushing yards in a game (237), most rushing yards in a season (1,686), and most rushing TDs in a game (4) and season (17).

"It all started up front," Alexander said, crediting his offensive line, which was nicknamed the Root Hogs. "You can have all the ability in the world, but you really don't have anything if you don't have the guys up front."

The four biggest games of Alexander's career came during that junior season in 1977. He rushed for 237 yards against Oregon, 231 against Wyoming, 199 against Tulane, and 183 against Vanderbilt, all Tigers victories.

"My junior year was my favorite," he said. "My senior year was disappointing because I pulled a hamstring and wasn't healthy for about half the year. But as a whole, my time at LSU was the best four years of my life."

91 The Football Operations Center

It all started with Nick Saban's initial contract negotiations when LSU was searching for a new head football coach after firing Gerry DiNardo at the end of the 1999 season. Since 1991 LSU had had a 100-yard indoor practice facility—a climate-controlled 83,580-square-foot facility adjacent to the Tigers' four outdoor 100-yard football practice fields. But Saban, as a condition of accepting LSU's job offer, had then–school chancellor Mark Emmert commit to build a football operations complex to connect with the indoor field.

Eventually, in 2003, then–LSU athletic director Skip Bertman unveiled a plan to pay for Saban's requested facility improvements. His idea was creating the Tradition Fund, in which the right to purchase season tickets included a donation ranging from $85 to $400 above the cost of the ticket. It was designed to generate $7.5 million in revenue annually, used to retire debt and build Saban's $15 million football complex.

Just prior to the 2003 season, Bertman was crossing his fingers Saban would have a good season so donations would flow without protest. "I'm counting on him, not just to have a winning season but to win nine games minimum," Bertman said of Saban. "Never before have I rooted for the football coach as much as I'm rooting for [Saban] now." All Saban did that season was coach the Tigers to the national championship.

By 2006, two years after Saban had moved on to coach the NFL's Miami Dolphins, LSU opened its football operations center, which included a locker room, players' lounge, weight room, a training room, an equipment room, a video operations center, coaches' offices, and individual position meeting rooms. It also had the Shirley and Bill Lawton Team Room, which had 144 theater-style seats for team meetings and a lobby featuring all of LSU's national championship and bowl trophies and major national individual awards.

It all had a "wow factor" until July 2019, when LSU revealed its $28 million football operations building renovations that made the Tigers the envy of college football. The building, renamed the LSU Football Operations and Performance Nutrition Center, is the most cutting-edge functional practice facility in college football.

Yes, it has its share of bells and whistles designed to turn heads in recruiting, such as a walk-through room featuring a state-of-the-art projection system and a 20-foot projection wall for players to participate in a virtual walk-through of game simulations. There's the Mathieu Players Lounge, a $1 million upgrade funded by a donation by former LSU All-American cornerback Tyrann Mathieu. The lounge has virtual-reality racing games, video game consoles, theater seating, HD TV, refreshment stations, and a Ping-Pong table. The LSU experience room showcases a 4-D experience that allows visitors to experience the feeling of running out in Tiger Stadium on game day.

But what truly sets the building apart is the athletes-only training building called the Performance Nutrition Center, which features an executive chef and a first-of-its-kind locker room that includes high-tech sleep pods. Executive chef Michael Johnson, formerly with the NFL's Seattle Seahawks, oversees the nutrition center. "It's a chef's dream to have variety in menu and not see the same thing every day," Johnson said. "It's why you want to go in this business, to see difference daily. It's a wonderful challenge."

The Phillips-Bordelon Locker Room contains the 150 sleep pod lockers in an area that continually has fresh air pumped into it. LSU trainer Jack Marucci and Tigers equipment manager Greg Stringfellow kicked around ideas on how to accommodate players taking naps without leaving the premises, especially during preseason practice, when players are basically at the football ops building for at least 12 hours a day. Stringfellow said in past years players would often attempt to sleep on the locker room floor instead of leaving the building. "It's not the cleanest place to sleep," he said.

But then Marucci saw the sleep pods in the first-class section of airplanes. "When I brought it to the architects [the Kansas City–based firm HNTB], their eyes got big," Marucci said. "My vision for the pods was finding a way we could put something in the dressing room that would help them with hydration, relaxation, meditation, sleep, and recovery."

The LSU lockers also have fresh air pumped into the storage that players pull out underneath the lockers and above the lockers.

LSU coach Ed Orgeron said the sleep pods allow him to schedule a nap time for his team daily during the preseason. "Now they can shower, walk in our cafeteria to eat, and then walk to the locker room to sleep," he said. "We'll dim the lights, keep it quiet so they can nap."

Orgeron has been thrilled with the finished product after he, his staff, and his players were displaced for a year while the renovations were completed. "The one thing we wanted to do when we started to build the facility was put most of the money into the players," Orgeron said. "It turned out absolute unique.

"You have to have great facilities to compete; I believe this is the very best. It's helping in recruiting. I think there's going to be a lot of locker rooms [at competing colleges] torn up fast and replaced with ones that include the visionary renovations we implemented."

92 Battle for the Rag

The series record of the Battle for the Rag is a debatable subject. LSU officials claim they lead the series over Tulane at 69–22–7. Tulane officially has the series record at 68–23–7. What would a rivalry clash be without disagreement? LSU-Tulane has that, or at least *had* that.

Take 1948 as an example. After a victory over the Tigers, Green Wave fans raised the Tulane flag on the LSU campus, according to a Nola.com story published in 2017, and they painted, in green, the final score of the game on some campus buildings: 46–0.

In retaliation, a group of former LSU players in 1949 planted fast-growing rye seed on the Tulane field in the weeks leading up to game day, the Nola.com story said. By kickoff time, it had sprouted, spelling out the letters *L-S-U*.

These were the most heated days of LSU's original rivalry series. A decade before the Tigers' clash with Ole Miss bubbled up and well before the yearly meetings with Alabama began, LSU's chief, bitterest rival resided in its own state about 80 miles from Baton Rouge.

LSU and Tulane met for the first time in 1893, the first football game for both schools. The Green Wave and Tigers series became one of the most enduring in all of college football. They met every year from 1911 to 1994, aside from a one-year interruption in 1918 because of World War I. The stretch of 76 consecutive games is still the 24th-longest uninterrupted series in NCAA Division I history, according to a 2005 story on LSUSports.net.

They even fought over a prize starting in 1939: the Rag. The Rag was a rectangular flag divided diagonally, with LSU's school colors and emblem on one side and Tulane's colors and emblem on the other, and also bearing the seal of Louisiana. The Rag, like the series itself, vanished, said to have burned in a fire on the Tulane campus.

The annual meetings ended in 1994, and the teams have only played six times since then. A variety of reasons signaled the end to this once-intense rivalry, none greater than Tulane's exit from the SEC in 1966.

The series lost its luster. A tight rivalry between evenly matched foes became yearly blowouts between two schools that poured resources into football in vastly different ways. The Green Wave has won only 4 of the last 52 meetings, and 3 of those came in a 4-year stretch, from 1979 to 1982.

The two schools renewed their rivalry in 2006, agreeing to alternate home fields (the Superdome in New Orleans and Tiger Stadium in Baton Rouge). They didn't even make it halfway through the 10-year agreement. LSU pushed to shift all remaining matches to Tiger Stadium for financial reasons. The contract was canceled after the fourth game in 2009, with the two sides agreeing to play one game at an unspecified future date in New Orleans. That still hasn't happened as of 2020, and still the schools squabble over the series record.

The disputed game was a 22–0 Tulane win, but the game was forfeited to LSU via a ruling from the Southern Intercollegiate Athletic Association, the conference of which both were a part at that time. The SIAA ruled that Tulane fielded an ineligible player.

The schools aren't always fighting. In fact, in 1973 a friendly tradition began. Fans of both LSU and Tulane would meet Uptown in New Orleans at Norby's Bar on game day for a wheelbarrow parade. Fans of the losing team got the dubious honor of pushing the winning team's fans, Nola.com wrote in a 2017 story.

93 Derrius Guice

In life, Derrius Guice ran right instead of left, he says. This has nothing to do with his exploits in football—those school and conference records he shattered, the 32 touchdowns he scored, that electrifying running style, his tackle-breaking ability. This is about life—not about surviving a season of physical battering in the game's toughest conference but surviving a childhood of poverty and tragedy.

"Walking outside my house, you look left, you got people getting jumped and beat up, and you see people, pants at their kneecaps, you see guns," Guice told ThePostgame.com in 2018. "You look right, you see opportunity. And I always went out the house and walked right because I was going to walk to my football field."

Guice's feel-good story supersedes sports. Raised in one of the most rough-and-tumble neighborhoods of Baton Rouge— the Bottoms—Guice emerged as a superstar running back from Catholic High School, signed with LSU knowing he'd play second fiddle to sensation Leonard Fournette and, in many ways, surpassed his teammate in LSU lore. He set three school rushing records, carried the Tigers on his back through the somewhat disappointing seasons of 2016 and 2017, and led the SEC in rushing yards as a sophomore.

Bubbly and engaging with a mean, exciting running style, Guice captivated the LSU fan base almost immediately, showing bursts as a true freshman before taking the conference by storm in 2016 while replacing an injured Fournette. His 1,387 yards not only led the league, but he averaged 7.6 yards a carry, one of the best marks in school history and the fifth-best in the country that year.

In the last regular-season game of that year against Texas A&M, he set the single-game rushing mark, 285 yards, eclipsing Fournette's previous record of 284. He was also responsible for the longest touchdown run in school history, a 96-yard jaunt against Arkansas, and he set the mark for single-season yards per carry at 7.6, an insane record that is more than half a yard more than second place. He left LSU as the only player in SEC history with three career games of 250 or more rushing yards.

Guice's combination of speed, size, and agility made him one of the most difficult in the country to tackle. He was elusive enough to dance around opponents, fast enough to run by them, and strong enough—he could squat 650 pounds while at LSU—to rumble over them. In fact, Guice broke 106 tackles during his career at LSU with more than 55 percent of his yards coming after contact, according to *Pro Football Focus*, the statistical analysis outlet. "He's a rolling ball of butcher knives," said his high school coach, Dale Weiner.

Guice described his running style as "angry," stemming from the hardships of his youth. Guice's father, Derek, was gunned down and killed in an incident at a Baton Rouge Denny's restaurant when Guice was only five. Guice's older brother, Derrick, was sentenced in 2018 to two years in prison after pleading guilty to a weapons charge in a 2016 drive-by shooting. "My brother definitely went left, and that was my best friend growing up. He just kept drifting and drifting off," Guice said. "You know, peer pressure is real. Once you get in that game, it's just hard to get out."

Football was a needed distraction in Guice's life, and it soon became a career passion. Projected as a first-round pick in the 2018 NFL Draft, Guice slipped into the second round—a stunning set of events for a prospect who was invited and came to the NFL Draft site only to leave disappointed after the opening day. The Washington Redskins eventually chose Guice with the 59th pick.

Several outlets attempted to explain Guice's fall to the second round. Before the draft, teams had learned about unreported off-the-field incidents involving Guice, NFL.com reported. Another account questioned Guice's maturity and attitude.

"It did surprise me, because a lot of the things came out of nowhere and weren't true," Guice told reporters after being drafted. "I just didn't understand why me, out of all people, because I'm great to everybody, I have a great personality and I just didn't understand why everything just hit so hard with me out of everybody."

94 The Night the Barn Burned

Inside Jordan-Hare Stadium, defensive back Raion Hill scored more points (8) than any other offensive player in the game between LSU and Auburn in September 1996. This was a career night, his highlight during an otherwise ho-hum LSU career.

Outside Jordan-Hare Stadium, shooting flames and black smoke overshadowed his sparkling performance. "The fire became the story that night because it was such a truly unique experience," Josh Bean, a sportswriter covering that game, told AL.com in an interview in 2016.

Hill returned one interception for a touchdown and another for a two-point score, picking off a potential game-tying two-point conversion attempt in the waning minutes of his team's 19–15 win over Auburn.

The fire stole his show in one of the most legendary games in LSU history. A nearby fire on campus, visible to millions at home watching on ESPN and thousands in the stadium, raged throughout most of the game, its billowing smoke and orange flames creating a scary but incredible portrait on a bizarre night on the Plains.

The Associated Press's story from that game began, "While a piece of Auburn's athletic past went up in flames outside of Jordan-Hare Stadium on Saturday . . ." A headline in the local newspaper read, LSU BURNS AUBURN.

"It was a tough loss for us against LSU, but it was an interesting night," former Auburn coach Terry Bowden told AL.com in 2016. "It's one you never forget for weird reasons."

Auburn's former basketball arena, positioned only feet away from the southeast corner of Jordan-Hare Stadium, caught fire after a hot tailgating grill was left too close to the 50-year-old facility. The building, nicknamed the Barn, was scheduled for demolition and was made out of heart of pine, a highly flammable wood. It took nearly an hour for firefighters to control the blaze, and it burned all night and into the next morning—well after the visiting Tigers had used Hill's heroics to escape 15th-ranked Auburn with a victory.

Bowden's Auburn team outgained LSU and coach Gerry DiNardo 363–241 but had four turnovers, missed three field goals, had a PAT blocked, and played much of the second half without quarterback Dameyune Craig, who was concussed.

It was tough to concentrate on the game. The west side of the stadium, including Auburn's sideline and the press box, got the best view of the blaze. "When it happened, I thought the stadium was on fire," Craig told Nola.com for a 2016 story. "We could see it coming from the back of the stadium. It was a pretty scary ordeal."

"That's the most terrified I've ever been in a stadium," Bean said. "You just don't expect to see that kind of a fire so close to you and 80,000 other people."

Fans lined the ramps in the southeast corner of the stadium, eyeballing the shooting flames and smoke plumes arising from an ordeal that could have been much worse. "What if the wind had been blowing differently and brought that fire and that ash and smoke into the stadium?" former Auburn athletic director David Housel asked. "We could have had a disaster on our hands."

In the broadcast booth, ESPN broadcaster Ron Franklin had a perfect view of the fire. "I'm trying to do play-by-play and I've got producers talking in my ear from Bristol," Franklin said. "They're getting all these phone calls because our camera angles made it look like the stadium was on fire. It made for an unusually quiet Auburn crowd for a time, I do remember that. Very, very quiet."

Meanwhile, Hill led the Tigers to victory on the field in a game they nearly tossed away. Leading 17–9 late, an LSU interception—on a first-and-21 play call that DiNardo still regrets—gave Auburn life. Bowden's team scored with 38 seconds left and was poised to tie the game with a two-point try. Hill stepped in front of AU backup quarterback Jon Cooley's slant pass and returned it for the two points. "Thank you, Jesus. Thank you, Coach Carl Reese," Hill said of LSU's then–defensive coordinator in the Nola.com story. "We were in a 30 package and he had me in the perfect place. I was in the throwing lane."

95 Joe Dean

It might have been one of the most unusual yet appropriate wakes ever held. At Rabenhorst Funeral Home in Baton Rouge on the night before former LSU athletic director and basketball star Joe Dean's funeral after he died at age 83, the noise level at his visitation sounded like a cocktail party.

A crowd that ranged from three Final Four coaches to family, friends, and just about anybody whose life the personable Dean touched was telling stories about him and laughing through their tears. It was just the way Dean would have wanted it. Nobody loved people more than Dean, which is why he was a success in everything he tried.

For 40 years, his careers with Converse, as an SEC basketball television analyst, and as LSU's athletic director seemed to blend effortlessly together along with his summer basketball camp in Mississippi.

Once upon a time, before Sonny Vaccaro became the fastest-talking basketball shoe salesman in America, there was Dean, extolling the virtues of Converse Chuck Taylor All Stars. Not only did he persuade most college teams to wear Converse, especially in the South, but he also was instrumental in signing NBA legends Julius Erving, Larry Bird, and Magic Johnson to Converse endorsements, as well as tennis greats Chris Evert and Jimmy Connors. "You have to understand that in the shoe business," Dean once said, "there are people who can sell shoes and people who cannot. You've got to try to figure out who has that marketability."

Dean's job with Converse provided him countless contacts. But it was his weekly work as one of the original TV analysts on the SEC's *Game of the Week* telecasts starting in 1968 that made him the guy college basketball coaches and athletic directors called when there were coaching vacancies. Dean was a one-man search committee, a walking Rolodex. "I'd call home each night from the road," Dean said, "and Doris [Dean's late wife] used to say to me, 'They must be firing coaches.' I'd say, 'Why?' She said, 'Because they're all calling.' I don't know if I could get a guy hired, but I could get him in the hunt. Athletic directors would call me asking if this coach or that coach would be a good fit for their school."

For the next 20 years until he resigned his announcing job to become LSU's athletic director in 1987, Dean was the voice of SEC basketball, first working with John Ferguson and later Tom Hammond. "I didn't have any training," Dean said. "They stuck a mic in my hand and told me to start talking. No one ever came to me and said, 'You need to do this' or 'You need to do that.' No one ever tried to do anything to help me get better. I was flying by the seat of my pants."

He had a folksy style and a nasal tone. His unforgettable catch phrase was "String music" (which came from his childhood on the playgrounds of New Albany, Indiana) when someone hit a shot. Dean's style and tone were so popular that eventually various cities throughout SEC country would stage Joe Dean soundalike contests, such as one year when the league tournament was played at Rupp Arena in Lexington. Whoever could imitate Joe Dean the best would get prizes.

"I hear about the contest a couple of hours before the game when I'm at the arena," Dean said. "A couple of newspaper guys tell me about it, and say, 'Why don't you call in, say you're somebody else, enter the contest, and have a little fun?'

"I did. I gave a fake name and address, and I didn't win the contest. There were people who called in who did Joe Dean better than Joe Dean. Not only did I not win, I didn't finish in the top three."

Dean's 15-year tenure is the longest of any AD in LSU history. "I'm not sure if anybody has had as big an impact over several generations on LSU like Joe Dean did, and I don't know if anybody had a deeper love for LSU as Joe Dean did," said SEC associate commissioner Herb Vincent, who Dean hired as LSU's sports information director in 1988. He continued, "With Joe, it was much more than that. He was a friend. He was somebody who, besides being your boss, was always interested in your personal development and personal life. He believed in family and he wanted to foster that kind of environment so you could thrive professionally. The relationship I had with him outside of LSU was a lot more important to me than the one we had in the office."

Dean's last official hire as LSU's athletic director was Nick Saban as the Tigers' head football coach in 2000. It was a hire that would change the face of the LSU program forever, pushing it to the level of being consistently competitive for SEC titles and national championships that it enjoys today.

But to understand the true essence of Dean and his love and compassion for people, there is this: Gerry DiNardo has never forgotten what Dean said to him on the day in November 1999 when LSU chancellor Mark Emmert fired DiNardo. "I was to Mark's left, Joe was to the right, and after Mark fired me, Joe shared his feelings about the decision," said DiNardo, who Dean hired from Vanderbilt in 1995. "When we were done, I stood up and then Joe stood up and he hugged me and told me loved me. Then we walked out together, and I thought that was extraordinary that Joe would do that in front of his boss under those circumstances."

96 World Series Champs

Rising above Alex Box Stadium's right-field bleachers, the giant purple billboard is unmistakable. NATIONAL CHAMPIONS, it reads, with six years listed underneath: 1991, 1993, 1996, 1997, 2000, and 2009. To LSU fans, the billboard is known as the Intimidator, reminding all opponents of this program's storied history. In the modern era, no school has reigned over college baseball quite like LSU. The six national championships, all falling inside a 20-year window, are more titles than all but two college programs in the history of the sport. Texas also has six, while USC leads all schools with 12, all but one of those coming before 1980.

Skip Bertman, head coach from 1984 to 2001, laid the foundation for what LSU baseball is today: the rare money-making college baseball program with an intense, passionate fan base and a winning edge. Depending on the year, the Tigers generate around $1 million in revenue per season, when many other schools lose hundreds of thousands on their baseball teams. Since 1996 the school has led all programs in attendance, normally averaging more than 10,000 tickets sold per game, a remarkable number for a sport whose average attendance nationally is less than one-third that figure.

LSU's attendance streak began amid its dynasty under Bertman in the 1990s. In his first eight years as coach, he took the Tigers on five College World Series trips, finally winning it all on the fifth try in 1991. That team had pitchers such as Chad Ogea and Rick Greene and sluggers such as right fielder Lyle Mouton and catcher Gary Hymel, the College World Series MVP that year. It was a magical ride. The Tigers became the first team since Miami (Florida) in 1982 to win the national title without a loss in the NCAA Tournament, winning eight consecutive games in the tournament.

Two years later, LSU did it again. Second baseman Todd Walker delivered a walk-off single in a College World Series elimination game against Long Beach, and then the Tigers took care of Wichita State in an 8–0 rout to claim the title in Omaha. Behind the pitching of Mike Sirotka and hitting from Walker and Armando Rios, the 1991 hero, LSU finished the season 53–17–1 and became the first team in SEC history to win four straight league championships.

LSU won the 1996 championship in amazing and historic fashion. The Tigers trailed Miami in the national championship game with one out remaining in the season when second baseman and pinch-hitter Warren Morris rocketed a two-out, two-run homer to send LSU to the title. Morris's shot lives on in LSU lore, and as of 2020, it remains the only walk-off home run to win a World Series, college or pro. It was the only home run of the season for Morris. The Alexandria, Louisiana, native had missed 39 games that season due to a broken bone in his right hand.

The College World Series championship capped a long list of achievements for the big-swinging 1996 Tigers, many of them on offense. They established an SEC record with 131 home runs. Shortstop Jason Williams became the SEC career leader in runs scored (270), and first baseman Eddy Furniss set the SEC single-season mark for RBIs (103).

In June 1997 a then-record crowd of more than 24,000 fans watched LSU beat SEC rival Alabama in the National Championship Game at historic Rosenblatt Stadium in Omaha. Ironically, a month before the title match, the Crimson Tide had humiliated the Tigers 28–2 for the worst loss in LSU's 104-year baseball history. In the College World Series, the Tigers built a 9–0 lead after two innings and coasted to a 13–6 victory, capping off a season that started with 19 consecutive wins, then an NCAA record winning streak. LSU completed the year with an NCAA record 188 home runs, breaking the previous mark of 161 homers set by Brigham Young in 1988.

Shortstop Brandon Larson's 40 long balls led the way and broke the SEC record. Meanwhile, Eddy Furniss, Mike Koerner, and Tom Bernhardt each smashed at least 17 dingers. On the mound, righty Patrick Coogan struck out 144 batters, and Doug Thompson sat down 158 more.

In 2000 LSU needed key strokes from three seniors in a championship bout with Stanford in Omaha. Down 5–2, team captain Blair Barbier and outfielder Jeremy Witten each launched home runs, and catcher Brad Cresse drove in the eventual winning run in the ninth inning for a fifth national title in 10 years and the final under Bertman.

Nine years later, a different coach would win a crown on the diamond in Baton Rouge. Paul Mainieri, in his third season as coach, directed the Tigers to SEC regular-season and tournament titles before his team went 10–1 in the NCAA tournament, beating Texas 11–4 in a winner-take-all rubber match of the best-of-three championship series. The 2009 Tigers leaned heavily on right-handers Louis Coleman, Anthony Ranaudo, and Matty Ott, while getting pop at the plate from speedster Jared Mitchell, home-run hitter Blake Dean, and first baseman Ryan Schimpf.

97 Patrick Peterson

LSU has a long history of producing some of the country's best defensive backs. The university prides itself on being a sort of secondary mecca, a site to which talented high school cornerbacks and safeties flock. So rich is the defensive backs culture there that the program touts itself as DBU, an NFL-producing factory for DBs.

Who's best of them all? There is a litany of names: Tyrann Mathieu, Morris Claiborne, Jamal Adams, LaRon Landry, Grant Delpit. But there is little debate over the most decorated. That's Patrick Peterson. "He's not just a corner or a safety," fellow NFL defensive back Eric Berry said in an ESPN interview years ago. "He can do it all."

Among a host of highly touted LSU defensive backs, Peterson is the only one to have won both the Chuck Bednarik Award, given to the nation's best defender, and the Jim Thorpe Award, given to the nation's best defensive back, claiming both prizes during a magical 2010 season in which he even received some Heisman Trophy attention.

One of the most dynamic athletes in school history, Peterson served not only as a lockdown corner but a special teams kingpin. His final season included four interceptions, a school record in kickoff return yards, two punt returns for touchdowns, and a blocked field goal. He created one of the most iconic images in LSU history, striking the Heisman pose after returning a punt against West Virginia for a touchdown. "It's something that just happened," he said in an interview years later.

The Florida native was involved in one of the most hotly debated officiating calls in LSU history. Down by six points in a game at Alabama with six minutes left, Peterson appeared to intercept Tide quarterback Greg McElroy in what would have potentially been a game-changing play. Officials ruled that Peterson stepped out of bounds before possessing the football. A video review confirmed the ruling despite many people, including CBS broadcasters, siding with the Tigers. Alabama would go on to kick a field goal on that drive and win 24–15, but the call has become infamous in the LSU-Alabama rivalry, and still Peterson often mentions it in interviews.

But perhaps above anything else, Peterson's legacy at LSU resides in his jersey number. He's often considered the first in a line of high-profile LSU players to don No. 7. After leaving early for the NFL Draft, he passed the digit to fellow defensive back Tyrann Mathieu. Years later, running back Leonard Fournette wore the number before passing it to receiver DJ Chark. Safety Grant Delpit wore the number in 2019. "No. 7 is the number for big-time playmakers from the program like myself, Patrick Peterson, Tyrann Mathieu," Fournette said in a 2017 interview on InsidetheTigers.com. "That number changes the program, and there's a lot to come for players wearing that number."

Like many talented defensive backs, Peterson found his way to Baton Rouge despite growing up a distance away, in Pompano Beach, Florida, near Fort Lauderdale. He chose the Tigers over his home-state schools Florida, Florida State, and Miami, the last of which he was committed to for months.

Three years after signing with LSU, Peterson became the first of a run of five defensive backs in an eight-year span to be selected in the first round of the NFL Draft.

98 Jimmy Taylor

You won't find running back Jimmy Taylor sprinkled throughout the LSU record book; he may be in only a couple places. Such as being ranked 10th in career yards per game, averaging 65.7 yards, or 10th in career attempts per game with 13.94, all in only 20 games in the 1956–57 seasons.

"I thought I was a better linebacker than running back coming out of college," the late Taylor once said before his death at age 83 in 2018. "I didn't develop the necessary skills to become a pro running back. I was running from tackle to tackle in college, did very little pass receiving and very little blocking. I wasn't utilized much."

But 10 years after a 10-year pro career—mostly as the hard-nosed fullback of four-time NFL champ Green Bay Packers, who retired at the end of the 1967 season as the NFL's No. 2 career rusher—Taylor was elected to the Pro Football Hall of Fame. How? How did someone who had only moments of brilliance in college become one of the cornerstones of legendary coach Vince Lombardi's championship Packers dynasty? How did he become the first running back in NFL history to rush for more than 1,000 yards for five consecutive seasons? Because of Taylor's football credo: "Football is a contact sport. You've got to make them respect you. You've got to punish tacklers. You've got to deal out more misery than the tacklers deal out to you."

Such a hard-nosed approach for the 6-foot, 215-pound Taylor began in his days as a young, thick-legged natural athlete growing up in Baton Rouge. Taylor's dad died when he was 10 and his mother worked in a laundry. So bicycling what he once jokingly estimated as "a million miles," he earned three dollars per week throwing newspaper routes in the morning and afternoon.

By the time he enrolled at Baton Rouge High School, he was dazzling as a basketball player. He didn't go out for the BRHS football team until he was a 5'9", 155-pound junior. "I didn't like the game," he said. "I don't like anything unless I can do it real well." By the time he graduated from BRHS, he was a 5'11", 212-pound bruiser who signed to play football with LSU.

"Jim could have played anything and been good at it," said Bat Gourrier, the BRHS track coach. "If you had stuck a tennis racket in his hand, he would have been great. If you bought him a set of golf clubs, he could outdo you in that too. He was just natural as an athlete."

LSU freshman football coach Pop Strange said, "Taylor was the finest freshman athlete I've ever seen."

Unfortunately, Taylor flunked out of LSU after his freshman year and spent his sophomore year regaining his eligibility at Hinds Community College in Mississippi. Once he returned to LSU as a junior in 1956, it took him half the season to become acclimated to the Tigers' new offensive system. In the final five games of the season, Taylor scored 51 points to lead the SEC with 59, and the Tigers won three games.

LSU closed that season with consecutive wins over Arkansas and Tulane, thanks to Taylor. Against the Razorbacks, he ran for 170 yards in a 21–7 upset. The next week, in a 7–6 win over the Green Wave, he scored LSU's lone touchdown, kicked the extra point, made a TD-saving tackle, and intercepted a Tulane pass late in the game.

In the Tigers' 1957 season in which LSU's team fought the Asian flu, Taylor, a senior, was named first-team FWAA All-American after leading the SEC in rushing with 762 yards and 86 points. His college finale was a 171-yard, two-TD performance in a 25–7 win over Tulane that enabled LSU to finish 5–5 and quiet critics of third-year Tigers coach Paul Dietzel. The very next season, when Taylor had moved on to the NFL, LSU won the national championship. "With the ball under his arm, Jimmy Taylor was the best runner I've ever been associated with," Dietzel said.

In Taylor's final game with the Packers in 1966, before playing one last year with the expansion team the New Orleans Saints, Taylor ran for 56 yards and scored the first rushing TD in Super Bowl history as Green Bay beat Kansas City 35–10 in the first AFL–NFL World Championship Game, known retroactively as Super Bowl I.

99 Ben McDonald

Ben McDonald, at least for one season, was probably the most unique two-sport athlete in LSU. There have been football/track athletes and football/baseball athletes. But a basketball/baseball athlete? How can that even work with the two seasons overlapping?

The truth is it didn't during McDonald's freshman season. That year, he was a reserve 6'7" forward on the 1986–87 LSU basketball team that lost to Indiana by a point in the regional finals and a pitcher on LSU's 1987 College World Series team who reported late and started only four games after missing more than a third of the season.

It took that one year of not really doing either sport well—he averaged 2.8 points and 2 rebounds per game in basketball and was 2–3 with a 4.06 ERA in baseball—for McDonald to realize he had to pick one sport. He chose baseball, and he chose wisely.

Two summers later, after leading LSU to third place in the 1989 College World Series, he was drafted by the Baltimore Orioles as the first player picked in the Major League Baseball draft.

After three months of contract negotiations and only two starts in the Class A Carolina League, McDonald was promoted to the Orioles, where he stayed for seven of his nine seasons before calling it a career after compiling a 78–70 record with a 3.91 ERA in 211 appearances, including 198 starts. "It took me a couple years to adjust to the major leagues," said McDonald, who was raised in the Baton Rouge suburb of Denham Springs. "I was just a country boy who loved playing baseball, but suddenly I was in a grown man's world."

But McDonald wasn't intimidated in the least. If anything, he welcomed the challenge. He was, as LSU teammate Pete Bush once described him, "ultra-competitive in everything he did, whether it was wrestling on the team bus on the way to Mississippi State or to see who could hit a golf ball the farthest with a fungo bat."

At Denham Springs High School, McDonald was a man for all seasons as an All-District punter in football and an All-State selection in basketball and baseball. He actually signed a basketball scholarship with LSU and coach Dale Brown in 1986.

LSU baseball coach Skip Bertman stayed patient, knowing he could accelerate McDonald's progress if he ever stuck with baseball, which finally happened. "Ben was a good player for Dale," Bertman said, "but it was clear baseball was his sport. Still, he might be the best overall athlete LSU has ever had.

"He's arguably LSU's best-ever pitcher. In my 30 years as a coach and athletic director, I never had anyone who could pitch like Ben."

In his final two seasons at LSU, when he solely concentrated on baseball, McDonald had a combined record of 27–11 with a 2.89 ERA, 18 complete games, 5 saves, 346 strikeouts, and 67 walks. He was the ultimate definition as the bell cow of the staff, emerging as a star as a sophomore in 1988 when he was 13–7 for the Tigers and then won two games for the USA's gold medal–winning team in the Seoul Olympics.

As a junior in what became his final college season, in 1989, McDonald averaged nearly 12 strikeouts per 9 innings and threw 44.2 consecutive scoreless innings. It was a Southeastern Conference record that stood for more than 15 seasons.

Though his college career ended with two losses in the College World Series, the Tigers wouldn't have made it to Omaha without his performance as the Most Outstanding Player in the regional finals at Texas A&M, where he had two wins and a save. LSU had to fight its way back through the losers bracket and was faced with the prospect of having to beat the Aggies twice on a broiling hot Texas afternoon in late May. All McDonald did was throw seven innings as a starter in a 13–5 win over the Aggies to immediately force a Game 2. When LSU took a 5–4 lead over A&M in the 11th inning, McDonald entered as a closer who got the game's final out with a runner on first base.

As a winner of the Golden Spikes Award as the college baseball's best player, he found himself in a bidding war of sorts once he was drafted by Baltimore. He and his agent, Scott Boras, met in New York City with associates of Donald Trump. Trump was attempting to form a pro baseball league, and he wanted to make McDonald his first steal of a marquee player from Major League Baseball.

McDonald reportedly left a $2 million offer on the table and the Trump league never materialized. Finally in mid-August, McDonald signed with the Orioles. He received a $350,000 bonus as part of a three-year deal that could pay as much as $1.1 million.

He made six appearances as a reliever at the end of the season and joined Baltimore's starting rotation in 1990. He threw a 4–0 complete-game shutout against the Chicago White Sox and won his next two starts to become the first No. 1 overall draft pick in major league history to win his first three starts.

He signed a free-agent deal with the Milwaukee Brewers in 1996. After going 12–10 that season, shoulder problems limited him in 1997 and he was traded to Cleveland. McDonald never played with the Indians. After unsuccessful shoulder surgery in February 1998, he eventually retired with few regrets. In 2008 he was elected to the College Baseball Hall of Fame, and in 2010 he was inducted into the Louisiana Sports Hall of Fame.

McDonald and his family live once again in Denham Springs, where he lives the life of an outdoorsman and a college baseball TV analyst for ESPN's SEC Network.

Bertman is extremely proud of McDonald, more so as a person than as one of LSU's best-ever players. "He's always been about his family and his community, choosing to coach his kids in soccer, softball, and baseball rather than pursing a full-time national TV analyst job," Bertman said. "He's talented enough to do that, but the path he chose doesn't surprise me. Ben has made great choices all his life."

100 Tommy Hodson

Tommy Hodson didn't have an overwhelmingly strong throwing arm. He wasn't the biggest, fastest, or quickest quarterback ever to start for LSU. "I'm as average and plain as you get," Hodson said when he was inducted into the Louisiana Sports Hall of Fame in 2013.

So how did Hodson manage to become one of the greatest quarterbacks in LSU history? Perhaps Bob Gros—Hodson's head coach at Central Lafourche, where Hodson threw for 4,361 yards and 36 TDs—had the most accurate description of his protégé. "Tommy was the purest quarterback I ever coached," Gros said. "He had a great touch and picked up things very easily."

The crazy thing about Hodson is that basketball, not football, was his favorite sport for the longest time. His idol growing up was former LSU basketball star Pete Maravich, college basketball's all-time leading scorer. "I never worked hard at football in high school," Hodson said. "I picked up a football when football season was there."

He averaged 27.4 points per game as one of the best high school basketball players in the state. "I really wanted to play basketball, but I eventually caught the fever for football when LSU started recruiting me," Hodson said. "I couldn't have asked for a better college career."

He also couldn't have dreamed of a better situation. From the outset, when he stepped into the starting lineup as a freshman in 1986, he was surrounded by veteran talent. "We were set in a lot of spots, so it was an ideal situation for me," Hodson said. "I was a role player because we had a lot of playmakers on offense. It allowed me to have some success early in my career."

In both Hodson's freshman and junior seasons, LSU won the SEC championship. The Tigers were a combined 27–8–1 in his first three seasons as a starter. "Whether a game was going good or if it was going bad, Tommy's demeanor never changed," said Mike Archer, who was LSU's head coach in Hodson's three final seasons. "He never deviated from the game plan. Our team never panicked and never gave up because of Tommy's attitude."

Hodson started 46 of 47 games in his college career and was 5–3–1 against top 10 opponents. His most memorable win was in 1988, when his 11-yard game-winning TD pass to Eddie Fuller with 1:41 left to play gave LSU a 7–6 win over No. 4 Auburn. The explosion of sound at Tiger Stadium when Fuller scored was so loud that it registered as an earthquake on a seismograph at LSU's Howe-Russell Geoscience Complex about 1,000 feet from the stadium. "I'm thankful the guy running the geology department left the seismograph on," Hodson said. "It's just adds to the great folklore of LSU football."

Hodson left a lot of lore and legacy in Baton Rouge by the time he was taken in the third round of the 1990 NFL Draft by the New England Patriots. Chosen All-SEC for four consecutive years, Hodson became the first 9,000-yard passer in league history (9,115) and was the first SEC player ever to throw for more than 2,000 yards in four straight seasons. He held the LSU records for total yards with 8,998 (minus-117 yards rushing, 9,115 yards passing), career touchdown passes (69), and most yards per game passing (203.1 yards per game) in a career. Also, he threw for 200 or more yards 26 times.

Hodson was a 58 percent career passer, something Archer marveled over at the time. "I'm not quite sure where he gets his touch from, but he has great accuracy," Archer said. "He knows that instant when there's going to be a window. That's when the ball is there."

Because of Hodson's college success, it was a surprise that his NFL career lasted only six seasons. He played for the New England Patriots, the Miami Dolphins, the Dallas Cowboys, and the New Orleans Saints.

He was the third quarterback selected in the 1990 NFL Draft behind first-round picks Jeff George of Purdue and University of Houston Heisman Trophy–winning quarterback Andre Ware. The Patriots were so bad—1–15—in Hodson's rookie season that he started the last six games of the season. He also started six games over the next two years before he was cut during the 1993 training camp.

After bouncing to the Dolphins and then the Cowboys, he landed with the Saints, where he played in four games before retiring. "I didn't have the career that I would have dreamed of having, but I got to play six years," Hodson said. "I met a lot of great people, and I have friends today from my NFL days. I have no regrets."

Online Resources

AL.com
AndtheValleyShook.com
BleacherReport.com
ChicagoTribune.com
ESPN.com
Gannett.com
InsidetheTigers.com
LSU.edu
LSUReveille.com
LSUSports.net
NBCSports.com
Nola.com
OutkicktheCoverage.com
NYTimes.com
Panthers.com
SBNation.com
SI.com
TheAdvocate.com
TheARDA.com
TheAthletic.com
ThePostgame.com
TigerDetails.com
TigerRag.com
TheCommercialAppeal.com
247Sports.com
WAFB.com
WBRZ.com
Yahoo.com
YouTube.com